TEACH YOURSELF BOOKS

MALTESE

Maltese is a very interesting language, with
a complex, but logical and rational, structure.
Having mastered the basic rules, one need
not worry about the exceptions.

TEACH YOURSELF BOOKS

MALTESE

JOSEPH AQUILINA
LL.D., Ph.D. (Lond.)
Professor of Maltese
in the Royal University of Malta

TEACH YOURSELF BOOKS
ST. PAUL'S HOUSE, WARWICK LANE, LONDON E.C. 4

First printed 1965
This impression 1970

ISBN 0340 05805 6

Printed in Great Britain for The English Universities Press Limited by Stephen Austin & Sons Ltd., Hertford, Herts.

PREFACE

Maltese is a very interesting language with an Arabic morphology and a very mixed vocabulary. It is the language of a people who have been Christian since 60 A.D. when Malta was a Roman colony. Before the Romans, Malta was inhabited by the pre-Phoenicians with whom are associated the famous megalithic temples of the Island, such as the Hypogeum at Ħal Safiieni, a sort of underground temple (about 2400 B.C.), *Borġ in-Nadur* (1350 B.C.) and *il-Baħrija* (about 900 B.C.) The Phoenicians colonised Malta in about 800 B.C. After the Phoenicians came the Carthaginians (about 700 B.C.), then the Romans (218 B.C.), the Arabs (870-1090), the Normans, Suabians, Angevins, Aragonese and Castilians (1090-1530), the Order of St. John (1530-1798), the French (1798-1800) and last the British (1800-1964). This shows that though the Maltese speak a morphologically Arabic language (North African branch), a continuous political connection with the Arabic world came to an end about 875 years ago, while linguistic influence continued till 1224 when the Arabs were expelled from Malta by Frederick II, the Suabian king of Sicily (1197-1250). One may assume that very probably a number of Arabs became Christians in order to acquire the right to remain in the island and keep their property. With the arrival of the Normans, the Maltese language began to absorb a large number of Romance loan-words expressing new ideas and requirements. This explains why spoken Maltese, like modern English, which is basically Anglo-Saxon where Maltese is largely Semitic, has so many loan-words. But so strong is the Semitic morphology of the language that these have been adapted to Maltese morphological word-patterns.

The present volume differs from Sutcliffe's *A Grammar of the Maltese Language* and May Butcher's *Elements of Maltese* in that it considers Maltese without any arbitrary exclusion of the Romance element of the language; this is, in fact, as absurd as writing a grammar of the English Language including only the lexical and morphological Anglo-Saxon element, leaving out all the linguistic Romance element. Every language has its own limits, within which the author of a *Teach Yourself Book* has to work. These frontiers and limits differ from one language to another in more than one aspect. The Maltese language, like Arabic and the other Semitic languages, has a complex, but very logical and, I would say, rational structure. Having mastered the basic rules, one need not worry about the exceptions, because irregular formations are very few. The advice to the user of this grammar is: "Make sure you understand the basic rules governing the formation of a word-pattern, and you can form more words on this model yourself." That is why, in this grammar I have made frequent use of word-models, which I called patterns, with the warning that these word-patterns are not meant to be memorised, but to be treated as sign-posts, models, showing the interaction governing the semantic relationship between a group of consonants, generally 3, sometimes 4 or 2, which never vary their order, and one or more vowels, a change in which brings about a change in meaning.

Though the Maltese language is spoken by a numerically small people, it is none the less a very interesting language both because it provides the key to direct access to the literature, social life and background of a Mediterranean Semitic-speaking Christian people, and, if you are a linguist, because it provides good material for comparative linguistics in the field of Semitic and Romance languages.

What kind of people are the Maltese? Like all small peoples they need more publicity in the large and competitive world of today. Professor A.J. Arberry of Pembroke College, Cambridge, has written two books which give English readers a good idea of the growth of Maltese Literature. These two books are *A Maltese Anthology* (O.U.P., 1960) and *Dun Karm — Poet of Malta* (C.U.P., 1961).

Malta, a British Colony since 1813, became an independent member of the Commonwealth on the 21st of September, 1964. Though this is Malta's first experiment in democratic freedom in a new world of free nations, her history bears witness to her ancient civilization. As far back as the 1st century B.C., the Greek historian Diodorus Siculus described the Maltese as a colony planted by the Phoenicians, "whose inhabitants are blest in their possessions, artisans skilled in every manner of craft." St. Luke, in the Acts of the Apostles (xxviii. I), in his account of St. Paul's shipwreck in Malta, in 60 A.D., described the Maltese as a courteous people. In more recent times, after the 2nd World War, President Franklin D. Roosevelt, in the name of the people of the U.S.A., saluted the people of the Island of Malta, who "in the cause of freedom and justice and decency throughout the world, have rendered valorous service far above and beyond the call of duty."

The other tribute is the award of the George Cross by King George VI, "to bear witness to a heroism and devotion that will long be famous in history."

I am, of course, aware that all this has no relevance to the rules of Maltese grammar. But I hope it serves to introduce the user of this book to both the Maltese language and the people who speak it. The two go together.

J. AQUILINA.

Floriana, Malta.
6th March, 1965.

CONTENTS

viii

PART III

THE VERB

PART I

THE SOUNDS AND LETTERS

THE ALPHABET

The Maltese alphabet consists of the following 24 consonants and 5 vowels:—

A a; B b; Ċ ċ; D d; E e; F f; Ġ ġ; G g; H h; Ħ ħ; I i; J j; K k; L l; M m; N n; Għ għ; O o; P p; Q q; R r; S s; T t; U u; V v; W w; X x; Ż ż; Z z.

THE CONSONANTS

(Pronunciation and Phonetic Notation)

The whole list of Maltese sounds and letters is given in the form of a table divided into five columns on pp. 12-15.

To those to whom phonetic notation is unfamliar, and perhaps a deterrent, columns 2 and 5 could be sufficient for a general knowledge of Maltese sounds and letters . But columns 3 and 4, especially the latter, as well as the supplementary description of consonants on pp. 17-18, though not indispensable, are worth the time one could give to them because together they enable the user of this book to get as close an imitation of Maltese sounds as it is possible to do so without the guidance of a native speaker of the language.

For examples given in the fifth column in phonetic notation, note that symbol (') means that the stress, or tonic accent, falls on the syllable following it, and that repeated vowels (exx. aa, ee, etc.) indicate a long vowel. An alternative method of indicating vocalic length is by symbol : (exx. fuːl or fuul 'beans'; buːt or buut 'pocket'), the former being used by A.S. Tritton in his *Teach Yourself Arabic* (Classical Arabic), and the latter by T.F. Mitchell in his *Teach Yourself Colloquial Arabic* (Egyptian). These two companion books are useful for the student of Comparative Arabic dialectology.

No.	Letter	Class and Manner of Articulation	Phonetic Notation	Approximate Pronunciation
1.	B b	Voiced bilabial plosive.	b	like Eng. 'b'. Exx. **blu** (**bluu**) 'blue'; **but** (**buut**) 'pocket'.
2.	Ċ ċ	Unvoiced palato-alveolar affricate.	tʃ	like Eng. 'ch' in 'church'. Exx. **ċatt** (**tʃatt**) 'flat'; **ċoff** (**tʃoff**) 'bow' (tie).
3.	D d	Voiced dental plosive.	d	as in Eng. Exx. **demm** (**demm**) 'blood'; **Dott** (**dott**) 'Dr.'
4.	F f	Unvoiced labio-dental fricative.	f	as in Eng. Exx. **ful** (**fuul**) 'beans'; **fomm** (**fomm**) 'mouth'.
5.	Ġ ġ	Voiced palato-alveolar affricate.	dʒ	like Eng. 'j' in John. Exx. **ġab** (**dʒaap**) 'he brought'; **ġenn** (**dʒenn**) 'insanity'.
6.	G g	Voiced velar plosive.	g	like Eng. 'g' in 'gun'. Exx. **goff** (**goff**) 'rough'; **garr** (**garr**), 'he grumbled'.

7.	**H h**	Unvoiced pharyngal fricative.	**h**	like Eng. 'h' in 'horse', but comparatively stronger, occurring not only initially but also medially and finally. **Exx. habb (happ)** 'he loved'; **bahar ('bahar) 'sea'; ruh (ruuh)** 'soul'.
8.	**H h**	Unvoiced glottal fricative in Arabic.	**h**	unpronounced like Eng. 'h' in 'heir', except when it occurs at the end of a word. When silent in a medial position it merely lengthens the preceding and/or the following vowel. **Exx. hemm (emm)** 'there'; **hena ('ena)** 'happiness'; **deher ('deer)** 'he appeared', **dehra ('deera)** 'a vision'.
9.	**J j**	Voiced palatal semi-vowel.	**y**	like Eng. 'y' in 'yes'. **Exx. jaf (yaaf)** 'he knows'; **jum (yuum)** 'a day'.
10.	**K k**	Unvoiced velar plosive.	**k**	like Eng. 'k' in 'kite'. **Exx. kif (kiif)** 'how'; **kieku ('kieku)** 'if'.
11.	**L l**	Voiced alveolar lateral.	**l**	approximately clear 'l' of 'life', 'live', etc., and never like dark 'l' of seal. (See supplementary description, p. 18).
12.	**M m**	Voiced bilabial nasal.	**m**	as in Eng. **Exx. mil (miil)** 'mile'; **mhux (muuʃ)** 'he is not'.

No.	Letter	Class and Manner of Articulation	Phonetic Notation	Approximate Pronunciation
13.	N n	Voiced dental nasal.	n	as in Eng. Exx. naf (naaf) 'I know'; nefah ('nefah) 'he blew'.
14.	GH gh	(i) Voiced velar fricative g, or (ii) voiced pharyngal fricative ʕ in Arabic.(N.B. the information is useful for etymological purposes only).	y (symbol used in Maltese phonetic notation only when necessary).	unpronounced, like Eng. 'gh' in 'thorough' and 'through'. Like h (No. 8), it serves to lengthen the preceding and/or following vowel in any position. Exx. gherf ('eerf) 'wisdom'; boghod ('boot) 'distance'. Alternative phonetic notation not used in this book, ('yerf; 'boyot).
15.	P p	Unvoiced bi-labial plosive.	p	as in Eng. but without any aspiration. Exx. papa ('paapa) 'pope'; prezz (pretts) 'price'.
16.	Q q	Unvoiced glottal plosive.	ˀ	this is a glottal stop or catch. (See supplementary description, p. 18).
17.	R r	Voiced rolled al-veolar.	r	like rolled Scottish 'r', never unrolled as in Eng. (See supplementary description, p. 18).

18.	S s	Unvoiced alveolar (sometimes dental) fricative.	s	as in Eng. 'sea', Exx. sab (saap) 'he (it) found'; sann (sann) 'he sharpened'.
19.	T t	Unvoiced dental plosive.	t	like dental Italian or French 't'. (See supplementary description, p. 17).
20.	V v	Voiced labio-dental fricative.	v	as in Eng. Exx. venven ('venven) 'it whirred'; iva ('ĭiva) 'yes'.
21.	W w	Voiced bilabial semi-vowel.	w	like Eng. 'w' in 'war'. Exx. wasa' ('wasa) 'it contained'; wiċċ (witt∫) 'face'.
22.	X x	Unvoiced palato alveolar fricative.	∫	like Eng. 'sh' in 'shoot'. Exx. xita ('∫ita), 'rain'; xemx (∫em∫), 'sun.'
23.	Ż ż	Voiced alveolar fricative.	z	like Eng. 'z' in 'buzz', but comparatively stronger. Exx. żift (zift) 'pitch'; żiffa ('ziffa) 'breeze'.
24.	Z z	Unvoiced alveolar affricate.	ts	like Eng. 'ts' in 'bits'. Exx. zokk (tsokk) 'trunk'; zopp (tsopp) 'lame'.

(1) Orthographic Notes on h (no. 8)

H h is silent when it occurs at the beginning of a word or inside it. It is pronounced like ħ (no. 7) when it occurs at the end of a word or inside a word when it occurs in the feminine pronoun suffix ha (her) or hom (their) preceded by ħ or għ. Exx. ruħ 'soul', ruħha ('ruħħa) 'her soul', ruħhom ('ruħħom) 'their soul'. Ma' 'with' (for magħ) magħha ('mahħa), magħhom ('mahħom) 'with her/them'. The following is a list of the more important words containing h (i) *at the beginning of a word*: Exx. huwa ('uwwa) 'he'; hija ('iyya) 'she'; hemm ('emm) 'there'; hawn (aun) 'here'; huma ('uuma) 'they'; hemeż ('emes) 'he fastened with pins'; hewden ('euden) 'he raved'; herra ('erra) 'rudeness'; hena ('ena) 'happiness'; hekk (ekk) 'so' (ii) *in the middle of a word*: deheb ('deep) 'gold'; dehen ('deen) 'intelligence'; fehem ('feem) 'he understood'; dahar ('daar) 'back' to be distinguished from dar ('daar) 'house'; nhar ('naar) 'day' to be distinguished from nar ('naar) 'fire'; żahar ('zaar) 'blossoms' to be distinguished from żgħar ('zaar) 'small' pl. and żar (zaar) 'he visited' (iii) *at the end of a word*: boloh ('boloħ) 'foolish' pl., but bluha 'folly' ('bluwa, h silent) koroh ('koroħ) 'ugly' pl., kruha ('kruwa) 'ugliness'; xebħ (ʃeph) 'resemblance' but xbieha ('ʃbiǝa) 'an image'; uċuħ (u'tʃuuħ) 'faces' pl. of wiċċ (witʃ) 'face'; sabuh (sa'buuh) 'they found him' for sabu ('saabu)+pron. suffix h (ħ).

(2) Orthographic Notes on "għ" (no. 14)

1. When għ preceded by the vowel a is the third (radical) consonant of a verb, it is silent and is represented by the symbol '. Exx. sama' ('sama) for samagħ 'he heard'; tala' ('tala) for talagħ 'he went up'. But when morphological extensions are added, the third radical shown by the symbol ' is written out in full as għ.

Exx. bala' ('bala) for balagħ 'he swallowed' but belgħu ('beleu) 'they swallowed'; tefa' ('tefa') 'he threw' but tefgħu ('tefeu) 'they threw'. Also 'belou, 'tefou.

Final għ is pronounced ħ in verbs forogħ 'it (the sea) ebbed away'; and żebagħ 'he painted'.

2. għ at the end of a word preceded by a vowel other than a is pronounced ħ.

Exx. smigħ (smiəħ) 'hearing' from sama' 'he heard'; tfigħ (tfiəħ) 'throwing' from tefa' 'he threw'; qlugħ ('luuħ) 'sails'; biegħ ('biəħ) 'he sold' and bejgħ ('beiħ) 'sale'.

3. Final a' in ta' 'of' for tagħ, and ma' 'with' for magħ, and in verbs ending in a' + pron. suffix ha 'her' and hom 'them' phonetically become double consonant ħ i.e. ħħ; but they are written with the original spelling. Thus ta' 'of' + ha or + hom, though pronounced 'taħħa 'taħħom respectively, are written tagħha 'her, hers' and tagħhom 'their, theirs'. Similarly tefa' 'he threw' (for tefagħ) + ha 'her', + hom 'them' are pronounced te'faħħa, te'faħħom but are written tefagħha, tefagħhom.

4. għ + i or u are pronounced like long diphthongs, approximately as Eng. *ay* in *day* and as Eng. *o* in *hole*. For further explanation see *Diphthongs* on p. 25.

5. agħa, egħe, ogħo inside a word between two consonants are pronounced like a long a, e, o.

Exx. qagħad ('aat) 'he stood'; lagħab ('laap) 'he played'; xagħar ('ʃaar) 'hair' (to be distinguished from xahar [ʃaar] 'month') ċagħak ('tʃaak) 'pebbles'; xogħol ('ʃool) 'work'; logħob ('loop) 'games'.

6. If għ occurs between ie - e, it is pronounced ie + long e.

Exx. wiegħed ('wiəeet) 'he promised'; qiegħed ('iəeet) 'he put'; biegħed ('biəeet) 'he removed'.

SUPPLEMENTARY DESCRIPTION OF CONSONANTS

(1) (t) and (d) are pronounced with the tongue in contact with the teeth and the ridge behind them, unlike Eng. t and d, which are pronounced with the

tip of the tongue in contact with the ridge of the teeth only.

Compare and contrast (i) M. **te** (tee), Eng. 'tea'; M. **tim** (tiim), Eng. 'team'; M. **fitt** (fitt), 'importunate', Eng. 'fit'; (ii) M. **dejn** (dein), 'debt', Eng. 'Dane'; M. **dum** (duum) 'tarry', (imperative) Eng. 'doom'; M. **medda** ('medda) 'extent', Eng. 'madder'.

(2) Maltese **l**, which is always clear like l in 'love' and never dark like l in 'seal', is formed by the tip of the tongue touching the ridge of the upper teeth with the front part of the tongue raised towards the hard palate.

Exx. **miljun** (mil'juun) 'million'; **linja** ('linya) 'line'; **ballu** ('ballu) 'ball'.

(3) (**q**). This is a glottal stop produced by completely closing the vocal cords and then suddenly separating them. In Cockney, this **q**- sound (glottal stop or catch) replaces medial **t**, sometimes **p** in words like 'water', 'fortnight', and 'paper'. It also occurs in standard English between words beginning and ending with a vowel as in 'Malta oranges'; 'sea air'.

Exx. **qalb** (ʔalp) 'heart' or 'amongst'; **qanqal** ('ʔanʔal) 'he moved (something heavy)'; **qroqqa** ('ʔroʔʔa) 'brooding hen'.

(4) (**r**) is always rolled in Maltese, also in English loanwords with unrolled r (ɹ). Initial r of **rabbejt** (rab'beit) 'I have brought up (a child)', is quite different from initial unrolled r of English 'rabbit' ('ɹæbit).

Exx. r:— **razza** ('rattsa) 'race'; **fiera** ('fiəra) 'fair'; **renju** ('renyu) 'reign'.

(5) (**z**) is pronounced as **ds** in English buds (bʌdz) in the following words; **gazzija** (gad'dziyya) 'acacia'; **zona** ('dzoona) 'zone', **mezza** ('meddza) 'a measure'; **mezzanin** (meddza'niin) 'mezzanin'; **Nazzarenu**

Naddza'reenu) 'Nazarene'; **gazzetta** (gad'dzetta) 'newspaper'.

THE CLASSIFICATION OF CONSONANTS

The consonants may be classified in correlative groups into (i) *Voiced* and (ii) *Breathed* or *Unvoiced* as follows:

	(i) *Voiced*	(ii) *Breathed* or *Unvoiced*
(1)	b	p
(2)	v	f
(3)	d	t
(4)	z (ż)	s
(5)	dʒ (ġ)	tʃ (ċ)
(6)	g (g)	k
(7)	g (għ)	ħ (ħ)
(8)	—	ʔ (q)
(9)	ʒ (x)	ʃ (x)

Voiced Velar fricative sound no. 7 is still heard in some villages of Gozo, but it is dying out.

When a consonant from group (i) is followed by a consonant from group (ii), it changes into its corresponding sound in column (ii). Similarly, when a consonant from group (ii) is followed by a consonant from group (i), it changes into its corresponding sound in column (i).

Taking **B** for the Breathed, that is, unvoiced consonants and **V** for Voiced consonants, we can formulate the principle of:

1 — PARTIAL ASSIMILATION

$$B + V = V$$
$$V + B = B$$

It must be borne in mind, however, that the phonetic change heard in the spoken language is not recorded in the spelling of the written language. For example, **b** which becomes a voiceless consonant **p** in the word 'ptiəhi, plural of **bitħa** 'courtyard', is retained in the spelling **btieħi** / **bitħa**. Similarly **s** in **sdieri** ('zdiəri) 'waistcoats' though pronounced **z**, is written **s** as in the singular **sidrija** (sid'riyya).

Also in the spoken language only, voiced consonants at the end of the word are unvoiced, unless in continuous speech they are immediately followed by a word beginning with a voiced consonant.

Exx. **bieb** (biep) 'door'; **trid** (triit) 'you (she) want(s)'; **raġġ** (rattʃ) 'ray'; **mitfugħ** (mit'fuuħ) 'thrown'; **liv** (liif) 'leave'; **mizz** (miss) 'rancid' but **sab barra** (saab‿'barra) 'he found outside'; **trid dar** (triid‿'daar) 'you (she) want(s) a house'.

2 — COMPLETE ASSIMILATION

Complete assimilation takes place in the case of one or two or more consonants making the other consonant or consonants sound completely like them. This happens in the case of **l-**, which is the definite article, and **t-**, a verbal preformative, when these are followed by consonants with which they assimilate.

In the case of monosyllabic words which become dissyllabic as a result of the prefix definite article **l-**, the accent falls on the second syllable. Exx. **il-kelb** (il'kelp) 'the dog'; **id-dell** (id'dell) 'the shadow'.

The following exemplified tabulation illustrates this phonetic law:—

Assimilation of **l** (+ **ċ, d, n, r, s, t, x, ż, z**).

*(Note how **l** loses its own sound and takes instead the sound of the consonant which follows it + euphonic vowel **i** before it).*

(1) **l + ċ = iċċ**. Exx. **iċ-ċella** (it'tʃella) for **il-ċella** (il + 'tʃella) 'the cell'; **iċ-ċirasa** (ittʃi'raasa) for **il-ċirasa** (il + tʃi'raasa) 'the cherry'.

(2) l + d = idd. Exx. id-dar (id'daar) for il-dar (id + 'daar) 'the house'; id-demm (id'demm) for il-demm (il + 'demm) 'the blood'.

(3) l + n = inn. Exx. in-nar (in'naar) for il-nar (il + naar) 'the fire'; in-nifs (in'nifs) for il-nifs (il + nifs) 'the breath'.

(4) l + r = irr. Exx. ir-ras (ir'raas) for il-ras (il + raas) 'the head'; ir-ruħ (ir'ruuħ) for il-ruħ (il + ruuħ) 'the soul'.

(5) l + s = iss. Exx. is-silġ (is'sildʒ) for il-silġ (il + sildʒ) 'the ice'; is-suq (is'suuʔ) for il-suq (il + suuʔ) 'the market'.

(6) l + t = itt. Exx. it-trab (it'traap) for il-trab (il + 'traab) 'the dust'; it-tin (it'tiin) for il-tin (il + tiin) 'the figs'.

(7) l + x = ixx. Exx. ix-xahar (iʃ'ʃaar) for il-xahar (il + ʃaar) 'the month'; ix-xagħar (iʃ'ʃaar) for il-xagħar (il + ʃaar) 'the hair'.

(8) i + ż = iżż. Exx. iż-żir (iz'ziir) for il-żir (il + ziir) 'the pitcher'; iż-żarbun (izzar'buun) for il-żarbun (il + zar'buun) 'the shoe'.

(9) l + z = izz. Exx. iz-zokkor (it'tsokkor) for il-zokkor (il + tsokkor) 'the sugar'; iz-zalzett (ittsal'tsett) for il-zalzett (il + tsal'tsett) 'the sausage'.

Assimilation of t (+ ċ, d, ġ, s, x, ż, z)

(Note how t like l assimilates with the consonant that follows it adding euphonic vowel i before the word).

(1) t + ċ = iċċ. Exx. iċċanfar (itʃ'tʃanfar) for t + ċanfar (t + 'ʃanfar) 'you (she) reprimand(s)' or 'he was reprimanded'; iċċempel (itʃ'tʃempel) for t + ċempel (t + tʃempel) 'you (she) ring(s)'.

(2) t + d = idd. Exx. iddawwar (id'dauuar) for t + dawwar (t + 'dauuar) 'he was late'; iddewwa

(id'deuua) for t + dewwa (t + deuua) 'he received medical treatment'.

(3) t + ġ = iġġ. Exx. iġġib (idȝ'dȝiip) .for t + tġib (t + 'dȝiip) 'you (she) bring(s)'; iġġennen (idȝ'dȝennen) for t + ġennen (t + dȝennen) 'he became mad'.

(4) t + s = iss. Exx. isserva (is'serva) for t + serva (t + 'serva) 'he was accommodated'; issellef (is'sellef) for t + sellef (t + 'sellef) 'he borrowed'.

(5) t + x = ixx. Exx. ixxabba' (iʃ'ʃabba) for t + xabba' (t + 'ʃabba) 'you (she, it) satiate(s)' or 'he (it) had enough'; ixxengel (iʃ'ʃengel) for t + xengel (t + 'ʃengel) 'he (she) swings' or 'he (it) was swung'.

(6) t + ż = iżż. Exx. iżżerżaq (iz'zerzaʔ) for t + żerżaq (t + zerzaʔ) 'he (it) slid'; iżżelleġ (iz'zelledȝ) for t + żelleġ (t + zelledȝ) 'it was blurred'.

(7) t + z = izz. Exx. izzappap (it'tsappap) for t + zappap (t + 'tsappap) 'you (she) limp(s)' or 'he was lamed'; izzekzek (it'tsektsek) for t + zekzek (t + tsektsek) 'you (she) hiss(es)'.

Remark: t + t = itt. Exx. ittaffa (it'taffa) for t + taffa (t + taffa) 'it was mitigated'; ittertaq (it'tertaʔ) for t + tertaq (t + tertaʔ) 'he (it) was shattered'.

Other complete assimilations: s + final x and ż + x = ʃʃ. Exx. ħass (ħass) 'he felt', ma ħassx (ma‿'ħaʃʃ) 'he did not feel'; ħażż (ħass) 'he scribbled', ma ħażżx (ma‿'ħaʃʃ) 'he did not scribble'.

Note also l + n within the word = nn. Exx. kellna ('kenna) 'we had'; ġralna ('dȝraalna) 'it happened to us'; but għamilna (a'milna or a'minna) 'we have done'.

n + b = imb. Exx. nbid (mbiit) 'wine'; għenba ('eemba) 'a grape'.

t or d + x = tʃ. Exx. għatx (aattʃ) 'thirst'; ma qagħadx (ma—'ʔaatʃ) 'he did not stay'.

t or d + s = tts. Exx. mqaddsa ('mʔattsa) 'sacred' (f.); mqartsa ('mʔartsa) 'packed up'.

NOTE ON LENGTHENED OR DOUBLED CONSONANTS

All Maltese consonants except h, għ, but including semi-consonants w and j, can be reduplicated in writing and lengthened phonetically at the beginning of a word or inside it. As consonantal reduplication in English does not involve phonetic lengthening, the English student of Maltese must practise this lengthening by *doubling the length of the twice-written consonant as* s + s in KiSSeR and d + d in HaDDeM which must be pronounced not with one s or d as in English *fussy* and *bladder*, but with the first 's' or 'd' *closing* the first syllable and with the second s or d *opening* the second syllable.

Practise first with the following pairs of English words, then pass on to the list of Maltese words for further practice:—

stab—breast (bb); Church—chimes (tʃʃ); mad—dog (dd); rough—form (ff); pledge—John (dʒʒ); big—gun (gg); may—you (yy); sick—cat (kk); full—life (ll); some—men (mm); gun—night (nn); stop—pay (pp); far—road (rr, both r's rolled); glass—soldier (ss); a bit—tired (tt); love—volume (vv); how—well (ww); flash—shine (ʃʃ); buzz—zoom (zz).

Now try the following M. words for further exercise:— ħabat ('ħabat) 'he struck'; ħabbat ('ħabbat) 'he knocked'; ċass (tʃass) 'fixed (stare)'; iċċassa (itʃ'tʃassa) 'he stared'; feda ('feda) 'he redeemed'; fidda ('fidda) 'silver'; iġib (i'dʒiip) 'he brings'; iġġib (idʒ'dʒiip) 'you (she) bring(s)'; garr (garr) 'he grumbled'; iggroggja (ig'groggya) 'he swigged'; baħar ('baħar) 'sea'; baħħar ('baħħar) 'he sailed'; ħaj (ħai) 'alive' (m.); ħajja ('ħaiyya) 'alive' (f.); **siker** ('siker) 'he got drunk'; **sakkar** ('sakkar) 'he intoxicated); **qaleb** ('ʔalep) 'he turned over (the page of a book, etc.)'; **qalleb** ('ʔallep) 'he upset'; **demel** ('demel) 'manure'; **demmel** ('demmel) 'he manured'; **papa** ('paapa) 'pope'; **pappa** ('pappa) 'piece of bread (child's word)'; **baqa'** ('baʔa) 'he remained'; **baqqa** ('baʔʔa) 'a bug'; **qargħa** ('ʔara) 'a pumpkin'; **qarrħa** ('ʔarra) 'he heard her confession'; **nesa** ('nesa) 'he forgot'; **nessa** ('nessa) 'he caused to forget'; **xitel** ('ʃitel) 'plants'; **xettel** ('ʃettel) 'he planted'; **iva** ('iiva) 'yes'; **ivvota** (iv'voota) 'he voted'; **sewa** ('seua) 'it was worth while' or 'it cost'; **sewwa** ('seuua) 'he mended'; **baża'** ('baza) 'he feared'; **bażża'** ('bazza) 'he frightened'; **ziju** ('tsiyyu) 'uncle'; **mazza** ('mattsa) 'mace'; **biha** ('biya) 'with her'; **bija** ('biyya) 'with me'.

THE DIPHTHONGS

The union of two vowels pronounced in one syllable gives rise to the following diphthongal combinations with **w** and **j** (**y**) pronounced more energetically than **w** and **y** in similar English diphthongal combinations:

(1) **aw** (**au**), as Eng. *ow* in *cow, how, now*. Exx. **raw** (**rau**) 'they saw'; **babaw** (ba'bau) 'bogey'.

(2) **aj** (**ai**) as Eng. *igh* in *high, right*. Exx. **ħaj** (+ **ja**, f.) ('hai) (+ **yya**, f.) 'alive'; **rajt** (**rait**) 'I have seen'.

(3) **ew** (**eu**). This un-English diphthong arises from the combination of short vowel **e**, forming one syllable with **w**. Exx. **mewt** (**meut**) 'death'; **lewn** (**leun**) 'colour'.

(4) **ej** (**ei**) as Eng. *ay* in *lay, fay, jay*. Exx. **lej** (**lei**) 'towards'; **fej** (**fei**) 'where'; **ġej** (+ **ja**, f.) (**dʒei**) (+ **yya**, f.) 'he (she) is coming'.

(5) **ij** (**iy**). An un-English diphthong made up of the vowel **i**, pronounced in one syllable with semi-

vowel **y**, which phonetically is heard like lengthened **y**. Exx. **hija** ('iyya) 'she'; **ħija** ('ħiyya) 'my brother'.

(6) **iw** (iw). An un-English combination made up of **i**, pronounced in one syllable with semi-vowel **w**. Exx. **liwja** ('liwya) 'a bend'; **kiwja** ('kiwya) 'cauterization'.

When these diphthongs begin with silent vowel-lengthening (i) **għ** or (ii) **h**, we get the following combinations:—

(1) (i) **għaw** (ii) **haw** ('aau). Exx. (i) **għawm** ('aaum) 'swimming' which is slightly longer than **aw** in **sawm** ('saum) 'fasting'; (ii) **hawn** ('aaun) 'here'; **hawx!** (aauʃ) an exclamation, 'how nice!'.

(2) **għaj** ('aai). Ex. **rgħajt** ('raait) 'I have grazed' which is longer than **aj** in **rajt** ('rait) 'I have seen'.

(3) **għu** (eeu or oou dialectal variant of Valletta and Sliema, also uu in Birgu). Exx. **għum** (+ u, pl.) ('ooum + u, pl. with variants 'eeum + u and 'uum + u) 'swim' (impv.); **bgħula** ('booula, with variants 'beeula and 'buula) 'mules'.

(4) (i) **għi** (eei, also aai, dialectal variant of Valletta); (ii) **hej** (eci). Exx. (i) **għid** ('eeit, or 'aait) 'Easter' or 'say' (impv.); **tiegħi** ('tieei or 'tiaai) 'mine' or 'my'; **miegħi** ('mieei or 'miaai) 'with me'; (ii) **hejm** ('eeim) 'affectedness'; **hejja** ('eeiyya) 'he prepared' pronounced more often 'ħeiyya.

THE VOWELS

There are five vowels in Maltese, each of which can be long or short, according to its position in the word. A long vowel, like a lengthened consonant, approximately takes twice the length given to its single counterpart. As a rule, no diacritical marks are used to show length except occasionally when vocalic length makes a difference in the meaning: for example, **żina** ('ziina), with circumflex accent over **i**, means 'ornament' and **żina** ('**zína**), with the acute accent, means 'lechery'; and in the case of loanwords, generally from Italian, ending in a stressed vowel, shown by the *accent grave* `. Exx. **Università** 'University'; **it-Tre Rè** 'the Epiphany'; **Marì** 'Mary'; **xabò** 'the frill of a shirt'; **virtù** 'virtue'.

These five vowels in Maltese are **a, e, i, o, u**, which can be either close or half-close, open or half-open, according to the amount of space left open between the tongue and the roof of the mouth (the palate). N.B. Unstressed vowel **e** becomes **ə** when the primary stress of the word in which it occurs is moved forward to another syllable of another word following it. Exx. **'raadʒel** (**raġel** 'a man'); but, **ˌradʒəl—ma'riit** (**raġel marid** 'a sick man'). Unstressed vowel **e** in verbs becomes **i** when the accent falls on it. Exx. **kiteb** ('**kitep**) 'he wrote'; but **kitibli** (**ki'tibli**) not **kitebli** (**ki'tebli**) 'he wrote to me'. Similarly **għamel** ('**aamel**) 'he did or made'; **għamilt** (**a'milt**) not **għamelt** (**a'melt**) 'I did or made'.

APPROXIMATE PRONUNCIATION

(1)   (i) Short **a** (a) approximately like *u* in Eng. *shut* and *hut* but comparatively more fronted and closer. Exx. **xatt** (**ʃatt**) 'seaside'; **ħadt** (**ħatt**) 'I took'; **ħadd** (**ħatt**) 'nobody'; **ħatt** 'he unloaded'.

    (ii) Long **a** (aa) like short **a**, but about twice as long Exx. **far** (**faar**) 'rat'; contrast Eng. *far* (**faɑr**); **bar** (**baar**) 'bar'; contrast Eng. *bar* (**baɑr**).

(2)   (i) Short **e** (e), as Eng. *e* in *elf, shed*, but with lips less spread out, and therefore more like *e* in *bloodshed*. It is different from **ɛ** of Eng. *e* in *swear* (**swɛə**), *bear* (**bɛə**), and closer than Eng. *e* in *get* and *bet*. Exx. **bell** (**bell**) 'he wetted', **dell** (**dell**) 'shadow'; **elf** (**elf**) 'thousand'; **xedd** (**ʃett**) 'he put on (suit)'.

    (ii) *Long* **e** (ee) like short **e**, but about twice as

long. Exx. **xena** ('ʃeena) 'scene'; **żelu** ('zeelu) 'zeal'.

(3) (i) *Short* **i** (i) as Eng. *i* in *sit, fit*. Exx. **sitt** (sitt) 'six'; **sidt** (sitt) 'mistress'; **fitt** (fitt) 'importunate'.

    (ii) *Long* **i** (ii) as Eng. *ee* in *seed, jeep* but slightly diphthongized (iiy). Exx. **sid** (siit) 'owner'; **ġib** (dʒiip) 'bring'.

(4) (i) Short close back vowel **o** (o) does not occur in English, but is very close to the *o* in Scottish 'och'. This un-English vowel is different from English *o* in *hot* (hɔt) and *not* (nɔt). Exx. **dott** (dott), short for 'Doctor'. Contrast with Eng. *dot* (dɔt); but it is very close to a shortened form of ɔɔ in words like 'caught' (kɔot) and 'bought' (bɔot).

    (ii) *Long* **o** (oo). This is the above vowel, about twice as long.

    Exx. **sod** (soot) 'steady', compare with Eng. sought (sɔot); **cok** (kook) 'cook'. Compare with Eng. *cork* (kɔɔk).

(5) (i) *Short* **u** (u), as Eng. *u* in *pulpit, full*. Exx. **pulptu** ('pulptu) 'pulpit'; **kull** (kull) 'every'.

    (ii) *Long* **u** (uu), about twice as long as short *u*, pronounced like Eng. *oo* in *fool, hoot*. Exx. **ful** (fuul) 'beans'; **hut** (ħuut) 'fish'.

Remark: vowel **u** before **ħ** and **q** as in **ifuħ** (i'fu°ħ) 'it is fragrant' and **fuq** (fu°ᵍ) 'above' is slightly diphthongized with a sound tending from **u** to a very narrow **o**.

RULES GOVERNING THE LENGTH OF VOWELS

As a general rule .

(1) All vowels at the end of a word in open syllable, that is, one not closed by a consonant, are short and un-

stressed, except in a few loan-words from Italian ending in a stressed vowel.

Exx. **darba** ('darba) 'once'; **marti** ('marti) 'my wife'; **darbu** ('darbu) 'they struck' or 'he struck him'; but **karità** (kari'ta) 'charity'; **bidè** (bi'de) 'bidet' (Fr. bidet) (bi'dɛ); **Marì** (Ma'ri) 'Mary'; **repò** (re'po) 'refreshments'; **virtù** (vir'tu) 'virtue'.

(2) All vowels are long when followed by one consonant and carry the main stress. They are short when followed by more than one consonant. Vowels, originally long, remain so even when possessive pronominal suffixes are added.

Exx. **ras** (raas) 'head'; **rasna** ('raasna) 'our head'; **rass** (rass) 'he pressed'; **għera** ('eera) 'nakedness'; **herra** ('erra) 'rudeness'; **ġid** (dʒiit) 'wealth'; **ġidd** (dʒitt) 'generation'; **kor** (koor) 'choir'; **korra** ('korra) 'he hurt himself'; **kul** (kuul) 'eat' (sing. impv.); **kull** (kull) 'every'.

(3) A long vowel becomes comparatively shorter when the word in which it occurs is followed by another word which begins with one or more consonants, and carries the main stress. Thus long **a** in **dar** 'house' becomes shorter in the phrase **dar sabiħa** 'beautiful house', the main stress of which falls on the second syllable of the adjective.

DIGRAPH — ie (iə)

The special digraph **ie** represents the mutation of long **a** (aa) known as ʔimaala in Arabic. Some Maltese plural nouns end in long a (aa) or ie (iə) both stressed + t.

Exx. **xewqat** (ʃeu'ʔaat) or **xewqiet** (ʃeu'ʔiət), plural of **xewqa** ('ʃeuʔa) 'wish'; **werqat** (wer'ʔaat) or **werqiet** (wer'ʔiət) plural of **werqa** ('werʔa) 'a leaf'.

This special digraph which always carries the main stress is pronounced approximately as Eng. **ea** in fear (fiə).

Exx. **bierek** ('biərek) 'he blessed' the first syllable of which sounds like Eng. **beer** (biə); but with roller **r**, and **xierak** ('ʃiərek) 'he partnered', the first syllable of which similarly sounds like Eng. **sheer** (ʃiə), but with rolled **r**.

Remark 1: When the stress on **ie** moves onward to the next syllable after the addition of a suffix, **ie** becomes unstressed **i** or **e**.

Exx. **bniedem** ('bniədem) 'man'; **bnedmin** (bned'miin) or **bnidmin** (bnid'miin) 'people'.

Remark 2: For the phonetic value of **ie**, cp. **ġieb** (dʒiəp) 'he brought' and **ġib** (dʒiip) 'bring' (impv.); **żied** (ziət) 'he added' and **żid** (ziit) 'add' (impv.); **miel** (miəl) 'it leaned' and **mil** (miil) 'a mile'; **snien** (sniən) 'teeth' and **snin** (sniin) 'years'. The differentiating sound of **ie** lies approximately midway between long **i** (ii) and long **e** (ee).

Remark 3: **i** before **ħ**, **h** or **q** as in **riħ** (riəh) 'wind'; **fih** (fiəh) 'in it'; and **triq** (triəʔ) 'street' is pronounced like **ie**.

THE LIQUIDS

When one of the so-called liquid consonants **l, m, n, r**, and by analogy **għ**, occurs between two consonants, a vowel is inserted before the liquid consonant to break up the three consonant group. Any other consonant can occur in this position without having to insert a vowel as a syllable-breaker.

Exx. **midneb** ('midnep) 'sinner' (m.) but **midinba** (mi'dinba) 'a female sinner' not **midnba**, which would be unpronounceable. Similarly, **jitolbu** (yi'tolbu) 'they pray' not **jitlbu** ('yitlbu); **joqogħdu** (yo'ʔoodu) 'they stay' not **joqgħdu** (yoʔdu).

The rule does not apply to **m** if the consonant which follows it is another liquid.

Exx. **iżmna** ('izmna) 'times' and not **iżimna** (i'zimna) **iġmla** ('idʒmla) 'camels' and not **iġimla** (i'dʒimla).

THE STRESS

1. All long vowels are stressed but not all stressed vowels are long. Exx. issa ('issa) 'now'; isa ('iisa) 'hurry up'.

2. In the same word there can be one main or primary stress, either on the penultimate or the last syllable. The primary stress in the phonetic script is shown by an accent before, and on top of the stressed syllable.

Exx. kotba ('kotba) 'books'; kittieb (kit'tiep) 'writer'; riġlejha (ridʒ'leya) 'her legs'.

3. In quick continuous speech, the *Primary Stress* becomes *Secondary* when the main accent is carried forward to the more prominent syllable of the word which follows it. In the phonetic script, the secondary stress is shown by an accent placed before the stressed syllable, but at the bottom of its first consonant or vowel.

Exx. bniedem ('bniədem) 'man' but bniedem ħażin (ˌbniədem ħa'ziin) 'a wicked man'; idha ('iida) 'her hand' but idha mfekka (ˌiida 'mfekka) 'her hand is sprained'.

RULES GOVERNING PLACES OF STRESS

(a)

The stress falls on the last syllable.

(i) when it closes with one consonant preceded by long i, u and ie.

Exx. marid (ma'riit) 'sick'; baħrin (baħ'riin) 'sailors'; batut (ba'tuut) 'hard up'; vapur (va'puur) 'a ship'; inġinier (indʒin'iər) 'engineer'; ġennien (dʒen'niən) 'gardener'.

(ii) when the last syllable, either open or closed, ends in a diphthong. In the case of the phonetic diphthongal rendering of għu ('eeu) or ('oou) and għi ('eei), the syllables must be closed by a consonant.

Exx. ġarrew (dʒar'reu) 'they moved house'; ġarrewk (dʒar'reuk) 'they carried you'; semmew (sem'meu) 'they

mentioned'; **semmewni (sem'meuni)** 'they mentioned me';
mirghux (mir'eeuʃ or **mir'oouʃ)** 'affronted'; **mibgħut**
(mi'beut) or **(mi'boout)** 'sent'; but **'yibⁱou** not **yib'ⁱou**
for **jibqgħu** 'they remain'.

(iii)   when the final syllable ends in **a** or **i**, followed
by a consonant group, or by a long, that is, a repeated
consonant.

Exx.   **sammart (sam'mart)** 'I have nailed'; **ħabbatt**
(hab'batt) 'I (you, sing.) have knocked'; **tqarbint**
(t'ar'bint) 'I (you, sing.) have received Holy Communion';
iżżerżaqt (izzer'za'ⁱt) 'I (you, sing.) have slid down'.

(iv)   when the final syllable ends in a long **a** generally closed by a liquid consonant and the first vowel in
the sequence is **u, o** or **i**.

Exx.   **sultan (sul'taan)** 'sultan'; **burdnar (burd'naar)** 'an
ass or mule driver'; **sular (su'laar)** 'storey'; **ħortan**
(ħor'taan) 'bromegrass'; **liżar (li'zaar)** 'sheet'; **xitan**
(ʃi'taan) 'devil'; **tilar (ti'laar)** 'wooden frame'.

As all the vowels occurring in a final open syllable
are always unstressed, except in a few loan-words from
Italian or Sicilian which retain their original stress, it is
evident that the stress in all dissyllabic words falls on
the first syllable. But the position of the stress is not so
self-evident when the vowel in the final syllable is closed
by one consonant. Length and stress in this case are
determined by the grammatical function of the word
(morphological criteria). Remember the following rule:

If the word is a VERB, the stress falls on the first
vowel, but if it is an ADJECTIVE or the name of the
doer, it falls on the second vowel.

Exx. **qassam ('ⁱassam)** 'he divided'; **qassam ('ⁱas'saam)**
'one who divides'; **baħnan ('baħnan)** 'he stultified';
baħnan (baħ'naan) 'stupid'; **fartas ('fartas)** 'he made
bald'; **fartas (far'taas)** 'bald'.

(b)

(i)   The stress falls on the penultimate syllable in

words ending in any of the three vowels **a, i** or **u** in open syllable or in pronominal suffixes **ha,** (her) **hom** (them). Exx. **dara** ('dara) 'he got used to'; **darha** ('daara) 'her house'; **darhom** ('daarom) 'their house'; **travi** ('traavi) 'beams'; **bravu** ('braavu) 'courageous'.

(ii) Words originally dissyllabic with the accent on the first syllable, when they become trisyllabic by the addition of a suffix suffer a shift of stress by which from the first syllable it moves onward to the second syllable. In this manner, the trisyllabic word conforms to the general principle that as a rule a stressed syllable is not followed by more than one unstressed syllable. Thus in **kamra** 'room' the stress falls on the first syllable, but in **kamrithom** (kamrit + pr. suffix **hom** 'their'), less commonly **kamarthom** (kamart + pr. suffix **hom**), the accent moves onwards to the second syllable. If it remained on the first syllable as in the unincreased dissyllabic word, we would have two unstressed syllables after the stressed syllable.

The rule that the stressed syllable cannot be followed by more than one unstressed syllable has many exceptions in the case of loan-words generally used by educated people.

Exx. **statistika** (sta'tistika) 'statistics'; **fiżika** ('fizika) 'physics'; **kimika** ('kimika) 'chemistry'; **botanika** (bo'tanika) 'botany'; **mużika** ('muzika) 'music'. Some of these loan-words have been adapted to the stress pattern of Maltese.

Exx. **pulitka** (pu'liitka) 'politics'; from It. politica; **aritmetka** (arit'meetka) 'arithmetic' from It. aritmetica and **matematka** (mate'maatka) 'mathematics' from It. matematica.

RULES OF SPELLING

1. In every syllable there can be no more than one vowel. Vowel **i** and **u** become semi-vowel **j** and **w** when followed or preceded by another vowel with which they form a diphthong. Exx. **bejn** 'amongst' not **bein; twil**

'tall' not **tuil**; **dinja** 'world' not **dinia**; **ħelwa** 'sweet' not **ħelua**.

An exception to this rule are a number of loan-words which retain their original vocalic form.

Exx. **poeta** 'poet'; **poema** 'poem'; **beatu** 'blessed'; **poeżija** 'poem'; but village people say **poweta, powema, bijatu, poweżija**.

2. In words of more than one syllable semi-vowel **j** or **w** is inserted between the vowel which ends one syllable and the next vowel which begins the syllable following it within the same word.

Exx. **zija** 'aunt' not **zia**; **Marija** 'Mary' not **Maria** and **batterija** 'battery' not **batteria** as in Italian; **ħija** 'my brother' not **hia**; **hejja** 'he prepared' not **heiia**; **sewwa** 'well' not **seuua**.

3. Unstressed vowels **i** and **u** beginning a word become **j** and **w** when the preceding word ends in a vowel, as in continuous speech these vowels form a dipthong. For this reason we write **kien irid** (**kiən—i'riit**) 'he was willing' but **kienu jridu** (**kienu—y'ri:du**) 'they were willing'; **aħna wkoll** (**aħna—'wkoll**) 'also we'. The rule does not apply if the main stress falls on the initial vowel.

Exx. **ralu idu** not **jdu** (**ra:lu 'i:du**) 'he saw his hand'; **qallu ibnu** not **jbnu** (**ʔallu 'ibnu**) 'his son told him'; **ratu usa'**, not **wsa'** (**ra:tu 'uusa**) 'she saw it wider'.

4. Words beginning with **l, m, n** and **r** followed by another consonant or semi-consonant, or with a doubled consonant if the preceding word ends in a consonant require an additional vowel before them. This is generally vowel **i** which, not being an integral part of the word, is omitted when the preceding word ends in a vowel. It is not dropped after a pause shown by a punctuation-mark. In words having **għ** as a first radical in the singular and a few others, this prosthetic vowel is **e** which, unlike **i**, is not dropped when the preceding word ends in vowel.

Exx. **imsiebaħ** 'oil-lamps', **ħafna msiebaħ** 'many oil-lamps' but **ħafna erwieħ** (pl. of **ruħ**) 'many souls' or **egħruq** (pl. of **għerq**) 'roots'; **marru d-dar** (**marru 'dda:r**) not **marru id-dar** 'they went home'; **iġġieled** 'he fought' but **huma ġġieldu** 'they fought'; **it-tfal ingabru kmieni** 'the children went home early'; but **it-tifla ngabret kmieni** 'the girl went home early'. Other examples: **ilbies** 'clothes'; **ilwien** 'colours'; **illum** 'today'; **imtierah** 'mattresses'; **imwiet** 'deaths'; **immur** 'I go'; **inkejja** 'spite'; **injieb** 'eye-teeth'; **innifsi** 'myself'; **irtal** 'rotolos'; **irjieħ** 'winds'; **irrid** 'I want'.

5. Because **għ** and medial **h** are unpronounced, they present some difficulty as to their correct position in the written language. The best method is to compare their position with that of the corresponding consonants in words of similar structure (See Lesson 2). Should we write **mgħamul** or **magħmul** 'done' or 'made' both of which are pronounced **ma'muul**? A similar formation is **maqlub** 'overthrown' in which the first radical consonant follows **ma**. Following the same pattern we write **magħmul**. Similarly we write **wegħgħa** 'pain' and **fehma** 'opinion' as we write **werqa**. The rule is that silent **għ** and **h** fall into the same position and order of corresponding word-patterns as if they were fully pronounced consonants. The morphological rule of radicals in word-structure is explained in Lesson 2.

PART II

MORPHOLOGY

Lesson 1

THE ARTICLE

(N.B. From now on, words are given in the standard spelling. Phonetic notation is given only where necessary).

Maltese has only the definite article l- or il- (vowel i + article) preceding a noun or an adjective used as a noun for the two genders (m. and f.), and the two numbers (sing. and pl.) The mere absence of this definite article makes the (i) noun or (ii) any descriptive word used as a noun indefinite.

Exx. (i) **mara** 'a woman'; **il-mara** 'the woman'; **kelb** 'a dog'; **il-kelb** (+ a, f.) 'the dog (bitch)'; **bar** 'a bar'; **il-bar** 'the bar'; (ii) **marid** 'sick' (adj.); **il-marid** (+ a, f.) 'the sick man (woman)'; **twil** (+ a, f.) 'tall' (adj.); **it-twil** (+ a, f.) 'the tall man (woman)'; **ħafif** (+ a, f.) 'easy' (adj.); **il-ħafif** (+ a, f.) 'the easy one'; **maqtul** (+ a, f.) 'killed' (adj.); **il-maqtul** (+ a, f.) 'the killed person'; **bieżel** (m.) **bieżla** (f.) 'hard-working'; **il-bieżel** (m.) **il-bieżla** (f.) 'the hard-working man, woman'; **xiħ** (+ a, f.) 'old'; 'an old man (woman)', **ix-xiħ** (+ a, f.) 'the old man (woman); **miġnun** (+ a, f.) 'mad'; a mad man (woman).

Indefiniteness, in the sense of a certain person, is indicated also by **wieħed** meaning 'one' before a singular masculine noun, and **waħda**, before a singular feminine noun. Exx. **wieħed raġel** (**tifel, qassis**, etc.) 'a certain man (boy, priest, etc.)'; **waħda mara** (**sinjura, soru**, etc.) 'a certain woman (lady, nun, etc.)'.

The article is **il-** if the word following it begins with

35

a consonant or semiconsonant; l- if it begins with a vowel. It is l- or il- if it begins with għ or h both of which are silent.

Exx. il-bejt 'the roof'; il-ward 'the roses'; il-jum 'the day'; l-arja 'the air'; l-għonq or il-għonq 'the neck'; l-għerf or il-għerf 'the wisdom'; l-hena or il-hena 'the happiness'; l-hemm or il-hemm 'the grief'.

A euphonic i is added before nouns, or adjectives used as nouns, which begin with two consonants, the first of which is m, n, s or x.

Exx. mħadda, 'a pillow'; l-imħadda 'the pillow'; nsara 'Christians', l-insara 'the Christians'; skola 'a school', l-iskola 'the school'; xkora 'a sack', l-ixkora 'the sack'.

There are some nouns beginning with two consonants which either take il- before the first consonant or add euphonic vowel i to the first of these two consonants and use the l- form of the article.

Exx. Il-bdiewa or l-ibdiewa, 'the peasants'; il-bjar or l-ibjar, 'the wells'; ir-rjieħ or l-irjieħ, 'the winds'; il-bliet or l-ibliet, 'the cities'.

The i of the definite article and the i added to a word beginning with two consonants are both euphonic, and therefore both drop out when they are not required for ease of pronunciation, as happens when the definite article is preceded by a word ending in a vowel.

Exx. ktieb, 'a book'; il-ktieb, 'the book'; aqra l-ktieb, 'read the book' not aqra il-ktieb, where the i in il- is dropped.

The definite article l- in pronunciation and, unlike Arabic, also in writing, is assimilated to the consonants known as Xemxin (Sun-Letters) which are ċ, d, n, r, s, t, x, ż, z; but it does not assimilate with s followed by a consonant in all loan-words. In this case euphonic vowel i is inserted before s. Exx. is-sħab (native word) 'the clouds', but l-isptar 'the hospital' and l-isports 'the sports', both loan-words.

The article does not assimilate with the rest of the consonants known as **Qamrin** (Moon-Letters).

The classification of the consonants into Sun-Letters (**Xemxin**), and Moon-Letters (**Qamrin**), is only a mnemonic device based on the fact that l assimilates with x in **xemx** 'sun', but does not assimilate with **q** in **qamar** 'moon'.

NON-USE OF THE DEFINITE ARTICLE

Because the definite article by its very nature defines what would otherwise remain undefined, it is not used with words already defined in another manner. It is therefore not used with:

1. the word **Alla** as the one true God, but is used with the plural **l-allat** 'the gods'.

2. personal nouns and surnames. Exx. **Ġanni** 'John'; **Ebejer** (surname).

3. nouns defined by pronominal suffixes attached to them. Exx. **dar** 'house'; **id-dar** 'the house'; but **dari** for **dar + i** (my) not **id-dari** 'my house'.

4. the particles. (Lesson 12).

5. the noun in the Construct State. (Lesson 5).

6. nouns and adjectives after vocative **ja**. Ex. **ja nies ta' Malta** 'Ye people of Malta'.

EXERCISE 1 (a)

Memorise the following words and place the definite article before them:—

Arja 'the air'; **shab** 'clouds'; **dlam** 'darkness'; **ksieħ** 'cold' (noun); **art** 'earth' or 'land'; **gżira** 'island'; **lvant** 'east'; **xemx** 'sun'; **qamar** 'moon'; **ċpar** 'mist'; **ġlata** 'frost'; **shana** 'heat'; **silġ** 'snow'; **dawl** 'light'; **sema** 'sky'; **beraq** 'lightning'; **natura** 'nature'; **tramuntana** 'north'; **xita** 'rain'; **qawsalla** 'rainbow'; **dell** 'shadow'.

An interesting example of word-economy in spoken Maltese are a few weather-words given in the exercise above which, when preceded by the definite article, are equivalent to an impersonal sentence in English with the verb in the present tense. These are **il** (or its assimilated forms) + **ksieħ** (m.) or **kesħa** (f.), **sħab** (m.), **dlam** (m.), **xemx** (f.), **qamar** (m.), **ċpar** (m.), **sħana** (f.), **beraq** (m.), (also **ragħad** (m.) and **xita** (f.) meaning 'it is cold, cloudy, dark, sunny, moonlight, misty, hot, lightning (thundering) and raining'. The past tense is indicated by **kien** 'it was' before masc. nouns and **kienet** before fem. nouns. (Exx. **kien il-bard** 'it was cold'; **kienet is-sħana** 'it was hot') and the future by **ikun** 'it (he) will be' before masc. nouns and **tkun** 'it (she) will be' before fem. nouns. Exx. **Ikun il-bard** 'it will be cold'; **tkun is-sħana** 'it will be hot'.

USAGE OF THE DEFINITE ARTICLE

While the general rule in Maltese, as in English, is that the defined noun is accompanied by the defining article, there are usages which do not agree in the two languages. Unlike English, in Maltese the definite article is used with names of:—

(i) Minerals: Exx. **il-ħadid** '(the) iron'; **l-azzar** '(the) steel'.

(ii) Names of elements in daily use: Exx. **in-nar u l-ilma** '(the) fire and (the) water'.

(iii) Names of other substances: Exx. **xkora mimlija biz-zokkor, bit-tiben** 'a sack full of (the) sugar, straw'.

(iv) Collective nouns: Exx. **l-ilsna barranin** '(the) foreign languages'; **il-barranin** '(the) foreigners'.

(v) Abstract nouns: Exx. **is-sabar** '(the) patience', **it-tama** '(the) hope'; **l-għaqal** '(the) good sense'.

(vi) Colours: Exx. **l-aħmar (l-abjad, l-iswed, il-**

vjola, etc.) **lewn sabiħ,** '(the) red (white, black, violet, etc.) is a beautiful colour'.

(vii) Names of languages: Exx: **Il-Franċiż** '(the) French (tongue)'; **l-Ispanjol** '(the) Spanish (tongue)'; **l-Ingliż** '(the) English (tongue)'.

Note that these examples could also mean the Frenchman, the Spaniard and the Englishman, which become plural by the addition of suffix **i**. Exx. **il-Franċiżi, l-Ispanjoli, u l-Ingliżi;** 'the French, the Spanish and the English'.

(viii) Names of countries, of which some (a) take the definite article, and some (b) most of which are names of islands, do not Exx. (a) **L-Italja** 'Italy'; **l-Ingilterra** 'England'; **ir-Russja** 'Russja'; **il-Kanada** 'Canada'; etc.; (b) **Malta** 'Malta'; **Għawdex** 'Gozo'; **Kemmuna** 'Comino'; **Franza** 'France'; **Spanja** 'Spain'.

(ix) Names of villages: Exx. **Iż-Żejtun** (for **il-Żejtun**); **il-Ħamrun; l-Għasri; l-Għarb,** the first two being village-names in Malta, and the last two being village-names in Gozo.

(x) Names of week days and seasons (See Lesson No. 14 p. 124).

(xi) Nouns preceded by the demonstrative pronoun. Ex. **dan il-ktieb** 'this (the) book'. (See Lesson No. 11).

The definite article which accompanies the defined noun generally accompanies also the adjective which qualifies the same noun. But in many cases it does not do so.

Exx. **il-mara t-twila,** or more often **il-mara twila** 'the tall woman'; **il-ktieb il-ġdid** or **il-ktieb ġdid** 'the new book'.

But the second example is grammatically ambiguous, because it can mean both 'the tall woman' or 'the woman is tall'; 'the new book' or 'the book is new'. The reason is that Maltese has no verb for English *to be*, and that the word-combination, definite article + noun + adjective is equivalent to a sentence in English. The intended meaning is made clear in the spoken language by the intonation, and in the written language, by the context.

PERSONAL PRONOUNS

It is important to learn the personal pronouns right now because they have a verbal function which makes up for the absence of the verb 'to be' in Maltese and makes possible the formation of simple sentences. These personal pronouns can be negatived by **ma** (**m'** before a vowel or silent **h**) preceding the pronoun and the suffix **x** *which attracts the main stress*. These are:—

Sing: **jien** (also + a) 'I' or 'I am', **ma jiniex** or **m'iniex** (**mi'niəʃ**) 'I am not'; **int** (or **inti**) 'you' or 'you are'; **m'intix** 'you are not'; **hu** (or **huwa**) 'he' or 'he is', **mhux** (for **m'hux**) 'he is not'; **hi** (or **hija**) 'she' or 'she is', **mhix** (for **m'hix**) 'she is not'.

Plural: **aħna** 'we' or 'we are', **m'aħniex** 'we are not'; **intom** 'you' or 'you are', **m'intomx** 'you are not'; **huma** 'they' or 'they are', **m'humiex** 'they are not'.

The student of Arabic should note that in Maltese the gender-distinction has been maintained only in he/she (3rd. pers. sing.). **Exx. hu marid** (lit. he sick) 'he is sick'; **hi Maltija** 'she is Maltese'; **intom, huma Nsara** 'you, they (both genders) are Christians'.

Because personal pronouns have also a verbal function, they can be added after the subject to which they refer. This is often done either redundantly or for emphasis. They are left out when no emphasis is intended.

Exx. l-Italja hi art sabiħa 'Italy (lit. + she) is a beautiful land'; **l-Italja art sabiħa** 'Italy is a beautiful land'.

The personal pronouns and pronominal suffixes are treated more fully in Lesson 11.

SOME USEFUL WORDS

Memorise the following words useful as links in the formation of phrases and sentences:
u 'and'; **hemm** 'there is' or 'there are'; **hawn** 'here is' or 'here are'; **mhux** 'he (it) is not'; **għax** 'because'; **għaliex** 'because, why?'; **ta'** 'of'; **ma'** 'with'.

EXERCISE 1 b & c

Translate:

(a) **L-Italja qrib** (near) **Malta. It-Taljan ħafif; l-Ingliż inqas** (less) **ħafif. L-Ispanjoli jistudjaw** (study) **l-Ingliż u l-Franċiż. Il-Maltin jistudjaw ħafna** (very much) **l-Ingliż. Is-silġ abjad. L-Ingilterra hemm** (there is) **ħafna xita, ksieħ u ċpar. L-art u s-sema fid-dlam. Malta gżira xemxija. L-Ingliżi jħobbu** (love) **il-baħar. Il-Malti** (Maltese) **lsien semitku** (semitic).

c. He went (**mar**) to church (def. art. + **knisja**) and (**u**) to market (def. art. + **suq**). He is in prison (def. art. + **ħabs**). Man (def. art. + **bniedem**) is not eternal (**etern**). Only (**biss** after God) God is eternal. Vesuvius (def. art. + **Vessuvju**) is a volcano (**vulkan**) in Naples. They are not Christians (**Nsara**). Qrendi is a village (**raħal**) in (**f'**) Malta and Għarb is a village in Gozo. She is not Maltese and he is not French. Russia is a large country (**art kbira**). Malta and Gozo are (**huma** = they) islands (**gżejjer**).

Lesson 2

AN INTRODUCTION TO WORD STRUCTURE

Before we proceed further with grammar, it is important to understand the structural mechanism of Maltese Morphology. Most words consist of three, less frequently of two or four and rarely of five consonants forming a base called the Root which can be shown by the symbol √, each consonant of which is known as a radical.

Various forms are obtained by the correlation of these roots to a number of variable vowels or vocalic sequences. The following example illustrates this principle of Semitic word-mechanism. The three unvowelled consonants N-Ż-L do not convey a specific meaning, but they are connected with, and therefore suggest, the general idea of 'descending' which ceases to be vague and general as soon as the three consonants are related to the right vocalic sequence, or the appropriate vowel, as the case may be. One can therefore say that meaning is the joint product of the Consonantal Roots + Vocalic Sequence or + one particular vowel, as the case may be.

The three radicals N-Ż-L can be related to various vocalic sequences or vowels. These vowels sometimes with affixes define the word-meaning with reference to the complete identity of the object, animate or inanimate noun, its quality (adjective), action (verb) time and person connected with an action or state of being or the manner in which such action is carried out (adverb) and other grammatical modalities, which form the subject-matter of the third section of this book. Here are some examples of the derived forms:—

√N-Ż-L Exx. NiżeL 'he descended' (the original verbal pattern i.e. the Base or Root-Word); tNiżżeL 'it was brought down'; NżuL 'descent'; or 'the act of descending'; NiżLa 'a descent'; NieżLa (f) NieżeL (m.) 'descending'; miNżeL 'descending place'. The same radicals can associate with a larger variety of vocalic sequences unknown in Maltese, but known to Arabic or another Semitic language.

As words in Maltese (the rule applies to other Semitic languages) follow one or other pattern, we show such patterns by √K-T-B and √K-T-B-L for quadriliterals each of which, like x in Algebra representing an unknown quantity, stands for any in its own position. One or more of the radicals may be semi-vowel J or W in one or other of the three or four positions. An alternative method would be to use C for Consonant and V for Vowel. Thus KeTeB, the pattern of collective noun NeMeL 'ants' GeBeL 'stone' could be indicated by CvCvC or CeCeC.

What has been said so far is a general description of the chief characteristic feature of word-structure in Maltese. *The patterns which as such can be meaningless will be given to illustrate the construction of the various parts of speech and are not meant to be memorised.* But the student should memorise as many of the words given as possible to increase his vocabulary.

An important point to bear in mind is that a word-pattern may have multiple functions; i.e. it can be the pattern of a noun, of an adjective and also of a verb or some other part of speech. I have chosen √K-T-B as the three consonants for the patterns, because they are three consonants which form part of the English alphabet and are therefore easy to pronounce and memorise by an English-speaking person. The patterns will be accompanied with phonetic notations only where this is necessary, generally to indicate vocalic length and the prominent, i.e. the stress-bearing, syllable.

NOUNS AND ADJECTIVES

Nouns and adjectives may be either simple or derived. They are simple if they are original forms, that is, not obtained from another word-form by the addition of a suffix or a prefix. Naturally, derived nouns are those so obtained. Examples from English would be words like *man* (simple)+*hood, ly, liness* (derived forms); *un* (prefix)+*man*+*liness* (suffix); *clean* (simple)+*ly, liness, able, er,* (derived forms); *un* (prefix)+*clean*+*liness* (suffix).

The following are the main word-patterns of simple words common to (i) Nouns and (ii) Adjectives, which you should memorise as part of your growing vocabulary, *remembering that adjectives as attributes, unlike English, are placed after the nouns they qualify.* All examples are masculine except those indicated otherwise. The addition of vowel a to a noun or adjective gives the feminine form or the noun which indicates one object. The addition of the fem. suffix to dissyllabic words with the accent on the first syllable causes the omission of the second unstressed vowel.

In the following word-lists note how the different vowels and vocalic sequences in bold create the different word-patterns.

Patterns	Vocabulary

1. KaTiB
(ka'tiib)

(i) Nouns: **xadin** (+a, f.) 'monkey'; **haxix** (+a f.) 'grass'; **halib** 'milk'; **sadid** 'rust'; **tabib** (+a, f.) 'doctor'.

(ii) Adjectives: **hazin** (+a, f.) 'bad'; **qadim** (+a, f.) 'old'; **sabih** (+a, f.) 'lovely'; **marid** (+a, f.) 'sick'.

2. KTiB
(ktiib)

(i) Nouns: **iltim** (+a,f.) 'orphan'; **inbid** 'wine'; **zbib** (+a, f.); 'raisin'. [N.B. i in the first two nouns is euphonic]

(ii) Adjectives: **fqir** (+a, f.) 'poor'; **kbir** (+ a, f.) 'great', 'large'; **tqil** (+ a, f.) 'heavy' or 'difficult'.

This is pattern No. 1 with the first unstressed vowel omitted.

3. KaTeB (m)
KaTBa (f)

('kaateb/
'kaatba)

(i) Nouns: **ragel** 'man'; **ghazeb** 'bachelor'; **ghazel** 'linen'.

(ii) Adjectives: **gharef** (+a, f.) 'wise'; **ghageb** (+a, f.) 'fussy'; **qares** (+ a, f.) 'sour'. In the fem. form unstressed e of the singular is omitted.

4. KaTBa

(i) Nouns: **baqra** 'a cow'; **basla** 'an onion'; **hawha** 'a peach'.

(ii) Adjectives: ħadra 'green' (f.); ħamra 'red' (f.); safra 'yellow' (f.); bajda 'white' (f.).

5. KeTBa   (i) Nouns: sengħa 'art', 'craft'; werqa 'leaf'; xewqa 'a wish'.

     (ii) Adjectives sewda 'black' fem. of iswed; ħelwa 'sweet' fem. of ħelu. Fem. descriptives with semi-vowel J as second radical: sejra 'going away'; żejda 'superfluous'; mejta 'dead'.

6. KoTBa   (i) Nouns: ħorġa 'knapsack'; forka 'gallows'; borka 'a wild duck'.

     (ii) Adjectives: għolja 'high' (sing. f. & pl.); għomja 'blind' (pl.) torja 'tender' (pl.).

(N.B. The vowel o in the adjectives is longer than in the nouns).

7. KoToB   (i) Nouns: kobor 'greatness'; ġobon 'cheese'; ħoġor 'lap'; xogħol 'work'.

     (ii) Adjectives: ħomor 'red' (pl. m. & f.); boloħ 'foolish' (pl. m. & f.); sofor 'yellow'; (pl. m. & f.).

8. KaTT   (i) Nouns: ħall 'vinegar'; ġarr 'carriage'; ħass (+a, f.) 'lettuce'.

     (ii) Adjectives: samm (+ a, f.) 'very hard' (stone); ħarr (+ a, f.) 'acrid'; ċass (+ a, f.) 'fixed' (stare).

9. KoTT   (i) Nouns: ħobb 'bosom'; ħoss 'sound'; moħħ 'brain' or 'mind'.

     (ii) Adjectives: morr (+a, f.) 'bitter'; żorr (+a, f.) 'rude'.

10. KaTTuB   (i) Nouns: **qattus** (+a,f.) 'cat'; **sallur**
    (kat'tuub)   (+a, f.) 'eel'; **ballut** (+a, f.) 'oak
                      tree'; **maġġur** 'major'.

             (ii) Adjectives: **għajjur** (+a,.f.) 'jealous'.

Remark 1: **Għ** and **h**, occurring in a medial position as
2nd radicals of triradical words, having lost their consonantal sound, fall under patterns with a middle long
vowel between the 2nd and 3 rd radicals. Both letters are
retained in the written language to keep unimpaired the
regularity of word-structure. Thus words like **xogħol**,
bogħod, etc. classified under pattern no. 7 phonetically
should be classified under pattern KoB (**koob**) because
they are pronounced '**ʃool** and '**boot**; similarly, words like
bagħal ('**baal**) 'mule'; **lagħaq** ('**laaʔ**) 'he licked'; **saħar**
('**saar**) 'he worked overtime'; **xahar** ('**ʃaar**) 'month'; **xagħar** ('**ʃaar**) 'hair'. which would fall under pattern
KaTaB if the medial radicals were pronounced, phonetically fall under pattern KaaB.

EXERCISE 2

Translate:

   (a) **Raġel għaref u mara** (woman) **għarfa. Hemm
inbid tajjeb** (good) **Malta. Basla ħadra mhix tajba** (good).
Il-bandiera (flag) **ta' (of) Malta bajda u ħamra. Sallura
kbira u baqra sabiħa. Il-qattus annimal** (animal) **għajjur.
Ġanni** (John) **għażeb. Il-kafè** (coffee) **morr. Kafè morr.
Raġel żorr u mara għaġba. It-tabib u l-marid it-tnejn**
(both lit. the two) **għomja.**

   (b) The monkey (fem. and masc.) is jealous. The
learned doctor cured (**fejjaq**) the sick man and the sick
woman.   A white cow amidst (**fost**) the green grass of
Holland (**l-Olanda**).   The flag (**bandiera**) of (**ta'**) Malta
is an old flag. The vinegar is sour. Gozitan (**Għawdxi**)
cheese is good (**tajjeb**). The major is poor and old. Sour
wine becomes (**isir**) vinegar. The Italian language is not
difficult. I heard (**smajt**) a big sound.

Lesson 3

DERIVED NOUNS

Before we deal with derived nouns we must understand that there are other word-patterns common to (i) Simple nouns or (ii) Adjectives only. Remember that the addition of suffix **a** indicating the feminine gender or 'oneness' to dissyllabic nouns or adjectives causes the omission of the second unstressed vowel of the singular. The more common nominal ones are:—

Noun Patterns	Vocabulary

1. KaTB   Exx. **qalb** (+ a, 'kernel') 'heart'; **sajd** (+ a,) 'fishing'; **ħawt** 'trough'.

2. KeTB   Exx. **kelb** (+ a, f.) 'dog' (bitch); **belt** 'city'; **xemx** 'sun'.

3. KiTB   Exx. **ġild** (+ a, 'skin') 'leather'; **ġibs** (+ a,) 'chalk'; **bint** 'daughter'.

4. KoTB   Exx. **qorq** (+ a) 'sandals'; **ħolm** (+ a) 'dreams'; **borġ** 'heap'.

5. KaTaB   Exx. **laħam** (+ a) 'meat'; **baqar** (+ a) 'cows'; **xaħam** (+ a) 'lard'; **ħabaq** (+ a) 'basil'; **għadam** (+ a) 'bones'; **ħaġar** (+ a) 'stones'.

   N.B. A number of nouns conforming to this pattern are collectives.

6. KeTeB   Exx. **nemel** (+ a) 'ants'; **ġemel** 'camel'; **ġebel** (+ a) 'stone'.

The following are the more common patterns of derived nouns:

1. KTuBija (= pattern KTuB + ijja). This is the pat-
   (ktu'biyya) tern of abstract nouns derived from (i) Nouns and (ii) from Adjectives.

(i) *From Simple Nouns*

tfulija 'boyhood' from **tifel** (+ a, f.) 'a boy' (girl).

xbubija 'maiden-hood'   **xebba** 'a maid'.

żgħożija 'youth'   „   **żagħżugħ** (+ a, f.) 'a young man (woman)'.

(ii) *From Adjectives*

sbuħija 'beauty'   „   **sabiħ** (+ a, f.) 'lovely'.

kruħija 'ugliness'   „   **ikrah** (**kerha** f.) 'ugly'.

xjuħija 'old age'   „   **xiħ** (+ a , f.) 'an old man (woman)'.

2. **KTuBa** (This is a variant of the above pattern).
('ktuuba)

bluha 'silliness'   „   **iblah** (m.) **belha** (f) 'silly'.

rtuba 'softness'   „   **artab** (m.) **ratba** (f.) 'soft'.

bjuda 'whiteness'   „   **abjad** (m.) **bajda** (f.) 'white'.

ħmura 'redness'   „   **aħmar** (m.) **ħamra** (f.) 'red'.

N.B. Some colour words can also take the pattern **KTuBija**. Thus we say **bjuda** or **bjudija** 'whiteness'; **ħmura** or **ħmurija**; 'redness'; **sfura** or **sfurija** 'yellowness'; **smura** or **smurija** 'brownness', but **swidija** 'blackness' not **swudija** or **swuda**.

3. **KaTTaB** This is the pattern of nouns which indicate
(kat'taab) names of tradesmen or the doer of the action indicated by the triradical verb.

These word-forms have also an adjectival function. The addition of suffix **a** may indicate the feminine gender and the plural, and, in some cases only, one or the other according to usage.

This word-pattern of nouns and adjectives is obtained by the repetition of the middle radical of the triliteral verb between one of the following vocalic sequences with the main stress on the syllable containing **ie** or long **a**.

(i) a — long a; (ii) a — ie, (iii) e — ie; (iv) i — ie.

(i) **ħajjat** (+ a, f. & pl.) 'tailor' from **ħat** 'he sewed'; **bajjad** (+ a, pl.) 'whitewasher' from **bajjad** 'he whitewashed'; **tallab** (+ a, f. & pl.) 'beggar' from **talab** 'he asked'.

(ii) **qattiel** (+ a, f. & pl.) 'murderer' from **qatel** 'he killed'; **ħalliel** (+a, f.) 'thief' from **ħallel** 'he considered one a thief'; **ħaddiem** (+ a, f. & pl.) 'worker' from **ħadem** 'he worked'.

(iii) **kennies** (+ a, pl.) 'scavenger' from **kines** 'he swept'; **ġennien** (+ a, pl.) 'gardener' from **ġnien** 'garden'; **ġellied** (+ a, f. & pl.) 'quarrelsome' from **ġlied** 'fighting'.

(iv) **nissieġ** (+ a. f. & pl.) 'weaver' from **niseġ** 'he wove'; **giddieb** (+ a, f. & pl.) 'liar' from **gideb** 'he lied'; **kittieb** (+ a, f. & pl.) 'writer' from **kiteb** 'he wrote'.

4. **KeTTeJ** (**ket'tei**) This pattern is derived from verbs the third radical of which in the Root-Verb is semi-vowel **J**, quiescent in the third person singular, masculine, such as **mexa** 'he walked', the three roots of which are **M-X-(J)**.

Exx. **bennej** (+ ja, f. & pl.) 'a builder' from **bena** (j) 'he built'; **ġerrej** (+ ja, f. & pl.) 'a 'jockey', 'runner' from **ġera** (j) 'he ran'; but **qaddej** not **qeddej** 'servant' from **qeda** (j) 'he served'; **qarrej** not **qerrej** 'reader' from **qara** (j) 'he read', because the first radical is **q**, which is generally followed by **a**, and only less frequently by **e**.

Verbs ending in **a**, with third radical **J** quiescent, form the subject-matter of Lesson 24.

MORE DERIVED FORMS

Derived forms are also
(i) nouns obtained from other nouns by prefix **m** known as mimated nouns, dealt with in Lesson 10.

Exx. **mixtla** 'nursery bed' from **xitla** 'plant'; **mħabba** 'love' from **ħabb** 'he loved'.

(ii) diminutive nouns and adjectives (explained in Lesson 6).

Exx. **dwejra** 'small house' from **dar** 'house'; **sbejħa** 'pretty' from **sabiħa** 'lovely'.

(iii) verbal nouns (Lesson 18).

Exx. **rqad** 'sleep' from **raqad** 'he slept'; **ħelsien** 'freedom' from **ħeles** 'he freed'.

EXERCISE 3

Translate:

(a) **Il-bluha tax-** (of) **xjuħija u l-irtuba ta' l-għażż** (sloth). **Il-Kardinal Newman kittieb għaref. Il-bajjad xiħ u l-ħajjat żagħżugħ. Ix-xjuħija kerha u marida. Żagħżugħ u żagħżugħa hallelin. Il-kennies iblah u ġellied iżda** (but) **l-ġennien ħaddiem tajjeb** (good). **It-tallab giddieb u ħalliel. Il-qarrej qara ktieb ġdid** (new). **Il-bjuda tas-**

shab filgħodu (in the morning) u l-ħmura tas-shab fil-għaxija (in the evening) huma dehra (vision) sabiħa.

(b) The beggar is a sick man and the thief is wicked (ħażin) and quarrelsome. The dog of the (tal-) tailor is big and fierce. A week of (ta') hard (iebes) and difficult work. The greenness of grass and the beauty of (taż-) youth. The whiteness of blossoms (taż-żahar) and the enthusiasm (ħeġġa) of boyhood are the poetry (poeżija) of dreams (tal-ħolm). The ugliness of (tax-) old age frightens (tbażża') the young woman and saddens (iddej-jaq) the old woman. The beauty of the holy (qaddis m., qaddisa f.) city (belt f.) of (ta') Jerusalem (Ġerusalemm) The murderer killed the worker. A large (adj. after noun) plant in the (fil-) nursery bed.

Lesson 4

GENDER OF NOUNS AND ADJECTIVES

Nouns and adjectives are either masculine or feminine, according as they indicate males or females, or, in the case of inanimate objects, according to their gender-classification. In the case of inanimate objects, the main rules are:

(1) MASCULINE

(i) all nouns (including verbal nouns) and adjectives ending in a consonant.

Exx. karkur 'slippers'; għażiż 'beloved'; kiefer 'cruel'; taqbil 'versifying'; taħwid 'confusion'; twerwir 'panic'; qerq 'treachery'. The exceptions are (a) *some parts of the human body*:— id 'hand'; għajn 'eye; qalb 'heart'; ras 'head'; sieq 'foot'; żaqq 'belly'. But masculine are moħħ 'brain' or 'mind'; għarqub 'heel'; riġel 'leg'; qadd 'waist'; ġbin 'forehead'; sider 'breast'; dahar 'back' (b) *A few other nouns*: aħbar 'news'; art 'earth'; belt 'city';

dar 'house'; **qmis** 'shirt'; **xemx** 'sun'; **triq** 'road'; **mewt** 'death'; **ruħ** 'soul'.

(ii) Nouns (including verbal nouns) which end in vowels **i** or **u** in open syllable preceded by a short vowel in the previous syllable, with the exception of the names of cities which end in **i**, such as **Brindisi** (f) 'Brindisi'; **Kartaġni** (f) 'Carthage' etc., but not local village names ending in **i**, such as **Il-Qrendi** (m) and **Ħal Safi** (m) in Malta and **l-Għasri** (m) in Gozo. Exx. (i) **sabi** 'young man'; **qari** 'reading'; **ġiri** 'running'; **fili** 'inspection'; **ġeru** 'a pup'; **felu** 'colt'; **delu** 'bucket'; **tosku** 'poison'.

(iii) Verbal nouns ending in **a** in open syllable similarly preceded by a short vowel in the first syllable. Exx. **il-ħala** 'waste'; **il-kera** 'rent'; **il-ħefa** 'barefootedness'; **il-għana** or **l-għana** 'singing'; **il-għama** or **l-għama** 'blindness'; **il-għera** or **l-għera** 'nakedness'.

·(iv) All loan-words ending in **u** in open syllable generally preceded by a long vowel. Ex.. **żelu** 'zeal'; **velu** 'veil'; **kredu** 'creed'; **mertu** 'merit'; **ċertu** 'a certain (person)'; **seklu** 'a century'.

(v) Adjectives which end in **i** in open syllable, preceded by (a) a short or (b) long vowel in the previous syllable. Exx. (a) **tafli** 'clayey'; (b) **għoli** 'high'.

Remark 1: Words falling under group (b) are grammatically present participles of verbs having **J** as their 3rd. radical.

(vi) But of common gender are adjectives of Sicilian or Italian origin ending in **i** in open syllable.

Remark 2: Such adjectives are easily recognisable because most of them are also English loan-words. Exx. **nobbli** 'noble'; **abbli** 'able'; **fabbli** 'affable'; **fraġli** ('fraadʒli') 'frail'; **gravi** 'serious'; **rari** 'rare'.

(2) FEMININE

(i) All adjectives and nouns ending in **a** other than those which indicate males such as **papa** 'Pope'; **eremita** 'hermit'; **seminarista** 'seminarian'; **trappista** 'trappist'; **artista** 'artist'. As a word-termination a indicates (a) the feminine counterpart of the masculine, a single object or (b) unity of action (an action done once — fem. gender).

Exx. (a) **kelba** 'bitch', feminine of **kelb** 'dog' (masc.); **dundjana** 'she-turkey', feminine of **dundjan**; **ħobża** 'a loaf'; from collective noun **ħobż** 'bread'; **ġobna** 'a cheese'; from collective noun **ġobon** 'cheese'; **żarbuna** 'one of a pair of shoes' from **żarbun** 'a shoe' (b) **daħka** 'a laugh', single action from verbal noun **daħk** 'laughter'; **taħwida** 'a mess' from verbal noun **taħwid** 'confusion'.

Exceptions (*masculine nouns ending in* a):— **Alla** 'God'; **sema** 'sky'; **ħama** 'silt'; **hena** 'happiness'; **difa** 'fine cloudless sky generally in winter'; **ilma** 'water'; **mera** 'mirror', sometimes also feminine.

(ii) All nouns generally of Sicilian or Italian origin ending in **i** preceded by a long vowel in the previous syllable: Exx. **vuċi** 'voice'; **kriżi** 'crisis'; **frażi** 'phrase'; **raġuni** 'reason'; **funzjoni** 'function'; **kwistjoni** also **kustjoni** 'question'.

(iii) All nouns ending in **ti** which, like those in the foregoing section, are also of Sicilian or Italian origin. Exx. **arti** 'art'; **parti** 'part'; **xorti** 'luck'; (N.B. Final **ti** can also be the pl. of feminine loan-words ending in **ta**. Exx. **karta** 'paper', pl. **karti**, **santa** 'holy picture', pl. **santi**).

FORMATION OF FEMININE GENDER

The feminine of adjectives and nouns is formed by adding vowel **a** to the last consonant of the masculine form.

In accordance with the law of Maltese stress (p. 30) in dissyllabic words, when the stress falls on the first syllable, the addition of the termination **a** requires the dropping of the unstressed vowel of the original form.

Thus the feminine of armel 'widower' is not armela ('armel + a), but armla ('arm[a] l + a).

Exx. (i) Nouns: kelb (m.) 'dog'; kelba (f.) 'bitch'; tifel (m.) 'boy'; tifla (f.) not tifela 'girl'; seftur (m.) 'man servant'; seftura (f.) 'maid servant'; sieħeb (m.) 'male companion'; sieħba (f.) not sieħeba 'female companion'..

(ii) Adjectives: xiħ (m.) 'old man'; xiħa (f.) 'old woman'; rieqed (m.) 'asleep', rieqda (f.) not rieqeda; maqtul (m.) 'killed', maqtula (f.).

In the case of masculine adjectives ending in the vowel i in open syllable, or nouns so formed which were originally adjectives, the feminine is formed by the addition of ja, with the stress moved one syllable. onwards.

Exx. xemxi ('ʃemʃi) (m.) 'sunny', xemxija (ʃem'ʃiyya) (f.); mistħi 'timid', mistħija (f.); Għawdxi (m.) 'Gozitan', Għawdxija (f.); barrani (m.) 'stranger', barranija (f.); safrani (m.) 'palish' or 'yellowish', safranija (f.); temtumi (m.) 'stammering', temtumija (f.). Exceptions: ġelliedi (m.) 'quarrelsome', ġellieda (not ġellidija (f.); ħabrieki (m.) 'diligent', ħabrieka (f.); rebbieħi (m.) 'victorious', rebbieħa (f.).

In adjectives formed from verbs the third radical of which is j (y), constructed on the pattern KaTi(J) ('kaati(y) or KieTi(J) ('kiəti(y), the termination ja (ya) is added to the final consonant of the masculine adj. after dropping final i, that is, the fem. pattern is KaT or KieT + ja.

Exx. ħali (m.) 'spendthrift'; ħalja (f.) not ħalija; għani (m.) 'rich', għanja (f.); safi (m.) 'pure', safja (f.); miexi (m.) 'walking', miexja (f.); ġieri (m.) 'running' (water), ġierja (f.); but tari (m.) 'tender' has fem. tarja or tarija.

The feminine of the following nouns and adjectives ending in u in open syllable is formed by changing u to wa; Exx. felu (m.) 'colt', felwa (f.) 'filly'; ġeru (m.) 'male pup', ġerwa (f.) 'female pup'; ħelu (m.) ħelwa (f.) 'sweet'.

The following masc. and fem. nouns are formed from different roots:

Exx. għoġol (m.) 'calf', erħa (f.) 'heifer' (also għoġla); irġiel (m.) 'men', nisa (f.) 'women'; raġel (m.) 'man', mara (f.) 'woman'; bodbod (m.) 'he-goat', mogħża (f.) 'she-goat'; missier (m.) 'father', omm (f.) 'mother'; żiemel (m.) 'horse', debba (f.) 'mare'; serduq (m.) 'cock'; tiġieġa (f.) 'hen', gendus (m.) 'ox', baqra (f.) 'cow'; nagħġa (f.) 'sheep'; muntun (m.) 'ram'.

The following form their feminine by adding **t** to the masculine form, this **t** being grammatically known as **t-marbuta**. (See page 58).

Exx. **bin** 'son'/**bint** 'daughter'; **sid** 'master'; 'owner'/**sidt** 'mistress'; **ħu** 'brother'/**oħt** 'sister'; **xbin** 'god-father'/ **xbint** 'god-mother'; **ħaten** 'brother or father or son-in-law' / **ħtint** 'sister or daughter or mother-in-law'.

As in English, in the case of animals when there are no specific gender-designations, gender can be expressed by the words **raġel** ('raadʒəl) 'male' or **mara** ('mara) 'female' placed *after* the name of the animal. Exx. **kanarin raġel** (m.) 'a male canary', **kanarin mara** 'a female canary'.

The feminine of colour-words and some words describing physical quality beginning with a vowel, follows patterns KaTBa or KeTBa, the masculine pattern being variably aKTaB, iKTaB or iKTeB.

Exx. **aħmar** (m.) / **ħamra** (f.) 'red'; **abjad** (m.) / **bajda** (f.) 'white'; **aħdar** (m.) / **ħadra** (f.) 'green'; **isfar** (m.) **safra** (f.) 'yellow'; **ikħal** (m.) / **kaħla** (f.) 'blue'; **iswed** (m.)/**sewda** (f.) 'black'; **iblah** (m.)/**belha** (f) 'silly'; but **oħxon** (m.)/**ħoxna** (f.) 'stout'; or 'base (voice)'.

Remark 1: In **abjad/bajda**; **iswed/sewda**, medial **j** and **w** count as radicals corresponding to the second consonant of the pattern.

But some loan-words can be both singular and plural, masculine and feminine:—

Exx. **kannella** 'brown'; **vjola** 'violet'; **roża** 'pink'; **lelà** 'lilac'; but **griż** (m.), **griża** (f.) **griżi** (pl. both genders) 'grey'.

EXERCISE 4

Translate:

(a) **Din** (this) **aħbar tajba. L-art ta' Malta art għammiela** (fertile). **Valletta hija l-belt ta' Malta u Victoria jew** (or) **ir-Rabat il-belt t'Għawdex. Il-għana Malti u Għawdxi mhux bħall-** (like) **għana barrani. Xiħa temtumija u ġellieda. Il-ħaddiem ħabrieki sid** (the owner of) **din id-dar. Amorin** (budgerigar) **raġel u kanarin mara. Is-Salini triq twila u xemxija. Il-vuċi ħoxna tal-** (of) **baxx** (bass). **Kriżi kbira tax-xogħol u kwistjoni mħawda** (complicated) **ta' finanzi** (finance).

(b) The man is cruel and quarrelsome, but (**iżda**) the woman (=his wife) is bashful and diligent. The blue sky of (**ta'**) Malta is pure and sunny. This (**din** f. and **dan** m.) is good. The old man and the old woman are quarrelsome. The daughter is spendthrift but the father (**missier**) is rich. Grey eyes, rosy cheeks (**ħaddejn**) and brown (adj. after the noun) hair (**xagħar**). A dear son and a cruel daughter. The artist has (**għandu**) a sweet voice. The woman is the mother and the girl is the daughter. The father is the master of the (**tad-**) old house.

Lesson 5

NOUNS IN CONSTRUCTION WITH OTHER NOUNS

THE CONTRUCT STATE

Two nouns are said to be in the Construct State when they follow one another with the first noun governing the second in a genitival relation i.e. expressing possession or close association. The nearest English example is the use of the possessive case as in John's book, but in an inverted order in Maltese ktieb Ġanni. Similarly the advocate's wife, in Maltese mart l-avukat or mart avukat 'an advocate's wife'. Other examples: ġnien sultan 'a king's garden', ġnien is-sultan 'the king's garden'; leħen professur 'a professor's voice', leħen il-professur 'the professor's voice; sid il-għalqa u l-ġnien 'the owner of the field and the garden'; missier u omm il-mara 'the father and mother of the wife'.

The adjective qualifying the first noun follows the second noun. Ex. omm Alla ħanina 'the mother of God is merciful' or omm Alla l-ħanina 'the merciful Mother of God.

When more than one noun follows the first one, only the last noun can take the definite article.

Exx. għeluq snin it-tifla 'the completion of the girl's years' (i.e. the girl's birthday); bieb dar is-sultan 'the door of the Sultan's house'; għeluq snin bint ir-re 'the birthday of the king's daughter'.

But when the last noun is undefined or has a pronominal suffix attached to it, it does not take the definite article. Thus 'a girl's birthday' and 'his wife's birthday' are translated għeluq snin tifla; għeluq snin martu.

Also in the the Construct State is a noun + its possessive pron. suffix (Lesson 11).

Exx. ġar 'neighbour', ġarek 'your neighbour'; omm 'mother', ommha 'her mother'; xewqa 'wish', xewqti 'my wish'.

The Construct State is, however, giving way to the analytical usage of the preposition ta' (of). Exx. Il-mara ta' l-avukat; il-leħen tal-professur: id-dar tiegħi. But it survives in several place-names like Ġebel Ċantar 'Ċantar (surname) hill'; Għajn Tuta 'the fountain of the mulberry tree'; **Għajn Tuffieħa** 'the fountain of the apple tree', etc. **Iben** 'son' in the construct form becomes **bin**:— **Bin Alla** 'the Son of God'; **bin is-sultan** 'the king's son'; **binhom** 'their son'.

Note from the examples given that, while the first noun is never defined by the article, the second or third noun (the possessor) may or may not defiined by the article.

All or most feminine nouns which now end in **a** in open syllable, in classical Arabic ended in **at(un)**, which has been dropped in the dialects, including Maltese. This is the **t** which reappears in the Construct State.

Exx. **nagħġa** 'sheep' / cl. Ar. **'nadʒat(un)**; **mara** 'woman' **ʔimrat(un)**. It will be noticed that in cl. Ar. the **t** of the suffix known as **t marbuta** is bound up with the whole word. This **t** which is dropped in the singular reappears in the ·same feminine noun when this (i) either occurs in construction with another noun immediately following it, or (ii) has the pronominal suffixes attached to it. That is, when it is used in the construct state with another noun. Except in **mara** 'woman', final **a** becomes **et** in the Construct State. Exx. (i) **mara** 'woman' becomes **mart** (short form of **'marat**), when followed by another noun, as in **mart tabib** 'a doctor's wife' or **mart it-tabib** 'the doctor's wife'; **kelma** becomes **kelmet** as in **kelmet is-sultan** 'the king's word'; **reqqa** becomes **reqqet** as in **reqqet il-wiċċ** 'bashfulness'; (ii) **marti** 'my wife'; **martek** 'your wife'; **kelmti** 'my word'; **kelmtek** 'your word' (for **mar** (a) or **kelm**(a) + **t** + pron. suffix **i, ek,** etc.).

There are other combinations of a noun following another in apposition to it not to express possession as in the Contstruct State, but some sort of connection or association. The following are the main examples:—

1. Noun + Noun:— This construction covers a number of semantic functions indicating:

(i) *fullness*

Exx. **tazza birra** (lit. glass beer) 'a glass óf beer'; **qoffa laring** (lit. basket oranges) 'a basketful of oranges'.

(ii) *part of a whole.*

Exx. **felli laringa** (lit. slice orange) 'a slice of orange'; **bicca hobż** (lit. piece bread) 'a piece of bread'.

(iii) *large or small quantity.*

Ex. **hafna, ftit flus** 'much, little money'.

(iv) *measure of space, value or time.*

Exx. **modd raba'** 'a modd (measure) of cultivated land'; **lira kotba** 'a pound's worth of books.'; **xelin haxix** 'a shilling's worth of vegetables'; **kwarta mixi** 'a quarter of an hour walking'.

2. When the two nouns are the same noun repeated, the combination serves to indicate a sequence or distribution of the objects indicated by such nouns.

Exx. **dar dar** 'house to house' or 'one house after another'; **hamsa hamsa** 'five at a time' or 'in sequences of five'.

The second noun in the above construction Noun + Noun can have the function of a descriptive, like any adjective.

Exx. **ragel tabib** 'a medical man'; **ragel hanżir** 'a gluttonous or greedy man', literally 'man doctor'; 'man pig'.

NOUNS IN CONSTRUCTION WITH ADJECTIVES

While nouns can stand alone within the context of a phrase or sentence, adjectives have often to be used to describe them. The following are examples of idiomatic usages obtained by the joint construction of a noun and an adjective or, as one might say, a Nominal to indicate any word which can be used as a noun and a Descriptive to indicate any word which can be used as an adjective.

1. Nouns and adjectives agree in gender and number, the plural being common to both genders. The adjec-

tive follows the noun, except the superlative which precedes the noun it qualifies.

Exx. **suldat qalbieni** 'a courageous soldier'; **suldati qalbe-
nin** 'brave soldiers'; **raġel (mara) għaref (għarfa)** 'a
learned man (woman)'; **nisa għorrief** 'learned women';
l-ogħla sur 'the highest bastion'; **l-isbaħ mara, raġel, nisa,
irġiel** 'the most beautiful woman, man, women, men'.

2. The adjective, when it qualifies a verb, has also
the function of an adverb. A similar usage in English is
that of 'quick' and 'loud', which can be used both as an
adjective and as an adverb.

Exx. **jikteb** (he writes) **sabiħ** (beautiful) 'he writes beautifully'; **jimxi** (he walks) **mgħaġġel** (hurried) 'he walks
hurriedly'.

3. The repetition of the same adjective qualifying
a noun indicates (i) a characteristic quality of the noun:
Exx. **raġel mutu mutu** (lit. 'a man dumb dumb') 'a man
who hardly ever says a word'; **raġel twil twil** 'a very tall
man' (ii) the manner of action when it qualifies a verb:
Exx. **taħ l-aħbar ħażina ħelu ħelu** 'he gave him (broke)
the bad news very gently'; **jimxi ħafif ħafif** (lit. 'he walks
brisk brisk') 'he walks very briskly'; **tikteb pulit pulit** (lit.
'she writes neat, neat') 'she writes very neatly'; **daħal
baxx baxx** 'he entered stealthily or unobtrusively'.

4. When the noun is defined by the article, the
adjective may or may not be defined also by the definite
article.

Exx. **il-karrozza l-ġdida** or **il-karrozza ġdida** 'the new car'.
But the meaning of the latter is ambiguous on account
of the reason given in the following rule.

5. When the noun accompanied by the definite
article is followed by an adjective undefined by the article, the combination is equivalent to a sentence in English.
The reason is that already pointed out, namely, that
Maltese has no verb 'to be'. Hence, **il-karrozza ġdida**,

given in the above example could also méan 'the car is new'.

6. All descriptives can be used as nouns if they take the definite article and follow the general rules governing the adjectives.

Exx. il-maqtul ħalla familja ta' sitt itfal 'the murdered man left a family of six children'; il-marid għadda għall-agħar 'the sick man has grown worse'.

7. Collective nouns ending in a consonant other than those which are broken plurals (see Lesson 9) take the masculine adjective.

Exx. il-bajtar misjur 'prickly pears are ripe' or 'ripe prickly pears'; il-qamħ niexef 'the corn is dry' or 'the dry corn'.

EXERCISE 5

Translate:

(a) Xorob tazza ħalib (milk) aħjar minn tazza ilma. Mart is-sultan marida ħafna (very). Tal-ħalib, tal-ħaxix u tal-laħam qegħdin (are) is-suq (market). Martek xtrat ratal (= 28ozs) majjal (pork) u nofs artal (for nofs ratal) ċanga (beef). Fredu (Alfred) raġel ta' saħħa (strength) kbira. Il-Milied hu jum ta' ferħ għad-dinja Nisranija (Christian world). Għajn Tuta isem (name) post (place) f'Għawdex u Għajn Tuffieħa isem post f'Malta. Għall-(for the) Insara, Ġesù Kristu huwa Bin Alla. Bieb id-dar magħluq (shut). Illum (today) għeluq snin ommha.

(b) Give me (agħtini) a glass of wine. The soldier's wife is ill. I bought (xtrajt) a pound's worth (lira) of meat (laħam). It is a quarter-of-an-hour's walk from Valletta to Floriana. A woman of character (karattru). The milkman, the greengrocer and the butcher are friends (ħbieb). He talks (jitkellem) hurriedly but (iżda) writes (jikteb) beautifully. I saw the new car. A house to house visit (żjara, begins the phrase). Little money for much work.

Lesson 6

THE DIMINUTIVE AND COMPARATIVE FORMS

Maltese, like Arabic, has also the diminutive form of the noun and the adjective, a form which indicates (i) physical smallness or (ii) gracefulnes, English examples formed by suffixes being words like 'rivulet', 'lambkin', 'kitten', 'duckling' etc. Its usage in Maltese has become restricted to a few nouns and adjectives.

Masculine diminutives are formed by means of -ajja-, -ajje-, -ejja-, or -ejje- infixed between the second and third radicals of the word with the stress on the first syllable. The feminine is formed by adding -a to the masculine diminutive with the omission of the short unaccented penultimate -je or -ja according to the general rule of Maltese stress which does not permit two unstressed syllables after the stressed syllable. Many of the nominal and adjectival diminutive forms given in grammar books are not used in the spoken language. They form their plural by the addition of stressed suffix in (iin).

Memorise the following living survivals:—

PATTERN 1

KTajjaB ('ktayyab) more frequently **KtajjeB** (m.) ('ktayyeb)/**KTajBa** (f.) ('ktayba). (i) Nouns: ħmajjar/ ħmajra 'a little donkey', dim. of ħmar/ħmara 'donkey/ she-ass'; tfajjel/tfajla 'a young man/woman'; dim. of tifel/tifla 'boy/girl'. (Note that the connotation of this dim. form is affection and not physical smallness); xtajta 'shore', dim. form of xatt (connotation of grace). (ii) Adjectives: fqajjar (m.)/fqajra (f.) 'rather poor' dim. of fqir/fqira (connotation of sympathy); smajjar/smajra 'brownish', dim. of ismar/samra; dgħajjef/dgħajfa 'rather thin, weak', dim. of dgħif/dgħifa (unused).

PATTERN 2

KTejjaB (m.) ('kteyyab)/**KTejBa** (f.) ('kteyba). (i) Nouns: **ġnejna** 'a little garden', dim. form of **ġnien**; **dwejra** 'cottage', dim. of **dar** 'house'. (ii) Adjectives: **sbejjaħ** (m.)/**sbejħa** (f.) 'rather fine', dim. form of **sabiħ**/**sabiħa** (connotation of grace); **xwejjaħ/xwejħa** 'old', dim. of **xiħ/xiħa** 'old man/woman' (connotation of affection). A few words form their diminutive by suffix -a:

Exx. but 'pocket', **buta** 'a small pocket'; **fies** 'pickaxe', **fiesa** 'a small pickaxe'; **zappun** 'a mattock'; **zappuna** 'a small mattock'; **forn** 'oven', **forna** 'a small oven'.

THE COMPARISON OF ADJECTIVES

The main function of an adjective is that of qualifying the noun by merely describing it in itself or in its relation to another noun. Hence, the addition of three comparative degrees of the adjectives, namely, that of (i) equality or likeness (ii) relative superiority or inferiority to another term of comparison (iii) the absolute comparative degree of a noun described in itself by means of adverbs or adjectival phrases without any specific reference to other terms of comparison. Exx. **ħelu wisq** or **ħafna**, 'very sweet'; **raġel mill-aħjar** 'a very good man'; **palazz mill-isbaħ** 'one of the loveliest palaces' or 'a most lovely palace'.

The comparative degree of adjectives with or without reference to another term of comparison is formed by prefixing **a, e, i** or **o** to the first two radicals the second of which is separated from the third radical by **i** or **e** with the stress invariably on the first syllable.

The Maltese conjunction for English 'than' which introduces the second member of the comparison is **minn** 'from' the second doubled consonant of which (**nn**) assimilates with the definite article. The superlative which precedes the noun it qualifies is formed by prefixing the definite article **l-** to the comparative degree.

Exx. **it-tifel itwal mit-tifla** 'the boy is taller than the girl' (**mit = minn + it**); **l-itwal tifel fil-klassi** 'the tallest boy in the class'.

If the comparative adjective is followed by a clause, the conjunction used is **milli** (= **minn** 'from' + **li** 'which', 'that'). Exx. **aktar jitkellem milli jaħdem** 'he speaks more than he works'; **aħjar milli taħseb** 'better than you think'.

COMPARATIVE FORMS

Remark 1: Note that the following comparatives are invariable being applicable to both genders and numbers, and that the first vowel is stressed and therefore **i** is not changed into **j** when preceded by another vowel. Ex. **kienu itwal** 'they were taller' not **kienu jtwal**.

Patterns		Vocabulary
aKTaB or aKTa (J)	(i)	Exx. **akbar** 'greater', 'older'/**kbir** (m.) (+ a, f.) **anqas** 'less'/**nieqes** (m.) **nieqsa** (f.) **aktar** 'more'; no positive degree; **aqwa** 'stronger'/**qawwi** (m.) (+ ja, f.).
iKTaB	(ii)	Exx. **ibgħad** 'farther'/**bgħid** (m.) (+ a, f.); **idjaq** 'narrower'/**dejjaq** (m.) **dejqa** (f.); **ifqar** 'poorer'/**fqir** (m.) (+ a, f.); **iqsar** 'shorter'/**qasir** (m.) (+ a, f.); **iżgħar** 'smaller'/**żgħir** (m.) (+ a, f.) **irħas** (or **orħos**) 'cheaper'/**irħis** (m.) (+ a, f.); **irqaq** 'thinner'/**irqiq** (m.) (+ a, f.).
eKTeB	(iii)	Exx. **eħrex** 'fiercer'/**aħrax** (m.) **ħarxa** (f.); **eħżen** 'worse'/**ħażin** (m.) (+ a, f.); **eħxen** 'stouter'/**oħxon** (m.) **ħoxna** (f.); **eqdem** 'older'/**qadim** (m.) (+a, f.); **eqreb** 'nearer'/**qarib** (m.) (+ a, f.); **eħfef** 'lighter'/**ħafif** (m.) (+ a, f.); **egħref** 'wiser'/**għaref** (m.) **għarfa** (f.); **egħżeż** 'dearer'/**għażiż** (m.) (+ a, f.).;

iKTeB   (iv) Exx. iċken 'smaller'/ċkejkén (m.) ċkej-
               kna (f.);   ismen 'fatter'/smin (m.)
               (+ a, f.);   itjeb 'better'/tajjeb (m.)
               tajba (f.).

oKTa(J)   Exx.   oħla 'sweeter'/ħelu (m.) ħelwa
               (f.); ogħla 'higher'/għali (m.) għalja
               (f.); ogħna 'richer'/għani (m.) għanja
               (f.).

UNUSUAL FORMATIONS

The comparative of wiesa' (m.) wiesgħa (f.) 'wide' is
usa'. Aħjar 'better' (stress on the second syllable) and
agħar 'worse' (stress on the first syllable), have no posi-
tive degree from the same radicals. Note the spelling of
agħar 'worse', pronounced like, but to be distinguished
from, għar meaning 'cave', and also 'disgrace' in the
phrase għarukaża 'scandal', 'great shame', for għar
'shame' + u (and) + każa 'scandal'.

Exx. Ħuk akbar minnek 'your brother is older than you';
aħjar għasfur f'idek milli mija fl-ajru 'better a bird in
your hand than a hundred in the air'; il-jasar agħar mill-
mewt 'slavery is worse than death'; ftit aħjar minn xejn
'a little is better than nothing'. The pattern of the comparative aKTaB and other vocalic sequences + minn =
English comparative adjective + than.

The pattern of the Superlative is the definite article
l- + aKTaB with the other vocalic sequences + fost
'amongst', when followed by a noun indicating any object
other than a place, animal etc., or + fi 'in' when the
object indicated by the noun is a place.

Exx. Dun Karm hu l-akbar fost il-poeti kollha Maltin,
'Dun Karm is the greatest of (lit. amongst) all Maltese
poets'; Sant Anton hu l-isbaħ ġnien tal-Kavalieri f'Malta,
'San Anton is the loveliest grove of the Knights (of St.
John) in Malta'.

Adjectives which (i) begin with a vowel, such as the

colour words **aħmar** 'red', **isfar** 'yellow' etc., (ii) verbal descriptives other than adjectives proper; and (iii) adjectives of foreign origin as a rule form their comparative degree by taking **aktar** or **iżjed** 'more', **anqas** 'less' + the definite article for the superlative to indicate the higher or the highest, the less or the least degree of comparision.

Exx. **iżjed** (also **aktar**) or **inqas iebes, edukat, pulit, magħruf** etc. 'more, less hard, well-educated, polite, known, etc.'; and for the superlative degree **l-iżjed** (or **l-aktar**) **l-anqas iebes**, etc. 'the most, the least hard, etc.'.

OTHER COMPARATIVE FUNCTIONS

The comparison of (i) likeness is indicated by **bħal** ('like' also 'as') and (ii) of equality by **daqs** (as much as'), both of which can either be followed by the other term of comparison or are used independently with the pronominal suffixes attached to them.

Exx. (i) **Dan bħal dak** 'this is like that'; **jitkellem bħal wieħed għaref** 'he talks like a wise man'; **hi mhix bħalu u lanqas bħalhom** 'she is neither like him nor like them'; (ii) **twil daqs ħuh** 'as tall as his brother'; **xiħ daqsha** 'as old as she'.

An archaic comparative formed by the particle **ma** (**m'** before a vowel) + the comparative degree of the adjective survives in a few expressions.

Exx. **raġel m'ogħla sur'** 'a man as tall as a bastion' (hyperbolic) for 'a very tall man'; **m'isbaħ** (many say **l-isbaħ**) **l-indafa** (cleanliness) 'good riddance'; **m'oħxon saba'** 'as thick as a finger'.

SOME IDIOMATIC PHRASAL COMPARISONS

(a) *Colour*: **Iswed borma** (pot) 'as black as coal'; **abjad silġ** or **qotna** (cotton) 'as white as snow'; **aħdar busbies** (fennel) or **ħaxix** 'as green as grass'; **aħmar nar** (fire) 'as red as blood'; **isfar leliux** (garden chrysanthemum) 'as yellow as a guinea'; **iħkal nir** (indigo) 'sky blue'.

(b) *Palate*: **Ħelu manna** (manna) or **zokkor** 'as sweet as sugar'; **morr tosku** (poison) 'as bitter as gall'; **qares ħall** 'as sour as vinegar'.

(c) *Measure*: **Wiesa' baħar** (or **ħorġ**) 'as wide as an ocean (or knapsack)' (used in connection with baggy trousers etc.); **dejjaq katusa** (pipe) 'as narrow as a drainpipe'.

Other Comparisons: **Iebes għuda** (wood) 'as hard as stone'; **artab ħaxu** (soft cheese) 'as soft as butter'; **imxarrab għasra** (soaking), **fellus** (chicken) 'as wet as a drowned rat'; **niexef qoxqox** (parched) 'as dry as dust'; **ibleh karnival** (Carnival) (lit. as foolish as Carnival) 'stupid as a clown'; **xiħ għakka** (decrepit) 'as old as the hills'; **ħafif rix** 'as light as a feather'; **tqil ċomb** 'as heavy as lead'; **nadif tazza** (lit. as clean as a glass) 'as clean as a new pin'; **tari baqta** (curdled cream) 'as soft as butter'.

(i) Additional Usages of Nouns

1. Unlike English, the object possessed by more than one noun is put in the singular. Exx. **L-irġiel siefru u ħallew il-mara** (woman = wife) **Malta** 'the men emigrated and left their wives in Malta'; **malli fetħu ħalqhom** (their mouth) **sikkithom** 'as soon as they opened their mouths (i.e. tried to speak) he silenced them'.

2. Nouns of (i) *place* and (ii) *time* are often used without a preposition. Exx. (i) **Hu baqa' Malta** 'he remained in Malta'; **wasal l-Ingilterra ġimgħa wara** 'he arrived in England a week after'; **mort Londra s-sena l-oħra** 'I went to London last year'; **inħobb noqgħod iddar** 'I like staying at home'; (ii) **niġi l-Ħamis li ġej** 'I will come next Thursday'; **għamel sentejn jistudja l-lingwi** 'he spent two years studying languages'.

(ii)   Additional Usages of Adjectives

1. The rule that the adjective follows the noun applies to all other words with a descriptive function. Exx. **Tifel maħbub** 'a loved boy'; **it-tifel il-maħbub** 'the loved boy'.

2. The adjective before the noun occurs in a few formal or stereotyped phrases not accepted in good literature. Exx. **Egħżież uliedi** 'my dear children' (rhetorical); **il-maħub ibni** 'my beloved son'.

3. In the case of an absolute superlative degree formed by **l-aktar, l-iżjed** or **l-inqas**, the order is **l-aktar** etc. + the noun + the adjective of which is expressed the highest or least quality.

Exx. **l-iktar (l-iżjed** or **l-inqas) (superlative) tifel (tifla, tfal) intelliġenti** 'the most (least) intelligent boy (girl, children)'; also less effectively **it-tifel l-aktar intelliġenti**.

EXERCISE 6

Translate:

(a) **Xwejjaħ u xwejħa fi dwejra ħdejn** (near) **il-baħar. Il-ġnejna ta' Pietru** (Peter) **akbar minn dik** (that) **ta' Ġanni** (John). **Dante l-aqwa poeta** (poet) **tad-dinja** (world). **L-irħis għali** (is dear). **L-egħżeż ħabib** (friend) **tiegħi siefer** (emigrated) **ilbieraħ** (yesterday). **Iċ-ċkejken ħelu imma l-iċken oħla. L-anqas xogħol iebes** (hard work) **hu wkoll** (also) **l-eħfef. Tifel ħelu wisq u raġel mill-aħjar. Toni** (Anthony) **iblah karnival. Marija** (Mary) **mara nadifa tazza. L-iktar poeta Malti magħruf** (known) **hu Dun Karm Psaila.**

(b) Xlendi is a lovely bay (**bajja**) in Gozo. A little garden and a cottage in Marsalforn, a sunny bay in Gozo. This street (road) is wider than the old street of (**tar-**) my (**tiegħi** after noun) village (**raħal**). John is older than Anthony. Maltese is like Arabic, but it is not as difficult as Arabic. He was born (**twieled**) in Malta, but lived (**għex**) in Gozo. A rather poor and weak woman as old as the rocks. The tiger (**tigra**) is fiercer than the (**mill-**) lion (**ljun**) Peter is as old as Michael (**Mikiel**). "Good riddance" said (**qal**) Joseph (**Ġużè**).

Lesson 7

NUMBERS

Maltese has three numbers: (i) the singular which indicates one person or thing, (ii) the dual which indicates things in pairs, and (iii) the plural number indicating more than two things.

THE DUAL

The dual is formed by adding (i) suffix -**ejn** to the last consonant of the singular; (ii) -**ajn**, if this last consonant is **għ**, **h** or **q**; (iii) -**tejn**, if the singular noun is feminine and ends in the vowel **a** which is dropped. As these dual terminations attract the stress on to themselves, the original stress of the word is lost to conform to the stress pattern, according to which one word cannot have more than one main accent or stressed syllable.

Exx. (i) **elf/elfejn** 'a thousand/two thousand'; (ii) **siegħ** (siəh)/**sigħajn** (si'ain) 'a kind of Maltese measure for area or capacity/two such measures'; **ġewnaħ/ġwinħajn** 'wing/two wings'; **sieq/saqajn** 'foot/two feet'; (iii) **darba/darbtejn** 'once/twice'.

When the dual suffix -**tejn** is attached to feminine nouns, the 3rd consonant of which is **l**, **m**, **n**, **r** or **għ** (by analogy), the resultant triconsonantal group is broken up by the insertion of a vowel before the 3rd radical. This vowel can be (i) **a**, generally when the 3rd radical is **għ**. Exx. **fergħa/feragħtejn** 'branch/two branches'; **gimgħa/gimagħtejn** 'week/two weeks'; (ii) vowel **i** when the first vowel after the first consonant is

i. Exx. wiżna/wiżintejn '5 rotolos/10 rotolos'; **widna/
widintejn** 'ear/two ears'. (iii) vowel o when the first vowel
after the first consonant is o. Exx. **ħofra/ħofortejn** 'hole/
two holes'; **qoxra/qoxortejn** 'husk/two husks'.

The use of the dual is limited to:—

(i) *A few time-words*: Exx. **sena** ('sena)/**sentejn**
(sen'tein) 'one year/two years'; **jum/jumejn** 'one day/
two days'; **xahar/xahrejn** 'one month/two months';
siegħa/sagħtejn 'one hour/two hours'; **ġimgħa/ġimagħ-
tejn** 'one week/two weeks'.

(ii) *Some quantity and measure-words*: Exx. **mija**
('miyya)/**mitejn** (mi'tein) 'one hundred/two hundred';
elf/elfejn 'one thousand/two thousand'; **ħabba/ħab-
btejn** 'one grain/two grains'; **qantar/qantarejn** 'hun-
dred/two hundred rotolos'; **xiber/xibrejn** 'one span/two
spans'.

(iii) *Some nouns indicating food*: Exx. **bajda**
('baida)/**badtejn** (bat'tein) 'one egg/two eggs'; **ħobża/
ħbiżtejn** 'one loaf/two loaves'; **ġobna/ġbintejn** 'one
cheese/two cheeses'.

(iv) *A few odd words*: Exx. **darba** ('darba)/**darbtejn** (darb'tein) 'once/twice'; **daqqa/daqqtejn** 'one
stroke/two strokes'.

(v) *Some parts of the human body which exist in
pairs*: It must be noted, however, that though these are
grammatically dual formations, in actual usage they are
used as ordinary plurals for any number.

Exx. **id** (iit)/**idejn** (i'dein) 'one hand/hands' (lit. a pair
of hands); **difer/difrejn** 'a finger nail/finger nails' (lit. a
pair of finger nails); **saba'/subgħajn** 'a finger/fingers' (lit.
a pair of fingers); **ħadd/ħaddejn** 'one cheek/cheeks' (lit.
a pair of cheeks); **driegħ/dirgħajn** 'one arm/arms' (lit.
a pair of arms); **sieq/saqajn** 'one foot/feet' (lit. a pair of
feet); **ġewnaħ/ġwinħajn** 'one wing/wings' (lit. a pair of
wings); **koxxa** (from Italian coscia) **koxxtejn** 'thigh/
thighs' (lit. a pair of thighs).

(N.B. **mnifsejn** 'nostrils' and **minkbejn** 'elbows' are dual formations of **minfes** 'a nostril' (unused) and **minkeb** 'an elbow'. **Ħuġbejn** 'eye-brows' is the dual of obsolete **ħaġeb**).

(vi) *A few words ending in a which form their dual by termination* -ejn *not* -tejn *added to the last consonant.*

Exx. **spalla** ('spalla) from Italian/**spallejn** (spal'lein) one shoulder/shoulders' (lit. a pair of shoulders); **tomna/ tomnejn** 'two tumoli' (one **tomna**, a field measure = 0.278 acres); **widna / widnejn** 'one ear / ears' (lit. a pair of ears).

DETERMINATE AND INDETERMINATE PLURALS

The general plural can be either *Determinate*, and therefore must be preceded by the number of things, objects or persons counted or *Indeterminate*, that is uncounted, generally collective nouns.

(i) *Singular*	(ii) *Determinate*	(iii) *Collective*
bajda (f.) 'an (one) egg'	**żewġ, tliet bajdiet** (f.) 'two, three eggs'	**bajd** (m.) 'eggs'.
ġobna (f.) 'a (one) cheese'	**erba', ħames ġobniet** (f.) 'four, five cheeses'	**ġobon** (m.) 'cheese'
ħuta (f.) 'a (one) fish'	**sitt, seba' ħutiet** (f.) 'six, seven fish(es)'	**ħut** (m.) 'fish'.
kelma (f.) 'a (one) word'	**tmien, disa' kelmiet** (f.) 'eight, nine words'	**kliem** (m.) 'words'.
frotta (f.) 'a (one) fruit'	**għaxar frottiet** (f.) 'ten fruits'	**frott** (m.) 'fruit'.

NUMBER AND GENDER OF COLLECTIVE NOUNS

1. Collective nouns ending in a consonant, though not without some exceptions, are regarded as (i) singular

and masculine if the the object they indicate is *inanimate*
and as (ii) plural if the object indicated is *animate*,
generally animals other than those of small size and
insects.

Exx. (i) ħobż (ġobon, lariṅg, għeneb, frott, etc.) tajjeb
(sing. & masc.) 'good bread (cheese, oranges, grapes, fruit,
etc.)' but siġar sbieħ (pl. for both genders) 'beautiful
trees'; (ii) baqar (mogħoż, ngħaġ, etc.) sbieħ (pl.)
'beautiful cows (goats, sheep, etc.) but ħut sabiħ (sing. m.)
not sbieħ (pl.) 'beautiful fish', naħal bieżel (sing. m.) not
beżlin (pl.) 'busy bees'; nemel itir (sing. m.) not itiru
(pl.) 'flying ants'.

2. In both cases such collective nouns can be turned
into the expression of their units i.e. singular nouns, by
the addition of suffix a after the omission of the second
unstressed vowel in dissyllabic words which have the
stress on the first syllable.

Exx. ħobż/ħobża 'a loaf'; ġobon/ġobna 'a cheese-cake';
lariṅg/lariṅga 'an orange'; għeneb/għenba 'one berry of
a grape'; frott/frotta 'a fruit'; baqar/baqra 'a cow';
ngħaġ/nagħġa 'a sheep'.

Other Collective Nouns: These are mostly loan-words
ending in i some of which are regarded as (1) singular of (i) masculine or (ii) feminine gender or (2)
as plurals. Exx. (i) gawwi (abjad)/gawwija (bajda) 'white
seagulls/seagull'; ġiżi abjad/ġiża bajda 'white stocks/
stock'; lumi qares/lumija qarsa 'bitter lemons/lemon';
kaħli (from Maltese roots) frisk/kaħlija friska 'fresh
blacktails/blacktail' (name of a Mediterranean fish); (ii)
ċawsli (frawli, naspli, pitravi, piżelli, kaboċċi) friska/
ċawsla (frawla, naspla, pitrava, piżella, kaboċċa) friska
'fresh white mulberries (strawberries, medlars, beetroots,
peas, cabbages)/mulberry (strawberry, medlar, beetroot,
pea, cabbage)'; (2) papoċċi (buqari, gladjoli) bojod/papoċ-
ċa bajda (buqar abjad, gladjola bajda) 'white snap-
dragons (African lilies, gladioli)/snapdragon (African
lily gladiolus)'.

Also collectives are some names of fruits and plants ending in **a** either (i) with the definite article or (ii) without it but 'followed by an adjective or adjectival phrase or preceded by a quantity word. Exx. (i) **il-patata, il-banana, iċ-ċirasa,** which can mean either 'the potato', 'the banana', 'the cherry' or 'potatoes', 'bananas', 'cherries' in a collective sense fem. and sing. (ii) **ħafna patata (banana, ċirasa)** 'a great quantity of potatoes (bananas, cherries)'; **patata (banana, ċirasa) tajba (or ta' barra)** 'good (imported) potatoes (bananas, cherries)'.

EXERCISE 7

Translate:

(a) **Sentejn u xahrejn ta'** (of) **xogħol iebes** (hard). **Hu kellu** (he had) **bajda, jien kelli żewġ bajdiet, imma hi kellha erba' bajdiet. Għandu** (he has) **dirgħajn sħaħ ta' ġgant** (giant) **u għajnejn ta' seqer** (hawk). **Ġimagħtejn bla** (without) **xogħol agħar mill-mewt għal raġel fqir. Feragħtejn maqtugħa** (cut) **minn** (from) **siġra** (tree) **qadima. Qantarejn patata** (potatoes) **u elfejn tiġieġa** (hen). **Tkellem** (he spoke) **darbtejn; darba għal xejn. Għaxar laringiet** (oranges) **u seba' ħawħiet** (peaches). **Ġwinħajn l-għasfur miksura** (broken). **Badtejn, ġbintejn, ħobża u flixkun** (bottle) **inbid għall-ħaddiem.**

(b) I saw (**rajt**) the house twice. I want (**irrid**) two loaves, two eggs and two cheeses. Six fried (**moqlija**) eggs and nine grilled (**mixwija**) fishes. One word is better than two words. Words are dangerous (**perikoluż**). Strong arms and feet for hard work and running. A fine figure (**figura**), broad shoulders, clear (**safja** f.) eyes and rosy cheeks. A basketful (**qoffa**) of fruit for the orphans (**iltiema**). One bad fruit spoils (**tħassar**) a hundred. Fruit is scarce (**skars**) in winter (**fix-xitwa**). Her brothers (**ħutha**) bought her (**xtrawlha**) a big fish.

Lesson 8

THE FORMATION OF THE PLURAL

Maltese, like Arabic, has two types of plural formations for both nouns and adjectives, namely, (i) the plural obtained by the addition of suffixes called Sound or External Plurals: and (ii) plurals obtained by breaking up the internal structure of the singular form (Broken or Internal Plurals).

PLURAL BY SUFFIXES

Remark 1: Plural suffixes bear the main stress of the word. As a result of this, the original stress of the singular word is moved one syllable onward which is the last syllable formed by the plural suffix.

The plural suffixes are:—

(1) -n (2) in ('iin); (3) -at ('aat) or -iet ('iət); (4) -ijiet (iy'yiət); (5) -an ('aan) or -ien ('iən) and finally (6) unstressed -a.

(1) Termination **n** is used for the plural of adjectives ending in i in open syllable:—

Exx. **baħri** / **baħrin** 'sailor/s'; **Malti** / **Maltin** 'a Maltese / Maltese (people)'; **Għawdxi** / **Għawdxin** 'a Gozitan / Gozitans'.

(2) Stress-bearing **-in** is suffixed

(i) To some nouns and adjectives conforming to pattern KaTTieB and its variations:—

Exx. sing. **ħalliel**/pl. **ħallilin** 'thief/thieves'; **qattiel**/**qattilin** 'murderer/s'; **ġellied** / **ġellidin** 'quarrelsome'; **giddieb** / **giddibin** 'liar/s'.

(ii) To adjectives conforming to pattern KaTeB ('kaateb) or KieTeB ('kiəteb) after the elision of the 2nd unstressed vowel.

Exx. sing. **tajjeb** (m.) **tajba** (f.) **tajbin** (pl.) 'good'; **biered** (m.) **bierda** (f.) **berdin** (pl.) 'cool'; **nieżel** (m.) **nieżla** (f.)

neżlin (pl.) 'descending'. Note that ie which always bears the main stress in the sing, on losing the main stress which is attracted by the suffix, becomes unstressed i or e, according to the general rule.

(iii) To the third radical of the Passive participles conforming to pattern maKTuB, (mak'tuub) with variable vocalic sequences:—

Exx. sing. maqtul (m.) maqtula (f.) maqtulin (pl.) 'killed'; mahbub (m.) mahbuba (f.) mahbubin (pl.) 'loved'; mehlus (m.) mehlusa (f.) mehlusin (pl.) 'freed'; miksur (m.) miksura (f.) miksurin (pl.) 'broken'.

(iv) To singular adjectives ending in an or ien (alternative for ani or ieni):—

Exx. bahnan (m.) bahnana (f.) bahnanin (pl.) 'silly'; belhieni (m.) belhiena (f.) belhenin (pl.) 'foolish'; ghatxan (m.) ghatxana (f.) ghatxanin (pl.) 'thirsty'; xewqan (m.) xewqana (f.) xewqanin (pl.) 'desirous'.

(v) To the third radical of adjectives of the diminutive pattern KTajjeB (m.) KTajBa (f.) KTejjeB (m.) KTejBa (f.) (Lesson 6).

Exx. sing. twajjeb (m.) twajba (f.) twajbin (pl.) 'good'; sbejjah (m.) sbejha (f.) sbejhin (pl.) 'pretty'; fqajjar (m.) fqajra (f.) fqajrin (pl.) 'poor'. Note elision of 2nd unstressed vowel of the masc. adj. as in (ii).

(vi) To masc. adjectival forms ending in i (pattern m. KieTi/f. KieTja) from verbs the third radical of which is quiescent j (Lesson 24) changing final i into j which precedes the stress-bearing plural suffix or to final j of the fem. form.

Exx. hieni (m.) hienja (f.) henjin (pl.) 'happy' (from radicals H-N-[J]). Similarly hati (m.) hatja (f.) hatjin (pl.) 'guilty'; safi (m.) safja (f.) safjin (pl.) 'pure'; ġieri (m.) ġierja (f.) ġerjin (pl.) 'running' (water); mibni (m.) mibnija (f.) mibnijin (pl.) 'built'; mimli (m.) mimlija (f.) mimlijin (pl.) 'full'; minsi (m.) minsija (f.) min-

sijin (pl.) 'forgotten'; **mgħobbi** (m.) **mgħobbija** (f.) **mgħobbijin** (pl.) 'loaded'.

(3) The suffix **-at** or **iet** is added to the 3rd consonant of the singular feminine nouns ending in **a**:—

Exx. sing. **xewqa/xewqat** (pl.) also **xewqiet** 'wish/wishes'; **werqa/werqat** also **werqiet** 'leaf/leaves'; **felwa/felwiet** 'filly/fillies'; **xebba/xebbiet** 'young lady/young ladies'; **mħadda / mħaddiet** 'pillow/s'; **mgħażqa / mgħażqiet** 'spade/s'; plural of mimated nouns. (Lesson 10). An exceptional formation is **dnubiet**, pl. of **dnub** 'sin', which, in spite of its singular meaning, is the broken plural of an obsolete singular.

(4) **-ijiet (iy'yiət)** is suffixed to the last consonant of a few native words of both genders.

Exx. **aħbar/aħbarijiet** 'news'; **art/artijiet** 'land/s'; **ħsieb/ħsibijiet** 'thought/s'; **isem/ismijiet** 'name/s'; **missier/missirijiet** 'father/s'; **omm/ommijiet** 'mother/s'; **xogħol/xogħlijiet** 'work/s'; **żmien/żminijiet** 'time/s'.

(ii) Most loan-words which have not been adapted to the semitic word-pattern of Maltese:—

Exx. **radju/radjijiet** 'radio/s'; **soru/sorijiet** 'nun/s'; **patri/patrijiet** 'monk/s'; but **papa/papiet** 'pope/s' not **papijiet**.

(5) Suffix **an** or **ien** is attached to (i) a few words which show only the first and third radicals with either long **a** or **ie**, less frequently long **i** or the diphthong **aj**, between them or (ii) to a few words ending in **i** or **u** in open syllable after the second radical with the third radical **j** quiescent. The following examples are given under their respective patterns.

KiTBien (i) Exx. sing. **far** pl. **firien** 'rat/s'; **ġar** (kit'bien) (+ a, f.) **ġirien** 'neighbour/s'; **nar/nirien** 'fire/s'; **għar/għerien** 'cave/s'; **qies/qisien** 'measure/s'; **bies/bisien** 'hawk/s'; **bieb/bibien** 'door/s'; **wied/widien** 'valley/valleys'; **sid/sidien** 'landlord/s'.

KiTBan   (i)   Exx. siegħ/sigħan 'a kind of measure'
(kit'baan)   (a siegħ = 224.1 sq. yds.);   ħajt/ħitan
                'wall/s'; qiegħ/qigħan 'bottom/s'.

KoTBien   (ii) Exx. ħasi/ħosjien 'capon/s'; sabi/subien
(kot'bien)   (for subjien) 'lad/s'; għatu/għotjien
                'lid/s'.

Remark 2: Additional j in ħosjien and għotjien is the third radical corresponding to **B**, the third radical of the pattern.

(6) The suffix a is taken by descriptives in No. 2 (i) and (ii) as an alternative plural formation.

Exx. nies giddibin or giddieba 'lying people'; tfal niżlin or nieżla 'children coming down'; irġiel tajbin or tajba 'good men'.

THE PLURAL SUFFIXES OF WORDS OF FOREIGN (NON-ARABIC) ORIGIN

1. A large number of nouns and adjectives of Sicilian or Italian origin ending in (i) u (m.) or a (f.) or (ii) a consonant (m.) form their plural by adding suffix i in open syllable to the last consonant without affecting the original stress of the word.

Exx. (i) bravu (m.) brava (f.) bravi (pl.) 'clever'; travu (m.) travi (pl.) 'beam/s'; vara (f.) vari (pl.) 'holy statue/s'; (ii) suldat (m.) suldati (pl.) 'soldier/s'; vot (m.) voti (pl.) 'vote/s'; altar (m.) altari (pl.) 'altar/s'; buqar (m.) buqari 'jug/s'; fjur (m.) fjuri (pl.) 'flower/s'; xugaman (m.) xugamani (pl.) 'towel/s'.

2. Words ending in u preceded by a long (doubled) consonant form their plural by dropping u and adding suffix ijiet.

Exx. siġġu/siġġijiet 'chair/s'; ballu/ballijiet 'ball/s'; kallu/kallijiet 'corn/s'.

3. Words which end in ku (from It. *co* corresponding to English words ending in *ic*) change ku (sing.) to

ci (pl.), as in Italian but some purists and village people just change final u into i.

Exx. pubbliku / pubbliċi 'public'; kritiku / kritiċi 'critic/s'; prattiku / prattiċi 'practical'; fanatiku / fanatiċi 'fanatic'. But grammatika / grammatiki 'grammar/s'; or grammatiċi (adj.) 'grammatical' or 'grammarians'.

4. Names of occupation take a as the plural suffix, thus agreeing with examples given in No. 6.

Exx. arġentier/arġentiera 'silversmith/s'; parrukkier/parrukkiera 'barber/s'; infermier/infermiera 'hospital attendant/s'; xufier/xufiera 'chauffeur/s'.

5. Monosyllabic words ending in a doubled consonant form their plural by adding suffix (i) i or (ii) ijiet. Words of more than one syllable form their plural by suffix i.

Exx. (i): platt/platti 'plate/s'; brazz/brazzi 'branch/es (of a candlestick)'; raġġ/raġġi 'ray/s'; mazz/mazzi 'bunch/es'; rett/retti (adj.) 'upright'; fitt/fitti 'importunate'; fiss/fissi 'fixed'; moxx/moxxi 'soft (cheese)'; rozz/rozzi 'rude'; skoss/skossi 'jolt/s'; katnazz/katnazzi 'padlock/s'; kastell/kastelli 'castle/s'; kapriċċ/kapriċċi 'whim/s'; arloġġ/arloġġi 'clock/s'; papoċċ/papoċċi 'slipper/s'.

Exx. (ii): lazz/lazzijiet 'shoelace/s'; fatt/fattijiet story/stories' (also + i, 'fact/s'); gass/gassijiet 'gas/es'; tapp/tappijiet 'cork stopper/s'; xall/xallijiet 'shawl/s'; sett/settijiet 'set/s'; ċekk/ċekkijiet 'cheque/s'; ġlekk/ġlekkijiet 'coat/s'; gigg/giggijiet 'gig/s'; likk/likkijiet 'small ball/s'; skoll/skollijiet 'rock/s in the sea'; xott/xottijiet 'shot/s'; xokk/xokkijiet 'shock/s'.

EXERCISE 8

(a) Form the plural of the following nouns and adjectives

Sqalli (Sicilian); dħuli (easy to make friends with); ħabsi (goalbird); barri (a bull); għajjien (lazy); għar-

wien (naked); sajjem (fasting); diehel (entering); wieqaf
(standing); mahrub (fled); ferhan (happy); setgħan
(mighty); smajjar (brownish); ġwejjed (quiet); niedi
(wet); għali (expensive); hati (guilty); palju (a reed
fan, used by men); tank (tank); bank (bench or bank);
ballu (ball: dancing); sptar (hospital); taraġ (stairs);
għid (festival); furnar (baker); haddied (blacksmith).

Translate:

(b)   The Sicilian soldier is happy. Flowers on (fuq)
the altar. The silversmith bought (xtara) an old chair.
The hospital attendants are tired. The soldiers and the
sailors are very (hafna after adj.) clever. The jug is full
of wine. Jugs full of wine. The mothers are very happy
because (għax) the news is good. Men and women coming
(going) down (nieżel, sing.) the hill (għolja).

Lesson 9

BROKEN PLURALS OF NOUNS
AND ADJECTIVES

Broken plurals are those formed by breaking up the
internal structure of a word. The nearest English example would be words like *foot/feet*; *goose/geese*. They are
often regarded as collective nouns of fem. gender, though
the qualifying adjective can be variably fem. sing. or pl.
as in tfal imqarba, or imqarbin 'naughty children'. There
is no short cut to rules governing the formation of broken
plurals. Again, these are listed under a number of patterns *which are not intended to be memorised*, but the
student is advised to memorise as many plural formations
as he can, especially such words as he can expect to
be more frequently used.

The following lists include more patterns of simple
or underived singular nouns and adjectives not included
in Lesson 3.

(a) *Monosyllabic plurals starting with the first two radicals and ending with the third radical preceded by a long vowel or its mutated form* ie.

Patterns	*Vocabulary*

1. **KTaB**
   (ktaab)

(i) Nouns: pl. **bjar**/sing. **bir** 'well'; **braġ/ borġ** 'heap'; **djar/dar** 'house'; **dwal/ dawl** 'light'; **ħwat/ħawt** 'trough'; **qrar/qrara** 'confession'; **qtar/qatra** 'drop'; **rtal/ratal** 'rotolo = 28 ounces'; **swat/sawt** 'lash'; **tfal/tifel** 'boy' **tifla** 'girl'; **xbar/xiber** 'span'; **żrar/żrara** 'a very small stone'.

(ii) Adjectives: pl. **fqar**/sing. **fqir** (+ a. .f) 'poor'; **kbar/kbir** (+ a. f.) 'great, large'; **qsar/qasir** (+ a. f.) 'short'; **twal/twil** (+ a. f.) 'tall, long'; **żgħar/żgħir** (+ a. f.) 'small'.

2. **KTieB**
   (ktiəb)

(i) Nouns: pl. **bniet**/sing. **bint** 'daughter'; **bwiet/but** 'pocket'; **dnieb/denb** 'tail'; **dwieb/debba** 'mare'; **fniek/fenek** (m.) **fenka** (f.) 'rabbit'; **frieħ/ferħ** 'the young of an animal'; **ġfien/ġifen** 'galley (ship)'; **ħbieb/ħabib** (+ a, f.) 'friend'; **ħniek/ħanek** 'gum'; **ħrief/ ħaruf** (+ a, f.) 'lamb'; **ħtien/ħaten** 'brother - in - law'; **kmiem / komma** 'sleeve'; **mwies/mus** 'folding-knife'; **njieb/nejba** 'wisdom tooth'; **nwiel/ newl** 'loom'; **qfief/qoffa** 'basket'; **qrieq/ qorq** 'sandal'; **rjieħ/riħ** 'a cold, wind'; **rġiel/raġel** 'man'; **snien/sinna** 'tooth'; **żwieġ/żewġ** 'pair'.

Remark 1: Initial e of **erwieħ**, pl. of **ruħ** 'soul' unlike initial euphonic i in words like **irjieħ, imwies**, is not dropped when it occurs after a word ending in a vowel. Exx. **ħafna erwieħ** 'many souls', but **ħafna rjieħ** 'many colds'.

	(ii)	Adjectives: pl. ħfief/sing. ħafif (+a, f.) 'light'; qliel/qalil (+ a, f.) 'severe'; sbieħ/sabiħ (+ a, f.) 'beautiful'; smien/smin (+ a, f.) 'fat'.
3.	KTiB (ktiib)	Nouns: pl. ħmir/sing. ħmar (+ a. f.) 'donkey'; snin/sena 'year' (The only two examples).
4.	KTuB (ktuub)	(i) Nouns: pl. bjut/sing. bejt 'roof'; djun/ dejn 'debt'; dmugħ/demgħa 'tear'; flus/fils (a coin: unused); ġlud/ġild 'skin'; ġnub/ġenb 'side'; ħjut/ħajt 'thread'; Lhud/Lhudi (+ ja, f.) 'Jew' (+ess); mħuħ/moħħ 'brain'; qlub/ qalb (+a,) 'heart'; (kernel); qrun/ qarn 'horn'; qxur/qoxra 'husk'; sjuf/ sajf 'summer'; sejf 'sword'; tjur/tajr 'fowl'; truf/tarf 'end'; xhur/xahar 'month'; xmux/xemx 'sun'; xtut/xatt 'shore'.
		(ii) Adjectives: pl. xjuħ/sing. xiħ (+ a. f.) 'old'.

Remark 2: **Xhud** 'a witness' has a singular meaning, but it is grammatically a plural form of sing. **xiehed**, rarely used. **Qlugħ** 'sail' is used both as a singular and as the plural of **qala'** 'sail'.

In the case of nouns, the first consonant of which is **għ**, the pl. form **ktuub** is either **ek'tuub** or **ke'tuub**, that is, vowel **e** is prefixed to the first radical or inserted after it. As this does not make any phonetic difference, both forms of spelling are admissible in the written language. Exx. **għejun** or **egħjun**/sing. **għajn** 'fountain'; **għe-nuq** or **egħnuq**/**għonq** 'neck'; **għeruq** or **egħruq**/**għerq** 'root'; **għexur** or **egħxur** 'tithes'; **għaxra** 'ten'. By analogy the plural of **elf** 'a thousand' is **eluf**. [Note that initial **e** in this and other similar plural formations, though euphonic, as in the case of initial **e** in **erwieħ**, is retained also when preceded by a word ending in a vowel].

(b) *Dissyllabic plurals ending in vowels* **a** *or* **i** *in an open syllable.*

5. KTaBa   (This is pattern No. 1 + vowel a).
    ('ktaaba)   Nouns: **Nsara/Nisrani** 'Christian';
                 qraba/qarib 'relative'.

6. KTieBa   (This is pattern No. 5 with **ie** (iə)
    ('ktiəba)   instead of **a** (aa) between the second
                 and third radical).
                 Nouns: pl. **bdiewa**/sing. **bidwi** 'pea-
                 sant'; **lsiera/lsir** (+a, f.) 'slave';
                 ltiema/ltim (+ a, f.) 'orphan'; **xhieda/
                 xhud** 'witness'.

7. KTaBi   Nouns: **drabi/darba** 'one stroke', 'once';
    ('ktaabi)   **stali/satal** 'pail'; **trabi/tarbija** 'baby'.

8. KTieBi   Nouns: pl. **btieħi**/sing. **bitħa** 'yard';
    ('ktiəbi)   **bwieqi/bieqja** 'bowl'; **dwieli/dielja**
                 'vine'; **flieli/felli** 'slice (of an orange,
                 melon etc.)'; **friegħi/fergħa** 'branch';
                 grieħi/gerħa 'wound'; **griewi/geru**
                 'a pup'; **gwiebi/giebja** 'cistern'; **ħrieqi/
                 ħarqa** 'swaddling cloth'; **kliewi/kilwa**
                 'kidney'; **qtiegħi/qatgħa** 'a shock';
                 sdieri/sidrija 'waistcoat'; **swieni/sien-
                 ja** 'water-wheel'; **swieqi/sieqja** 'acque-
                 duct', **trieħi/terħa** 'a sash'; **xtiewi/
                 xitwa** 'winter'; **xwieni/xini** 'galley'.

Remark 3: As in the case of pattern 4, the plural
KTieBi becomes **eKTieBi** (ek'tiəbi) or **KeTieBi** (ke'tiəbi)
if the first radical is għ. Exx. **egħtiebi, għetiebi/għatba**
'threshold'; **egħlieqi, għelieqi/għalqa** 'field'; **egħwiedi,
għewiedi/wegħda** 'vow'.

9. KTuBa   Nouns: pl. **bgħula**/sing. **bagħal** (m.)
    ('ktuuba)   **bagħla** (f.) 'mule'; **ħbula/ħabel** 'rope';
                 ngħula/nagħal 'horse-shoe'; **qmura/
                 qamar** 'moon'; **rħula/raħal** 'village'.

Note **għeżula** or **egħżula** instead of **għżula** pl. of **għażel** 'fishing net'. (Pattern **eK'TuuBa** or **Ke'tuuBa** on account of initial **għ**).

(c) *Dissyllabic plurals with the 2nd and 3rd radicals which may be identical or different between vocalic sequence o and a in open syllable.*

10. **KoTBa** (**'kotba**)

   (i) Nouns: pl. **ġonna**/sing. **ġnien** 'garden'; **kotba/ktieb** 'book'; **tobba/tabib** 'doctor'; **xolfa/xlief** 'fishing line'.

   (ii) Adjectives: pl. **ġodda/ġdid** (+ a. f.) 'new'; **morda/marid** (+ a. f.) 'sick'; **għomja/agħma** (m.) **għamja** (f.) 'blind'; **għonja/għani** (m.) **għanja** (f.) 'rich'; **torja/tari** (m.) **tarija** (f.) 'tender'.

(d) *Dissyllabic plurals beginning with a variable vowel i or o and ending in a in open syllable.*

11. **iKTBa** (**'iktba**)

Nouns: pl. **ibħra/baħar** 'sea'; **iġfna/ġifen** 'ship'; **iġmla/ġemel** 'camel'; **iġsma/ġisem** 'body'; **ilħna/leħen** 'voice'; **ilsna/ilsien** 'tongue'; or 'language'; **isqfa/saqaf** 'ceiling'; **ishma/sehem** 'share'; **isqra/seqer** 'hawk'.

12. **oKTBa** (**'oktba**)

Nouns: pl. **oħtra**/sing. **ħatar** 'staff' (a stick); **oqbra/qabar** 'tomb'; **oqfsa/qafas** 'reed-cage'; **oqsma/qasam** 'farm'.

(e) *Dissyllabic plurals beginning with the first radical and ending with the third, the second radical between two vowels with the second and third radicals different or identical.*

13. **KaTaB** (**'katab**)

   (i) Nouns; (Words conforming to this pattern are generally collective nouns). pl. **baqar**/sing. **baqra** 'a cow'; **basal/basla** 'an onion'; **dagħa/dagħwa** 'a

swear-word'; ġarar/ġarra 'a jar';
labar/labra 'a pin'; naħal/naħla 'a
bee'; qasab/qasba 'a reed'; sarar/sorra
'a bundle'; tamal/tamla 'a date';
(fruit); taraġ/tarġa 'a step'; xagħar/
xagħra 'a hair'; xaqaq/xoqqa 'a cloth';
żahar/żahra 'a blossom'.

(ii) Adjectives: Għarab/Għarbi (+ ja, f.)
'Arabic' also 'an Arab'.

14. KaTeB   The second and third radical conson-
('kateb)   ants of these patterns are the same.
           Nouns: pl. ħalel/sing. ħalla 'billow';
           għases/għassa 'guard'; qatet/qatta
           'truss'; raded/radda 'furrow'.

15. KiTeB   (Also as in No. 14 with the second and
('kiteb)   third radical the same).

(i) Nouns: fided/fidda 'silverware'; sikek/
sikka 'ploughshare'; tikek/tikka 'dot'.

(ii) Adjectives: suwed (with 1st vowel u
instead of i)/iswed (m.), sewda (f.)
'black'.

16. KoToB   (i) Nouns: pl. qomos/sing. qmis 'shirt';
('kotob)   sodod/sodda 'bed'; toqob/toqba 'hole';
           toroq/triq 'street'.

(ii) Adjectives: pl. bojod/sing. abjad (m.)
bajda (f.) 'white'; boloħ/iblah (m.)
belha (f.) 'foolish'; ħomor/aħmar (m.)
ħamra (f.) 'red'; ħorox/aħrax (m.)
ħarxa (f.) ('haarʃa) 'harsh'; romol/
armel (m.) 'widower', armla (f.)
'widow'; sofor/isfar (m.) safra (f.)
'pale', 'yellow'; torox/trux (m.) truxa
(f.) 'deaf'.

(e) *Dissyllabic plurals with* ajja, ejje, *or* ejja *infixed
between the first two radicals and the third.*

17. KTajjaB
 (ktayyab)

Nouns: ġbajjar/ġbara 'poultice'; qlaj-ja'/qalgħa 'gossip'; qtajja'/qatgħa 'shock'; rqajja'/roqgħa 'patch'; snaj-ja'/sengħa 'trade'; xmajjar/xmara 'river'; żjajjar/żjara 'visit'.

Remark 4: When the first consonant of the sing. is għ, pattern KTajjaB becomes KaTajjaB. Exx. għadajjar/għadira 'pond'; għamajjar/għamara 'furniture'.

Remark 5: dgħajjes/dgħajsa 'boat'; blajjet/blata 'rock' and għarajjes (which conforms to patt. KaTajjeB on account of initial għ)/għarus (+ a, f.) 'bridegroom', 'bride' differ from the pattern in that they have vowel e instead of a in the second syllable.

18. KTejjeB
 ('kteyyeb)

Nouns: pl. bhejjem/sing. bhima 'beast'; gżejjer/gżira 'an island'; ħdejjed/ħadid 'iron'; ħġejjeġ/ħuġġieġa 'bonfire'; ħrejjef/ħrafa 'a fairy tale'; ħsejjes/ħoss 'sound'; ħwejjeġ/ħaġa 'thing'; ħxejjex/ħaxix 'herb'; or 'grass'; knejjes/knisja 'church'; nbej-jed/nbid 'wine'; rkejjen/rokna 'corner'.

Remark 6: Pattern KTejjeB becomes KeTejjeB or eKTejjeB if the first radical is għ. Exx. pl. għemejjel or egħmejjel sing. għamil 'deed'; għelejjel or egħlejjel/għalla 'product'; għebejjer or egħbejjer/għabura 'a year old sheep'; għerejjex or egħrejjex/għarix 'hut'.

19. KTejjaB
 ('kteyyab)

Nouns: pl. dwejjaq/sing. diqa 'anguish'; fwejjaħ/fwieħa 'fragrance'; ħlejjaq/ħlieqa 'creature'; qrejjaq/qroqqa 'brooding hen'.

(f) *Dissyllabic plurals with four consonants from triliteral verbs.*

20. KTaBaB
 ('ktaabab)

Note that in the exmaples the 2nd and 3rd radicals are identical, the third being a repetition of the 2nd radical of the singular.

Nouns: pl. **dbabar**/sing. **dabra** 'ulcer'; **ħwawar**/no sing. 'spices'; **sfafar/suffara** 'whistle'; **snanar/sunnara** 'fish hook'; **xfafar/xafra** 'blade'.

Remark 7: In **swaba'**, pl. of **saba'** 'finger', we have the insertion of an additional radical after the first.

21. (i) KTaBeB   Nouns: pl. (i) **dħaħen**/sing. **duħħan**
      ('ktaabeb)   'smoke'; **qtates/qattus** (+ a. f.) 'cat';
    (ii) KW[J]aTeB **slaleb / salib** 'cross';   **tlaleb / tallab**
      ('kw[j]aateb) (+ a, f.) 'beggar'; (ii) **xjaten/xitan**
                          'devil'; **xwabel/xabla** 'sword'; **twavel/**
                          tavla 'plank'; **twapet/tapit** 'carpet';
                          twaġen/taġen frying pan' — vowel a
                          in the last four sing. loan-words is
                          long.

22. (i) KTieBeB   Nouns: pl. (i) **dbieben**/sing. **dubbiena**
      ('ktiəbeb)   'fly'; **flieles/fellus** (+ a, f.) 'chicken';
                          rdieden/raddiena 'wheel'.

    (ii) KWieTeB   (ii) **dwiefer/difer** 'nail (finger)'; **qwie-**
      ('kwiəteb)   **bel/qabla** 'midwife';   **qwieleb/qaleb**
                          'cheese-form'; **twiebet/tebut** 'coffin';
                          żwiemel/żiemel 'horse'.

23. KoTTieB   Nouns: pl. **għorrief**/sing. **għaref** (m.)
      (kot'tiəb)   **għarfa** (f.) 'wise'; **għożżieb/għażeb**
                          'bachelor'.

   (g) *Dissyllabic Quadriliteral plurals from words with four different consonants.*

24. KTaBaL   ( )i Nouns: pl. **qnatar**/sing. **qantar** 'hund-
      ('ktaabal)   red rotolos'; **qratas/qartas** 'paper bag';
                          qratal/qartalla 'a large reed basket'.

              (ii) Adjectives: pl. **fratas/fartas** (+ a. f.)
                          'bald'; **żgħażagħ/żagħżugħ** (+ a. f.)
                          'young'.

The pattern KTaBaL ('kṭaabal) becomes ak'taabal if the first radical is
għ. The only example: għasafar or
agħasafar/għasfur 'bird'.

25. KTaBeL   (i) Nouns: pl. krafes/sing. karfusa 'celery';
    ('ktaabel)   slaten/sultan (+ a, f.) 'king', ('queen').

                 Adjectives: pl. fratas/fartas (+ a, f.)
                 'bald'; skaren/sikran (+a, f.) 'drunk'.

26. KTieBaL   Nouns: pl. bżieżaq/sing. bużżieqa
    ('ktiəbal)   'bubble'; ftietaq/fettuqa   'trifle';
                 ġwienaħ/ġewnaħ 'wing'; ħnicnaq/
                 ħannieqa   'collar';   sriedaq/serduq
                 'cock';   trietaq/tertuqa   'shred'   or
                 'celluloid'.

27. KTieBeL   Nouns: fkieren/fekruna 'turtle' or
    ('ktiəbel)   'tortoise'; grieżem/gerżuma 'throat';
                 kwiekeb/kewba written kewkba 'star';
                 qniefed/qanfud 'hedgehog'.

Remark 8: The pattern becomes eKTieBeL (ek'tiəbel)
or KeTieBeL (ke'tiəbel) when the first radical is għ. Exx.
egħnieqed or għenieqed/għanqud 'bunch of grapes'; egħ-
rieqeb or għerieqeb/għarqub 'heel'; egħsieleġ or għesieleġ/
għasluġ 'stick'.

ADDITIONAL REMARKS

1. Some singular nouns and adjectives can have
more than one broken plural.

Exx. foqra, fqar/fqir (+ a f.) 'poor'; ifħla, fħula/faħal
'stallion'; oqbra, qobra/qabar 'grave'; oqmra, qomra,
qmura/qamar 'moon'; qolol, qliel/qolla 'jar'; qtiegħi,
qtajja'/qatgħa 'shock'; rjieħ, rjiħat/riħ 'cold' (n.).

2. Some nouns can have both a broken and a strong
plural.

Exx. banek 'banks', bankijiet 'benches'/bank 'bank' or

'bench'; **drabi, darbiet** (determinate pl.)/**darba** 'once'; **frieghi, ferghat** (determinate pl.)/**fergha** 'branch'; **ġmieġhi, ġimghat** (determinate pl.)/**ġimgha** 'week'; **iżmna** 'seasons', **żmenijiet** 'times'/**żmien** 'time'.

3. The two forms of the broken and sound or external plurals can have different meanings.

Exx. **fqar** (adj.) 'poor', **foqra** (noun) 'poor people'/**fqir**; **qtajja'** 'large quantities' or 'shocks', **qtieghi** 'shocks', **qatghat** (determinate pl.) 'cuts' or 'slices'/**qatgha**.

4. The following are plural formations from different roots: **mara/nisa** 'woman/women'; **tifla/bniet** 'girl/s'; **tifel/subien** 'boy/s'; **iben** 'son', **bint** 'daughter'/**ulied** 'sons and daughters'. The plural of **hu** 'brother', always used with pronominal suffixes, is **ahwa**.

5. One might describe as also irregular, broken plurals to which are attached plural suffixes.

Exx. **truf** 'edges', **trufijiet** (**truf** + pl. suffix **ijiet**) 'loose ends'/sing **tarf** 'end'; **eluf** 'thousands', **elufijiet** (**eluf** + pl. suffix **ijiet**) 'many thousands'/sing **elf** 'a thousand'; **gheġubijiet** 'marvels' (**gheġub** + pl. suffix **ijiet**)/sing. **ghaġeb** 'marvel'; **drabi** 'times'/**drabijiet** 'some occasions' (**drab** + pl. suffix **ijiet**)sing. **darba** 'once'. **Dehbijiet** 'objects of gold', is formed of the singular (collective) **deheb** + pl. suffix **ijiet**.

The following plurals are considered as singular in the spoken and written language: **mnieher** 'nose' grammatically plural of unused mimated noun **minhar**. (The ungrammatical plural of **mnieher** in popular use is **mnehrijiet** 'noses'); **rdum** 'cliff' plural of **radam** (debris); **rwieh** 'gentle breeze' no sing. but Arabic has **rawh** 'breeze'; **xhud** 'witness' plural of **xiehed** (unused); **dnub** 'sin' (pl. **dnubiet**); in a plural sense it means "tails", singular **denb**.

EXERCISE 9

(a) *Form the broken plural of these non-Arabic nouns and adjectives which are easily recognisable as*

*such by those familiar with English and one or more
of the Romance languages. The number of the required
plural pattern is indicated in brackets. Check with the
key and memorise the correct forms*: **brama** (1) 'jelly
fish/es'; **serp** (2) 'snake/s'; **vers** (4) 'line/s'; **ċens** (4)
'ground-rent/s'; **qorti** (7) 'law-court/s'; **sala** (7) 'drawing-
room/s'; **banda** (14) 'musical band/s'; and (7) 'neighbourhood'; **kitla** (8) 'kettle/s'; **lanċa** (14) 'launch/es';
faxxa (14) 'bandage/s'; **pjazza** (14) 'square/s'; **niċċa** (15)
'niche/s'; **birra** (15) 'beer/s'; **pinna** (15) 'pen/s'; **borża**
(16) 'handbag/s'; **bolla** (16) 'postage-stamp/s'; **koxxa** (16)
'thigh/s'; **froġa** (18) 'omelette/s'; **spiża** (18) 'expense/s';
skuna (18) 'schooner/s'; **pastaż** (24) 'vulgar'; **qalfat** (24)
'caulker/s'; **kamra** (20) 'room/s'; **qartas** (24) 'packet/s';
tanbur (24) 'drum/s'; **suttana** (21) 'cassock/s'; **tavla**
(21) (ii) 'plank/s'; **virdun** (27) 'greenfinch/es'; **dublett**
(27) 'skirt/s'; **munzell** (27) 'stack/s of hay'.

Translate:

(b) The houses of Malta are large and beautiful.
The children are sick. New books and old pens. The
rich are harsh and the poor are foolish. The foolish girl
(**tifla**) is sick. Horses are beasts of burden (**tat-tagħbija**)
in Malta. The bachelors are wise. Malta has old and new
churches. The church of Mosta is the largest church
in the island (**gżira**). Great is the anguish of the poor.
Stars like (**bħal**) pins or dots in the sky. The widow
married (**iżżewġet**) a widower. The fragrance of the gar-
dens of Malta. The Maltese and the Gozitans are Christians. The Arabs are Moslems (**Misilmin**).

Lesson 10

MIMATED NOUNS: FORMATION AND
PLURALS

With the derived nouns given in Lesson 3 must be
included also the Mimated Nouns, so called because the

letter **m** is used as a preformative. These mimated nouns which are evolved from triradical verbs may indicate:

(i) *place-names*: Ex. **maħżen** 'magazine, storing place' (ħażen 'he stored');

(ii) *time*: Ex. **Milied** 'Christmas' (**wiled** 'to bring forth'), the only example;

(iii) *tools*: Ex. **maqbad** 'handle' (**qabad** 'he seized');

(iv) *abstract nouns*: Ex. **mibegħda** 'hatred' (**bagħad** 'he hated');

(v) *collectives*: Ex. **merħla** 'flock' (**raħħal** 'shepherd').

There are twenty-one patterns of singular mimated nouns. Of these, the following are patterns of words in common use, with the verbs from which they are evolved in brackets. Note the different vocalic movements in their relation to the consonants of the Root-Word in brackets.

Patterns	*Vocabulary*
1. maKTaB	Exx. **masġar** 'copse' (**siġar** 'trees'); **maġmar** 'brazier' (**ġamar** 'live coal').
2. maKTeB	Exx. **marden** 'spindle' (root unused); **magħlef** 'fodder' (**għalef** 'he fed'); **magħżel** 'distaff' (**għażel** 'he spun').
3. miKTaB	Exx. **mitraħ** 'mattress' (**teraħ** 'he stretched'); **minfaħ** 'bellows' (**nefaħ** 'he blew'); **misraħ** 'open air square' (**seraħ** obsolete in Maltese).
4. miKTeB	Exx. **minġel** 'scythe' (root unused); **minkeb** 'elbow' (**nikeb**, 'he turned'); **miżwed** 'pod' (no root).
5. muKTaB (**muk'taab**)	Exx. **musmar** 'nail' (**sammar** 'he nailed'); **munqar** 'beak' (**naqar** 'it

pecked'); **munxar** 'a saw', (**naxar** 'he cut off with a saw').

6. **muKTieB** (**muk'tiəb**)   Exx. **musbieħ** 'oil-lamp' (**sebaħ** 'it dawned'); **muftieħ** 'key' (**fetaħ** 'he opened').

7. **moKTieB**   Exx. **moħriet** 'plough' (**ħarat** 'he ploughed'); **moqdief** 'oar' (**qadef** 'he rowed').

8. **miKTBa**   Exx. **mitħna** 'mill' (**taħan** 'he ground'); **mixtla** 'a bed of plants' (**xitla** 'plant').

9. **mKaTT**   Exx. **mqass** 'scissors' (**qass** 'he cut'); **mdaqq** 'straw of thrashed barley' (**daqq** 'he beat cotton').

10. **mKeTT**   Exx. **mxedd** 'girth' (**xedd** 'he wore a dress'); **mleff** 'a child's cloak', obsolete, (**leff** 'he wrapped up').

11. **mKaTTa**   Exx. **mħakka** 'cheese-grater' (**ħakk** 'he grated'); **mħadda** 'pillow' (**ħadd** 'cheek').

12. **mKeTTa**   Exx. **mkebba** 'reel' (**kebb[eb]**) 'he wound threads'); **msella** 'packing needle' (**sell[el]**, obsolete).

13. **mi(W)TieB**   (from roots having w for first radical)

Exx. **miżen** 'scales' instead of **miWżieN** from **wiżen** 'he weighed'; **miżieb** 'gutter' instead of **miWżieB** from √**WŻB**. Note in the two examples the elision of the 1st radical semivowel W.

Remark 1: Roots not found in Maltese are generally still traceable in Arabic.

Remark 2: When the medial radical is l, m, n, r, or għ by analogy, a vowel is inserted before the second radical.

Exx. miżirgħa 'a sown field' (żara'); mibegħda 'hatred' (bagħad); maħanqa 'goat's collar' (ħanaq); mixegħla 'illumination' (xegħel); mterqa 'stone cutter's hatchet' for mitrqa [No. 8] (teraq); mselħa 'broom' for mislħa [No. 8] (selaħ).

IRREGULAR FORMATIONS

The following is a list of mimated nouns, generally abstract, which can be classified as irregular formations evolved from the verbal roots shown in brackets.

mogħdrija 'compassion' (għader); mibegħda 'hatred' (bagħad); mogħdija 'passage' (għadda); moħqrija 'oppression' (ħaqar); magħmudija 'baptism' (għammed); mistħija 'bashfulness' (staħa); mistoħbija 'concealment' (staħba); mistoqsija 'question' (staqsa); mera 'mirror' (ra 'he saw'); moħba 'hiding-place' (ħeba); mgħax 'profit' (għax); mrewħa 'fan' (rewwaħ); mreddgħa 'wet-nurse' (redda'); mgħallem 'master' (għallem); midneb 'sinner' (dineb); miġja 'coming' (ġie); mġiba 'behaviour' (ġieb); maħfra 'forgiveness' (ħafer); mkien 'a place' (kien) used in this sense in the written language only. In the spoken language it means 'nowhere'.

Also in use are the following adjectives with prefix m, muxgħar 'hairy' (xagħar 'hair'); muswaf 'woolly' (suf 'wool').

THE PLURALS OF MIMATED NOUNS

The following continues the list of broken plurals each with its singular form.

Patterns   *Vocabulary*

1. mKaTaB   Exx. pl. mgħażaq/sing. mgħażqa
   ('mkaatab)   'spade'; mqabad/maqbad 'handle'.

2. mKaTeB   Exx. pl. mħażen/maħżen 'storage
   ('mkaateb) place'; mqadef/moqdief 'oar'; mgħa-
                ref/mgħarfa 'spoon'; mħaret/moħriet
                'plough'.

Remark 3:**Mgħażqa** (patt. 1) and **mgħarfa** (patt. 2)
are written with għ before vowel a and not vice-versa
according to the rules of mimated patterns because when
precded by the def. article these two words take euphonic
vowel i which is characteristic of words beginning with
two consonants. We say l-imgħażqa, l-imgħarfa and not
il-magħżqa, il-magħrfa.

3. mKieTaB   Exx. pl. msieraħ/sing. misraħ 'open
   ('mkiətab) air square'; mtieraħ/mitraħ 'mat-
                tress'; msiebaħ/musbieħ 'oil-lamp'.

4. mKieTeB   Exx. pl. mnieġel/sing. minġel 'sickle';
   ('mkiəteb) mżiewed/miżwed 'bean pod'; msie-
                mer/musmar 'nail'; mxietel/mixtla
                'seed bed'.

5. mKaTeT   Note that the second and the third
   ('mkatet)   radicals are the same.

                Exx. pl. mqases/sing. mqass 'scissors'
                (plural more commonly used is mqas-
                sijiet); mħakek/mħakka 'cheese-
                grater'; mħaded/mħadda 'pillow'.

6. mKeTeT   Ex. pl. mselel/sing. msella 'packing
   ('mketet)   needle'; mkebeb/mkebba 'winding-
                reel'; mserek/mserka 'a quill to wind
                thread upon'.

7. mKieTi   Exx. pl. mdieri/sing. midra 'winnow-
   ('mkiəti)   ing fork'.

EXERCISE 10

(a) *Form (i) the singular mimated nouns according to the pattern shown by numbers in brackets and
(ii) their plurals also shown by numbers of the patterns.*

Check with the key and memorise the correct forms.
għalaq 'he shut' (1): (i) 'enclosure'; (ii) pl. pattern (1);
qagħad 'he sat'; (1): (i) 'seat'; (ii) no plural; **siġar** (1):
'trees' (i) 'copse'; (ii) pl. pattern 1; **ħabeż** 'he baked'
(2): (i) 'oven'; (ii) pl. pattern 2; **għaġen** 'he kneaded'
(2): (i) 'kneading basin'; (ii) pl. pattern 2; **debaħ** 'he
slaughtered' (a sacrificial animal) (3): (i) 'sacrificial
altar'; (ii) pl. pattern 3; **teraq** 'he shattered' (3): (i)
'stone cutter's hatchet'; (ii) pl. pattern 3; **ġibed** 'he
pulled' (4): (i) 'a beam which sets a mill in motion'; (ii)
pl. pattern 4; **rikeb** 'he rode' (4): (i) 'ship'; (ii) pl. pattern 4; **taħan** 'he ground wheat' (8); (i) 'mill'; (ii) pl.
pattern 4; **xitla** 'plant' (8): (i) 'a bed of plants'; (ii) pl.
pattern 4; **żibel** 'manure' (8): (ii) 'dunghill'; (ii) pl. pattern 4.

Translate:

'(b) In the museum (**mużew**) there are many old
oil-lamps. One Maltese mill and many Dutch (**Olandiżi**)
mills. One soft (**artab**) mattress and one hard (**iebes**)
pillow. Soft mattresses and hard pillows. The old Gozitan
woman has (**għandha**) a reel and a distaff. I have new
reels and distaffs. Compassion and love are the soul
(**ruħ**) of (**tar-**) religion (**reliġjon**). The peasant (**bidwi**)
has an old plough but (**iżda**) old ploughs are not good
for (**għax-**) work in the fields (**fl-egħlieqi**). There is a
great illumination in Mdina, the old city of Malta.

Lesson 11

THE PRONOUNS

THE PERSONAL PRONOUNS

1. There are two classes of personal pronouns: (1)
independent pronouns given in Lesson 1 and (ii) pronominal suffixes which will be explained in this lesson.

The Independent Pronouns can be used (i) *as the*

subject of a verb. Ex. **Jien kilt** 'I have eaten'; (ii) *with a verbal function when followed by another word which may be an adverb, a preposition, a nominal or a descriptive* ῾phrase*. Exx. **Hu fuq u hi isfel** 'he is upstairs and she is downstairs'; **hi fil-ġnien u missierek fuq ix-xogħol** 'she is in the garden and your father at work'; **hu professur l-Università** 'he is a professor at the University'; **aħna lesti** 'we are ready'; (iii) *elliptically (alone)*. Exx **Min qal hekk? Jien** 'Who said so? I (said so)'. As subject of a verb they may be used or omitted. Ex. **Aħna nħobbu** or just **inħobbu** 'we like'.

2. Personal Pronouns when repeated within the same sentence, have the value of the verb *to be*. Exx. **Intom, kemm intom mgħaġġlin?** (lit. you, how much (are) you in a hurry?) for 'What's all this hurry for?'; **hu min hu** 'whoever he is'; **inti x'inti** 'whatever you are'.

3. The singular and plural third person pronouns **hu, hi** and **huma** take the prefix **in** when they occur after **kif** 'how' or **xi** 'what' (**x'** before a vowel, **h** or **għ**). Exx. **Kif inhu** (not **hu**) **t-tifel?** 'how is the boy?'; **ma nafx kif inhi** (not **hi**) **sewwa l-istorja** 'I don't know the story well'; **x'inhuma** (not **huma**) **jgħidu?** 'what are they saying?'

4. These independent personal pronouns can also be repeated immediately after the subject of a sentence to which they refer, with a meaning corresponding to the verb *to be* in English. Note that in such sentences, subject and pronouns are identical. Exx. **It-tfal huma mgħaġġlin għax iridu jilħqu** (reach in time) **l-iskola** 'the children (+ they) are in a hurry because they want to reach school in time'; **it-tifel hu mill-aħjar fil-klassi** 'the boy (+ he) is one of the best in class'; **Marija hi mara tajba** 'Mary (+ she) is a good woman'. But when no emphasis is intended, the additional independent personal pronouns are left out.

5. The third person singular (**hu, hi**) and plural (**huma**) can also be used in the sense of *he, she, who is*

or *they, who are.* Exx. **Jien hu Alla Sidek** 'I am thy God, thy Master' (lit. I am he who is God, thy Master); **aħna huma dawk li ġġieldu għall-ħelsien** 'we are those (lit. they) who fought for freedom'.

Note that unlike in No. 4, here the pronouns are identical not with the subject but with its complement.

NEGATION OF STATEMENTS

While the idea of negation is conveyed in English by the verb *to be* + *not*, in Maltese (as already explained in Lesson 1), it is conveyed by **ma** (**m'** before a vowel, silent **h** or **għ**) + Pronoun or Verb + stress-attracting suffix **x**. Cp. similar use of French *ne .... pas.* Exx. **Jiena ma jiniex** (**jiena** + **x** becomes **jiniex**) **seftur tiegħek** 'I am not your servant'; **int, m'intix raġel** 'you are not a gentleman'; **hi m'hix** (or **mhix, m'hijiex**) **marida** 'she is not sick'; **hu mhux għaref** 'he is not learned'; **aħna Maltin, m'aħniex Taljani** 'we are Maltese, not Italian'; **intom m'intomx fqar** 'you are not poor'; **huma m'humiex minn Malta** 'they are not from Malta'; **irrid** 'I want'; **ma rridx** 'I don't want'.

QUESTION, STATEMENT, AND EMPHASIS

In Maltese one does not invert the order of subject and verb as in Eng. *I have/have I?* to produce a question. The wording remains the same, but the intonation changes. Questions are made on a rising intonation.

Exx. **Kelli flus biżżejjed** 'I had enough money'; **ma kellix flus biżżejjed** 'I did not have enough money'; **kelli flus biżżejjed? Ma kellix flus biżżejjed?**

As in English, emphasis on one particular word in a phrase or sentence calls attention to the particular word one wishes to emphasize or single out.

REFLEXIVE OR EMPHATIC PRONOUNS

These are expressed by (i) the personal pronouns + **innifs** + pronominal suffix or **stess** (invariable) and (ii) after a verb, by **ruħ** + pronominal suffixes.

Exx. (i) *Singular*   *Plural*
Jien innifsi I myself   **aħna nfusna** we ourselves
Int innifsek you yourself **intom** you
                               infuskom   yourselves
Hu nnifsu he himself   **huma** they
                               nfushom   themselves
Hi nfisha   she herself

Variants: **Jien, int, hu,** etc. stess. Exx. (i) **Jien innifsi**
(or **jien stess) rajtu Ruma** 'I myself saw him in Rome'.

Exx: (ii) **qatel** (he killed) **ruħu** 'he killed himself';
qatlet ruħha 'she killed herself' etc. often adding **b'id**
+ pronominal suffix. Exx. **Is-suldati qatlu ruħhom
b'idejhom** 'the soldiers killed themselves by their own
hands' i.e. committed suicide.

DEMONSTRATIVE PRONOUNS

These are:—
        Singular   *Plural*
Masc. **dan, dana** (this)   Both genders: **dawn, dawna**
Fem. **din, dina** (this)   (these)

Masc. **dak, daka** (that)   Both genders: **dawk, dawka**
Fem. **dik, dika** (that)   (those)

(i) *Optional forms*: **dal-** for **dan il-** or **dawn il-** and
dil- for **din il-** are obtained as a result of the assimilation
of **n** + the definite article with other variants as a result
of the assimilation of **l** with the sun-letters. Exx. **dal-
ktieb** or **dan il-ktieb** 'this book'; **dil-mara** or **din il-mara**
'this woman'; **dawl** (colloquially **dal-**) **kwiekeb** 'these
stars'; **dat-** (for **dawt-**) **tfal** 'these children'. (ii) *Archaic
forms*: These take preformative **he.** Exx. **hedan**(a),
hedin(a), etc.

Remark 1: Unlike English, the noun preceded by the
demonstrative pronoun can be accompanied by the definite article. Exx: **dan (dak) ir-raġel** 'this (that) man'.
If the definite article is omitted, the word-combination
can have the value of a sentence. Exx. **dan raġel** 'this
is a man' or 'a male'; **dawn sbieħ** 'these are beautiful'.

INDEFINITE PRONOUNS

These are: **xi** 'some'; **xi ħadd** 'some one'; **x'uħud** 'some' (pl.); **kull** 'every'; **kulħadd** 'every one'; **kull wieħed** (m.) **waħda** (f.) 'each one'; **wieħed (waħda)** . . . **lil ieħor (oħra)** 'one . . . another'; **kollox** 'everything'; **ilkoll** 'all (of persons)'; **ħaddieħor** 'someone else'; **kull min** 'whoever'; **kulma** 'whatever'.

Remark 2: **Kull** 'every' with **u** changed to **o** can also take the verbal pron. suffixes: **kollni, kollok, kollu, kollħa — kollna, kollkom, kollhom.** Exx. **raġel kollu (mara kollħa) ħeġġa** 'a man (woman) full of enthusiasm'.

THE RELATIVE PRONOUNS

1. This is **li** or the fuller form **illi** meaning *who, whom, that, which.* It introduces an adjectival clause and is used for both numbers and genders.

Ex. **raġel, irġiel, mara, nisa li**, 'a man, men, a woman, women who'.

2. **Li** or **illi** can be followed by a preposition + pronominal suffix.

Exx. **Li bih** 'with which'; **il-ħabel li$\overset{1}{}$ bih$\overset{2}{}$ tgħallaq$\overset{3}{}$**, more commonly **li$\overset{1}{}$ tgħallaq$\overset{3}{}$ bih$\overset{2}{}$** 'the rope with which he hanged himself'; **it-tifel li$\overset{1}{}$ għalih$\overset{2}{}$ għamel$\overset{3}{}$** (also 1, 3, 2) **kulma seta'** 'the boy for whom he did all he could'; **it-tabib li$\overset{1}{}$ miegħu$\overset{2}{}$ tkellimt$\overset{3}{}$ fuq il-marid** (also 1, 3, 2) 'the doctor with whom you spoke about the patient'; **il-kexxun li$\overset{1}{}$ fih$\overset{2}{}$ qegħidt$\overset{3}{}$ il-maktur** (also 1, 3 + obj., 2) 'the drawer in which I placed the handkerchief'.

3. **Li** + noun + **tiegħu** (his) **tagħha** (her) etc. expresses a relation of possession or property with **li** corresponding to English *whose*.

Exx. Il-kaptan li s-suldati tiegħu telquh qatel ruħu b'idejh 'the captain whose soldiers deserted him committed suicide' (lit. killed himself by his own hands).

4. **Li + ġej** (m.) **ġejja** (f.) = English 'next' (event).

Exx. Ix-xahar li ġej 'next month' (lit. the month which is coming); **is-sena li ġejja** (also **il-ġejja** for short) 'next year'.

INTERROGATIVE PRONOUNS

The Interrogative Pronouns are:— **min?** 'who?'; **xi** (or **x'** before words beginning with a vowel or semi-vowel, silent **h** or **għ** or single consonant) 'what?'.

Exx. Xi trid? 'what do you want?'; **x'jaf?** 'what does he know?'; **min hu dan?** 'who is this?'. **Min** can also mean 'he, she, they who' in an impersonal sense. **Ex. Min jitkellem ħafna jiżbalja** 'he who speaks too much errs'. These pronouns can also be used in affirmative statements. **Exx. Jien naf int xi trid** 'I know what you want'; **jien naf min ħa dak** 'I know who took that'.

Liema? 'which?' **Ex. liema ktieb?** 'which book?'; but **liema** can also be used in affirmative statements. **Ex. Jien naf liema ktieb trid** 'I know which book you want'.

Liema bħal + possessive pronominal suffixes indicates the best of the kind. **Exx. raġel liema bħalu** (lit. who like him?) 'a man without his equal'; **mara liema bħalha għall-pittura** 'a woman unexcelled (lit. who like her?) for painting'.

RECIPROCAL PRONOUNS

Xulxin used as the object of a verb preceded by **lil** (See Lesson 31, p. 222 para. 1) means 'one another'.

Ex. Ħobbu lil xulxin or **wieħed** (m.) **waħda** (f.) **lil ieħor** (**oħra** f.) 'love one another'.

POSSESSIVE PRONOUNS

These are the different forms of **ta'** 'of' + pronominal suffixes. For all its forms see Lesson 12, p. 108.

Other Possessive Usages: **Ta' min** expresses English "whose" in questions and statements. Exx. **Dal-ktieb ta' min hu?** also **Ta' min hu dal-ktieb? Ma nafx ta' min hu** 'Whose book is this? I don't know whose it is'; **minn ta' min int?** 'which is your family?' i.e. To whom do you belong? **Ta' min + verb** (3rd person masculine singular of the Imperfect) + pronominal suffixes = English "worthy of". Exx. **Ktieb ta' min jixtrih** 'a book worth buying'; **tifla ta' min iħobbha** 'a lovable girl'; **irġiel ta' min jobogħdhom** 'hateful men'; **ta' min imur jara t-tiġrija** 'it is worth going to see the race'.

Min preceded by a word in the construct state expresses also the idea of *property* or *belonging*. Exx. **Bin min hu Karlu u bint min hi Marija?** 'Whose son is Charles and whose daughter is Mary?'; **art min hi din?** 'whose land is this?'.

PRONOMINAL SUFFIXES·

The pronominal suffixes are attached to (i) nouns to indicate possession and (ii) to verbs and prepositions to indicate the object thereof.

The pronominal suffixes attached to nouns are:

Singular			*Plural*	
-i (suffixed to nouns ending in a consonant).	-ja (added to nouns and prepositions ending in a vowel).	my	-na	our
			-kom	your
			-hom	their
-ek	-ok, -k	thy		
-u	-h	his		
-ha		hers		

The Verbal Pronominal Suffixes are the same as those used for nouns with the exception of the verbal suffix of the first singular which is **ni**.

Exx. **Dar** 'house':- **dari** 'my house', **darek** 'your house',

daru 'his house', **darha** 'her house', **darna** 'our house', **darkom** 'your house', **darhom** 'their house'.

Seraq 'he robbed':- **seraqni** 'he robbed me', **serqek** 'he robbed you', **serqu** 'he robbed him', **seraqha** 'he robbed her', **seraqna** 'he robbed us', **seraqkom** 'he robbed you', **seraqhom** 'he robbed them'.

Hu 'brother' (never used alone):— **ħija** 'my brother', **ħuk** 'your brother', **ħuh** 'his brother', **ħuha** 'her brother'; **ħuna** 'our brother', **ħukom** 'your brother', **ħuhom** 'their brother'.

Oħt 'sister':— **oħti** 'my sister', **oħtok** 'your sister', **oħtu** 'his sister', **oħtha** 'her sister', **oħtna** 'our sister', **oħtkom** 'your sister', **oħthom** 'their sister'.

Remark 3: The plural of both **hu** and **oħt** is obtained by **ħut** + pron. suffixes (**ħuti, ħutek, ħutu, ħutha** etc. 'my, your, his, her brothers or sisters'). The plural of both without a pronominal suffix is **aħwa**. Thus we speak of **aħwa bniet u subien** 'sisters and brothers' and **ulied l-aħwa** 'female' or 'male cousins'.

Lil 'to':— **lili** 'to me', **lilek** 'to you', **lilu** 'to him', **lilha** 'to her', **lilna** 'to us', **lilkom** 'to you', **lilhom** 'to them'. These can be used as (i) *indirect objects*. Ex. **ġib il-kotba lili** 'bring the books to me' or as (ii) *objective pronouns of a transitive verb for emphasis*. Ex. **iħobbha** (**iħobb** 'he loves' + pron. suffix **ha** 'her') or **iħobb lilha** 'he loves her' (i.e. not someone else).

The three suffixes **-ja, -k, -h** are used after a vowel or a diphthong. In the case of dual nouns ending in **ejn** (exx. **riġlejn, idejn, għajnejn** etc.) the **n** is dropped. Exx. **ħija** (= **hi** + **ja**) 'my brother'; **għajnejja** (= **għajnej** +**ja**) 'my eyes'; **ħuk** (=**ħu**+**k**) 'your brother'; **għajnejk** (= **għajnej**+**k**) 'your eyes'; **ħuh** (=**ħu**+**h**) 'his brother'; **għajnejh** (= **għajnej**+**h**) 'his eyes'.

When the pronominal suffix is added to the last consonant or semi-vowel of a feminine noun ending in **a**, it is invariably preceded by **t** called the **t Marbuta** which originally formed part of the feminine word. (See Lesson 5, p. 58). A *stressed* vowel i is sometimes inserted before the t in the third person singular feminine and the three plural forms, but several such words have equally acceptable alternatives without this vocalic insertion. Examples:

xewqa 'wish' + pron. suffixes; mara 'woman' + pron suffixes.

xewqti	my wish	marti	my wife
xewqtek	your wish	martek	your wife
xewqtu	his wish	martu	his wife
xewqitha (or xewqtha)	her wish	—	—
xewqitna (or xewqtna)	our wish	martna	our wife
xewqitkom (or xewqtkom)	your wish	martkom	your wife
xewqithom (or xewtqhom)	their wish	marthom	their wife

Similarly for zija 'aunt'/zijiet 'aunts and uncles' — ziti 'my aunt' /zijieti 'my aunts and uncles'; zitek/zijietek; zitu/zijietu; etc. Ziju 'uncle' + pron. suffix gives zijuwi, zijuk, zijuh, zijuha, zijuna, zijukom, zijuhom, 'my, your his, her, our, your, their uncle'.

A euphonic vowel is similarly inserted when the pron. suffixes are attached to wieħed 'one' changing ie to a or e in the 3rd person feminine and in the plural forms.

Sing.	*Plural*
waħdi 'I alone'	weħidna or uħidna 'we alone'
waħdek 'you alone'	weħidkom or uħidkom 'you alone'
waħdu 'he alone'	weħidhom or uħidhom 'they alone'
weħidha or uħidha 'she alone'	(N.B. Also with a instead of e after w.)

Exx. Mara waħidha ħdejn il-baħar 'a woman alone near the sea'; it-tfal kienu weħidhom 'the children were alone'.

OTHER PRONOMINAL USAGES

1. The separate objective pronouns which can be used as alternative forms of Verb + direct pronominal suffixes when the verb is followed by one pronominal object as in għajjar lili or lili għajjar for għajjarni 'he insulted me', are the only forms that can be used when (i) the same verb occurs, or is understood, in two or more coordinate clauses or (ii) different verbs are used in different coordinate clauses.

Exx. (i) Iħobb lilnom u (jħobb verb understood) lilna (not iħobbhom u jħobbna) 'He loves them and us'; (ii) iħobb lilhom u jobgħod lilna 'he loves them and hates us'.

These objective pronouns are used also with verbs having as their object reflexive nifs + pronominal suffixes.

Ex. Iħobb lilu nnifsu mhux lilna 'He loves himself, not us'.

2. The (i) separate objective pronouns and (ii) the direct suffixes are often used redundantly for mere effect.

Exx. lilhom inħobbhom għax nies tajba 'I love them (lit. them I love) because they are good people'; (ii) min kitbu (kit[e]b 'he writes' + u 'it') dal-ktieb? 'who wrote this book?'; min ġiebha dil-ħamiema? 'who brought (her) this pigeon?'. (Note redundant use of *it* and *her*).

3. A peculiar usage is the employment of the third person feminine pronominal suffix -ha in an impersonal sense corresponding to a similar use of Italian *la* in *battersela* 'to run away'; or Eng. 'it' in 'to live *it* up'.

Exx. Taha (ta 'he gave' + ha 'her, it') għax-xorb 'he took to drink'; għamilha (għamel 'he made or did' + ha 'her, it') expresses some unusual daring, good or bad action.

The pronominal suffix -ha stands for a euphemistic omission of the action done. Waħda (f.) 'one' is similarly used euphemistically as in ġibed waħda 'he swore' with waħda used for dagħwa 'a swear-word'; x'waħda din! 'what a misfortune!' x'waħda ġratli! 'what ill-luck has befallen me!'.

EXERCISE 11

Translate:

(a) **Jien kilt larinġa ta' Malta tajba ħafna. Kiltu ħobż Malti** (question and answer). **Jien stess** (or **innifsi**) **u waħdi għamilt** (did) **dan. Dawn it-tfal Maltin; l-oħrajn** (the others) **jew** (either) **Taljani jew** (or) **Franċiżi. Dawn huma l-flus** (pl.) **li bihom ħallast** (paid) **il-ħaddiem.** (worker). **Il-mara li t-tifel tagħha marid ħafna** (much) **hi fqira u waħedha. Ta' min huma daż-żiemel abjad u dal-ħmar xiħ? Marti mara Maltija minn Tas-Sliema** (Sliema, a town name). **Hija u oħtok iħobbu lil xulxin. Taħa għall-qari** (reading) **ta' kotba bl-Ingliż u bil-Franċiż.**

(b) The palace (**palazz**) is old. Is the palace old? Which book is on the table (**mejda**)? My wife is Maltese; his wife is English (**Ingliża**). Which woman is your wife? I myself saw this man walking with that woman. These are the soldiers whose captain killed himself. Those are the men and women who abandoned (**telqu**) their children. This is the pen (**pinna**) with which he wrote (**kiteb**) these books. Good Christians love one another; bad Christians do not love one another. Whose house is this and whose sister is this? She is alone with (**m'**) God.

Lesson 12

PARTICLES

These are the indeclinable words which can be (i) adverbs (ii) prepositions (iii) conjunctions or (iv) interjections. The following is a functional list of the most common particles.

(a) THE ADVERBS

(i) *Adverbs of time*: **meta** 'when' in questions and statements; **la** in statements only; **qabel** 'before'; **issa** 'now'; **mbaghad** 'then'; **illum** 'today'; **dalghodu** 'this morning'; **illejla** 'tonight'; **dil-ġimgħa** 'this week'; **dax-xahar** 'this month'; **dis-sena** 'this year'; **qatt** 'never'; **ilbieraħ** 'yesterday'; **ilbieraħtlula** 'the day before yesterday'; **ilu** 'ago'; **għada** 'tomorrow'; **pitgħada** 'the day after tomorrow'; **pitpitgħada** (colloquial) 'two days after tomorrow'; **xħin** 'at what time' or 'when' in question and statement; **xi drabi** 'sometimes'; **fil-waqt** 'in time'; **għad** 'still', 'yet'.

(ii) *Adverbs of place*: **fejn** 'where'; **madwar** 'around'; **mnejn** 'whence'; **bejn** 'between'; **hawn** (also+**ekk**) 'here'; **hemm** (also + **ekk**), **hinn** (also + **ekk**) 'there'; **fuq** 'upwards'; **ħdejn** 'near'; **taħt** 'under'; **lura** 'backwards'; **wara** 'after'; **bogħod** 'far'; **kullimkien** 'everywhere'; **ġewwa** 'inside'; **barra** 'outside'; **kull fejn** 'wherever'; **biswit** 'opposite'.

These, except **hawn, hinn, bogħod, kullimkien, ġewwa, barra, lura** and **kull fejn**, can also be used as prepositions with pron. suffixes attached to them or before nouns.

(iii) *Adverbs of manner*: **kif** 'how'; **hekk** 'so'; **qajla** 'slowly'; **sewwa** 'right'; **għajr** 'except'.

(iv) *Adverbs of quantity*: **aktar** or **iżjed** 'more'; **anqas** 'less'; **ħafna, bosta** 'much', 'many'; **wisq** 'too much'; 'too many'; **biss** 'only'; **biżżejjed** 'enough'; **kemm** 'how much, how many'; followed by a plural noun, or **kemm-il** followed by a singular noun. Ex. **kemm tfal** or **kemm-il tifel** 'many a boy' (statement) 'how many boys?'; **kemm-il darba** 'many times' (statement) or 'how often?' (question).

(v) *Adverbs of negation*: **le** 'no'; **mhux** 'it is not'; **qatt** 'never'; ('ever' in a question); **ħadd** 'no one'; **xejn** 'nothing'; **mkien** 'nowhere'.

(vi) *Adverbs of affirmation*: **iva** 'yes'; **tajjeb** 'good'; **hekk** 'like this'; **tabilħaqq** 'truly'; **tassew** 'indeed', 'really'; **kollox sew** 'all right'.

(vii) *Adverbs of question*: **għala?** 'why'; **kif?** 'how?'; **jaqaw?** 'can it be by any chance?'; **biex?** 'with what?';

jewilla? 'by any chance?, can it be that (+ sentence)?';
għalfejn? 'for what reason?' mnejn? 'from where?';
safejn? 'till where?'; minn sa fejn?' 'by what right?';
għaliex? 'why?'.

They can also be used in statements, except jaqaw.

Of the above adverbs some are used always separately, and others sometimes separately and sometimes with
pronominal suffixes:—

1. għad 'yet, still'. Exx. għadni (for għad + verbal
suffix ni) 'I am still'; għadha 'she is still' etc., m'għadnix
'I am no longer' (+ adj. or verb); ma għadhiex also
m'għadhiex 'she is no longer' etc.

2. mnejn 'whence'. Exx. mnejni 'from my side';
mnejnek 'from your side' etc. used in Gozo.

3. daqs 'as much as' or 'of the same age'. Exx. daqsi
'of my age' or 'height'; fih daqsek 'he is as tall as you'.

4. qis. Though this is the singular Imperative of
qies/iqis 'he measured/measures', when attached to the
pronominal suffixes it has an adverbial function meaning like'. Exx. qisha belha 'she is like a fool'; qisu qed
jiblieh 'he seems to be growing foolish', (lit. consider her,
him, etc.).

5. Similarly għodd, Imperative of għadd/igħodd 'he
counted/counts' has also an adverbial function. Ex. il-
Milied għoddu wasal 'Christmas has nearly arrived', (lit.
count Christmas as if it had arrived).

6. Similarly donn (unused) + pron. suffix has an
adverbial function meaning 'like' or 'as if'. Ex donnu
bniedem fis-sakra 'he is like (lit. consider him) a drunkard'.

7. Il (never used alone) + pron. suffix indicates the
passing of time. Exx. ili (also ilni) siegħa nitkellem 'I
have been talking for an hour'; għaxar snin ilu 'ten years
ago'.

Remark 1: għad, qis, donn and il + verbal suffixes
can also be used negatively. Ex. m'għadnix etc.

(b) CONJUNCTIONS

u 'and'; jew 'or'; iżda 'however'; imma 'but'; jekk 'if'; għax 'because'; illi or li 'that'; meta 'when'; mela 'therefore, then'; biex, less commonly sabiex 'so that'.

(c) INTERJECTIONS

ja 'o'; jaħasra! 'what a pity!'; x'waħda din! 'O dear!'; jalla 'come on' 'quick!'; or 'would it were so!' uff (expression of annoyance) 'phew'; iff (expression of disgust) 'ugh'; jaqq (expression of physical distaste) 'ugh'; aħħ 'ouch' or 'ow'; ajma 'alas' also 'ouch'; i 'eh' (expression of wonder) as in i, x'waħda din! 'what a misfortune!'; i, x'għarukaża! 'what a shame!'.

(d) PREPOSITIONS WITH THEIR SUFFIXES

The following prepositions take the pronominal suffixes:

Exx. (i) BI 'with': bija 'with me', bik 'with thee', biħ 'with him', biha 'with her', bina 'with us', bikom 'with you', bihom 'with them'; (ii) FI, 'in': fija, fik, fiha, fina, fikom, fihom; (iii) WARA 'behind': warajja, (also urajja), warajk (urajk) warajħ (urajħ), warajha (urajha), warajna (urajna), warajkom (urajkom), warajhom (urajhom); (iv) ĦDEJN 'near': ħdejja, ħdejk, ħdejħ, ħdejha, ħdejna, ħdejkom, ħdejhom; (v) LEJN 'towards'; lejja, lejk, etc.; (vi) MINN 'from': minni, minnek, etc.; (vii) QABEL 'before': qabli, qablek, etc.; (viii) FUQ 'on': fuqi, fuqek, etc.; (ix) TAĦT 'under': taħti, taħtek, etc.; (x) BEJN 'between': bejni, bejnek, etc.; (xi) BĦAL 'like': bħali, bħalek, etc.; (xii) FOST 'amongst': fostna, fostkom, fosthom 'amongst as, you, them', (xiii) GĦAJR or ĦLIEF 'except'; għajri, għajrek, etc.; (xiv) QUDDIEM 'in front of'; quddiemi, quddiemek, etc; (xv) GĦAL 'for'; għalija, għalik, etc.; (xvi) MINFLOK or FLOK 'instead of' + i, ok, etc.

(e) OTHER PREPOSITIONAL USAGES

Ma' (with) Ta' (of) għand (at, in the possession of) + pronominal suffix.

When the pronominal suffixes are attached to the first two words, vowel a becomes stress-bearing ie in the singular, but remains stressed a in the plural and the word is written out in full, that is, with għ, according to the general rule. These three prepositions are very useful and should be memorised with their pronominal suffixes.

MA' 'with': **miegħi** 'with me', **miegħek** 'with you', **miegħu** 'with him', **magħha** 'with her', **magħna** 'with us', **magħkom** 'with you', **magħhom** 'with them'.

Ta' 'of': **tiegħi** 'my, mine', **tiegħek** 'your, yours', **tiegħu** 'his', **tagħha** 'her, hers', **tagħna** 'our, ours', **tagħkom** 'your, yours', **tagħhom** 'their, theirs'. Like adjectives these follow the nouns. (Affected forms used mostly in sermons are variants preceded by **MINN** 'from': **minn tiegħi** 'my, mine', **minn tiegħek** 'your, yours', etc.).

Għand 'at' 'to': (in the sense of Fr. chez) **għandi**, **għandek**, **għandu**, **għandha** **għandna** ('anna'), **għandkom**, **għandhom** 'at my, your (sing.) his, her, our, your (pl.) their house'. **Mar għand oħtu** 'he went to his sister's house'.

Għand + Pron. Suffix = 'To Have' or 'Must'

Maltese has no equivalent for the English verb *to have* or *must*, but its value is conveyed by the preposition **għand** followed by the pronominal suffixes.

Examples of verbal functions: **għandi** 'I have', **m'għandix** 'I have not'; **għandek** 'you have', **m'għandekx** 'you have not'; **għandu** 'he has', **m'għandux** 'he has not'; **għandha** 'she has', **m'għandhiex** 'she has not'; **għandna** ('anna') 'we have', **m'għandniex** (man'nieʃ) 'we have not'; **għandkom** 'you have', **m'għandkomx** 'you have not'; **għandhom** 'they have', **m'għandhomx** 'they have not'; **Għandi tlitt itfal** 'I have three children'; **it-tifla ż-żgħira għandha tliet snin** 'the youngest daughter is three years old', **m'għandekx tindaħal** 'you must not interfere'.

Kell + *Pron. Suffix* = *Had* + *Noun or* + *the Infinitive*
'Had to'

Maltese expresses the Past Tense of the verb *to have*
by **kell** + pron. suffixes. **Kell** is a modification of **kien**
'it was' + preposition l 'to'. It expresses the future by
ikollu, etc. (See Lesson 27 p. 200).

Memorise: sing. **kelli** (for **kien** 'it was' + **li** 'to me')
'I had'; **kellek** 'you had'; **kellu** 'he had'; **kellha** 'she had';
kellna ('**kenna**) 'we had'; **kellkom** 'you had'; **kellhom**
'they had'; **kelli ktieb** 'I had a book'; **kelli nitkellem** 'I
had to speak'.

The Use of Ħa/Biex

Two other particles in common use are **ħa** and **biex**.
Ħa, which is short for **ħalli**, grammatically imperative
of **ħalla** 'he permitted', and **biex** both introduce a clause
of purpose; but **biex** to the idea of purpose adds that of
the instrument with which that purpose is attained.
Exx. **Ħa** (or **ħalli**) **nara x'sa jagħmel** 'let me see what he
will do'; **agħtini l-flus ħa nħallas id-dejn** 'give me money
so that I may pay the debt'; **agħtini l-flus biex nixtri
l-ikel** 'give me money with which to buy food.'

EXERCISE 12

Translate:

(a) **Hemm 60 mil baħar minn Pozzallo fi Sqallija**
(Sicily) **għal Malta. Fejn hi t-tifla? Ħdejn it-tfal. Id-dar
tiegħi biswit** (opposite) **id-dar ta' ħuti. Kif int? Tajjeb
grazzi** (thank you). **Missierek tajjeb? Le, marid. Ommok?
Iva, tajba ħafna. Oħtok waslet?** (arrived) **Ilni siegħa
nistennieha** (waiting for her) **hawn; iżda huma ilhom
aktar minn sagħtejn weħidhom fejn il-bieb** (door) **tad-
dar. Dal-ktieb tiegħi; l-ieħor** (the other) **tagħha. Ġie
għandi bil-kelb miegħu. Biex ġejt** (you have come) **minn
Ruma? Bl-ajru jew bil-baħar? Bil-baħar. Ħa nara** (I see)
biex ġie huk u għalfejn. Hu donnu marid (sick) **u hi
qisha dejjem** (always) **imdejqa** (sad).

(b)   Where is your brother? I don't know (**ma nafx**) where he is. There are bastions (**swar**) around the city of Valletta. Sicily is an island whence we import (**nimportaw**) fruit and fish. How many girls are there in your class? (**klassi**). He is not as tall as you. She is still sick. Sit (**oqgħod**) near me. The boy is three years old. I have not been long here (**hawn**).

Lesson 13

PREPOSITIONS + DEFINITE ARTICLE OR + RELATIVE PRONOUN

The following particles are attached some to the definite article or its assimilated forms when the noun or adjective following them is preceded by the definite article and some to the relative pronoun **illi**.

bi 'with'; **bil-** 'with the'; **fi** 'in'; **fil-** 'in the'; **ma'** 'with'; **mal-** 'with the'; **ta'** 'of'; **tal-** 'of the'; **bħal** 'like'; **bħall-** 'like the'; **għal** 'for'; **għall-** 'for the'; **lil** 'to'; **lill-** 'to the'; **sa** 'till' or 'as far as'; **sal-** 'till the' or 'as far as the'; **ġo** 'in'; **ġol-** 'in the'; **minn** 'from'; **mill-** 'from the'.

Exx. **bħal ħmar** 'like a donkey', **bħall-ħmar** 'like the donkey', **lil tifla** 'to a girl', **lit-tifla** 'to the girl'.

The student must remember that the definite article assimilates with some consonants. (See pp. 20-21).

Exx. **bil-** becomes **bis-** before **sewwa**, 'by fair means'; **għall-** becomes **għax** in **għax-xahar**, 'for the month' and so on.

Bil- and **fil-** become **bl-**, **fl-** when the noun begins with a vowel, and in the spoken language also with **h** or **għ**.

Exx. **bil-baħar** 'by sea'; **bl-art** 'overland'; **fil-ħin** 'just in time'; **fl-aħħar mill-aħħar** 'in the long run'.

Ma', **ta'**, **dan**, **din**, **ġo**, **sa** are not attached to the definite article if the word starts with a vowel, but the rule is not followed consistently in the written language except in the case of the demonstrative pronouns.

Exx. mal-ktieb 'with the book' but ma' l-ishab or mal-ishab 'with the companions'; tad-deheb 'golden' or 'goldsmith' but ta' l-Indja or tal-Indja 'of India'; dal-gvernatur 'this governor' but dan l-iskultur or dan or da l-iskultur 'this sculptor'; dil-mara 'this woman'; din or di l-iskola 'this school'; ġol-but 'in the pocket'; ġo l-Afrika or ġol-Afrika 'in Africa'; sal-Hamrun, 'as far as Hamrun'; sa l-isptar or sal-isptar 'as far as the hospital'.

Bi, Fi, Mi, Minn, Ta' + Relative Pronoun Illi 'that'.

(i) Bi + illi = billi 'since' also 'with what'.

Exx. Billi m'għandekx flus, siefer (go abroad) sena oħra 'Since you have no money, go abroad another year'; billi tagħti tieħu 'what you do to others, others do to you'; billi (or b'li) tagħti tieħu 'with what you give you take' i.e. 'what you do to others, others do to you'.

(ii) Fi + illi + filli 'as soon as, no sooner than'.

Exx. Filli ħaj, filli mejjet (lit. No sooner alive than dead) 'he died very suddenly'; filli jidħaq filli jibki 'he begins to laugh and soon after to cry'.

(ii) Ma' + illi = malli 'no sooner than; when; as soon as'.

Ex.Malli rani ħarab 'As soon as he saw me he ran away'.

(iv) Minn + illi = milli 'from what'.

Exx. Dan biss niftakar milli qal 'I remember only this of (lit. from) what he said'; milli qed nara 'from what I am seeing'.

(v) Ta' + illi =talli 'because, for the reason that'.

Exx. Talli ġrejt waqajt 'because you ran, you fell'; talli ħdimt titħallas 'for the work you have done you will be paid'.

Note also the following combinations: għad li, għad illi, 'although'; waqt li 'while'; wara li 'after'.

Particles compounded with indefinite pronoun **ma**: **bħalma** (**bħal** + **ma**) 'as'; **bla ma** or **mingħajr ma** 'without'; **qabel ma'** 'before'. These are all followed by a verb in the Perfect or the Imperfect, which we shall explain further on. This **ma**, meaning 'what' which is suffixed to a few words, is not to be confused with the adverb of negation **ma** meaning 'not'.

Ex. **Kulma ma tgħidx inkun nafu minn għand ħaddieħor** 'Whatever you won't speak about, I shall know (it) from someone else'.

Other compounds similarly followed by verbs are: **daqs kemm** 'as much as'; **kull meta** 'whenever'; **la darba** 'since, seeing, considering that'.

Exx. **bħal ma qal Shakespeare** 'as Shakespeare said'; **daqs kemm ġera** (ran) **qata'** (cut) **nifsu** (his breath) 'he ran so much that he was out of breath'.

SOME PREPOSITIONAL USAGES

1. **Bi** or **B'** + Noun (with or without the definite article) = an adverb, adverbial or adjectival phrase in English.

Exx. **b'reqqa, bir-reqqa** 'with great attention', 'scrupulously'; **b'imħabba** 'with affection' or 'lovingly'; **bis-sewwa jew bid-dnewwa** 'by fair or foul means'; **bil-għatx** 'thirsty'; **bil-ġuħ** 'hungry'; **bi nhar** 'during the day'; **bil-lejl** 'at night'; **bl-ajru** 'by air'; **bl-art** 'overland'; **ktieb bil-Franċiż** (**bit-Taljan, bir-Russu,** etc.) 'a French (Italian, Russian, etc.) book'; **bil-qiegħda** 'sitting'; **bil-wieqfa** 'standing'; **bil-jedd** 'by right'.

2. **Fi** or **F'** + pron. suffix = 'it contains'; 'there is'.

Exx. **Malta fiha ħafna rħula** 'Malta contains (lit. in her) many villages'; **dit-tiġieġa fiha żewġ libbri** 'this hen weighs two pounds'; **din l-ittra ma fihiex żbalji** 'this letter has no mistakes'; **dar-raġel fih sitt piedi** (feet) 'this man is six feet tall'; **fl-aqwa, fl-isbaħ** or **fl-aħjar** 'at the height or best of'; **flimkien** 'together'; **fl-art** 'on the floor'; **fiex** (**fi** + **iex** 'what', unused) 'in what'; **fiex inqastek?** 'in what have I failed you?'; **fih** (**fi** + any other pronominal suffix) **x'tara** 'it is worth seeing'. **Din x'fiha!** 'what's wrong with this!' i.e. there is nothing to be ashamed of or offended at.

Note that **bi** and **fi** can also take verbal suffix **ni** (1st pers. sing.). Exx. **Bini l-għatx** (rare) 'I am thirsty'; **fini l-piż** 'I am heavily built'.

3. **Wara** 'behind' (adjectival form **warrani**).

Exx. **wara l-ħin** 'not in time', 'overtime'; **wara ftit** 'after a while'; **minn wara** 'from behind'; **ta' wara** 'the one coming after'; **wara kollox** 'after all'.

4. **Ħdejn** 'near' means also 'when compared to'.

Exx. **ħdejn darek** 'near your house'; **ħdejn dan, l-ieħor ma** (not) **jiswa** (is worth) **xejn** 'as (or 'when') compared with this, the other is worth nothing'

5. **Minn**: Exx. **dit-tfajla mill-Mosta** 'this girl is from Mosta'; **Toni** (Anthony) **jiġi** (comes) **mill-mara tiegħi** 'Anthony is a relative of my wife'; **raġel minn tagħna** 'a nice man'; **minn fejn int?** 'where do you hail from?'; **ħamsa minn tiegħi** 'five of mine'; **maħbub minn kulħadd** 'loved by everybody'; **minn issa 'l quddiem** 'from now onwards'; **oħtok aħjar minn ħuk** 'your sister is better than your brother'; **minnu** (m.) **minnha** (f.) **minnhom** (pl.) 'true'; **mhux minnu** 'it is not true'.

6. **Fuq**: Exx. **sabiħ fuq li sabiħ** 'couldn't be more beautiful'; **fuq tiegħu** (m.) **tagħha** (f.) **tagħhom** (pl.) 'smart, lively'; **fuq fuq** 'superficially'; **fuq ir-riħ** 'in an advantageous position'; **minn fuq** 'into the bargain'; **fuq il-qalb** 'unwillingly'; **fuq kollox** 'above all'; **riħ fuq** 'the North-West wind'; **fuq l-għoxrin** 'over twenty'.

7. **Taħt**: Exx. **minn taħt** 'in an unfavourable position'; **taħt l-età** 'under age'; **taħt il-kura tat-tabib** 'under medical attention'; **minn taħt** 'from below' or 'in an underhand manner' or 'in an unfavourable position'.

8. **Qabel**: Exx. **Qabel xejn** 'to begin with'; **minn qabel** 'beforehand'; **qabel il-waqt** 'before the time' or 'prematurely'; **ftit qabel** or **qabel ħafna** 'some time before' or 'long before'.

9. **Bejn**: Exx. **Bejn is-sitta u s-sebgħa** 'between six and seven o'clock'; **qal** (he said) **bejnu u bejn ruħu** 'he said in his heart of hearts'; **bejn ħaġa u oħra** 'between one thing and another'; **bejn wieħed u ieħor** 'approximately'; **bejnietna** 'in confidence' (between you and me and the bed-post). Note that **bejn** can also be followed by a verb. Exx. **Bejn ried jitkellem u bejn ma riedx** 'he would speak and at the same time would not'; **m'hemm xejn bejniethom** 'there is nothing (wrong) between them'.

10. **Lejn**: Exx. **lejn ix-xellug** or **lemin** 'towards the left or right'; **lejn l-art** or **il-baħar** 'towards the land or sea'.

11. **Bħal** 'as'; **bħallikieku** 'as if'; 'for example'. Note also that **bħal** when followed by a verb takes the indefinite pronoun **ma**. Exx. **Bħal ma qal l-avukat** 'as the advocate said'; **bħallikieku ma ġara xejn** 'as if nothing had happened'.

12. **Fost**: whence adjective **fustani** 'middle'.

Exx. **Jum fost l-oħrajn** 'once upon a time'; **fost kulħadd** 'of all people'; **fost ħwejjeġ oħra** 'among other things'.

13. **Għajr** or **ħlief** 'except', 'save that'.

Exx. **Alla wieħed; m'hemmx ieħor għajru** (or **ħliefu**) 'there is one God and no other except Him'; **mingħajr** (for **minn + għajr**) 'without'. Ex. **Mingħajr Alla ma nagħmlu xejn** 'without God we can do nothing'; **għajr jekk** 'unless'. Ex. **ma ninqdewx għajr jekk immorru aħna nfusna** 'we shall not be served unless we go ourselves'.

14. **Lil**: Besides being a preposition **lil** is also used before the object of a verb, regularly so when the object is a proper noun. When so used it must not be confused with the definite article **il-**.

Exx. **Iħobb 'l Alla** (**Alla** does not take the def. art.) 'he loves God'; **iħobb lil missieru** 'he loves his father'; **ra 'l Ġanni** 'he saw John'. It can be attached to the definite article.

Exx. **Spara lill-kelb** 'he shot the dog'. **Lill-** in this case stands for **lil** 'to' + **l-**, the definite article.

15. **Ma'**: Exx. **max-xatt ix-xatt** 'along the coast'; **ma' kullimkien** 'in every place'; **ma' ġenb** 'beside'; **ghandha mad-dsatax jew l-ghoxrin sena** 'she is about nineteen or twenty years old'; **mas-sebħ** 'at daybreak'; **mallejl** 'in the night'; **ma' nżul ix-xemx** 'at sunset'; **madwar** 'around', about'; **madwar il-belt** 'in the neighbourhood of the town'; **madwar ghoxrin ruħ** 'about twenty people'.

16. **Għal**: Exx. **għal-lum** 'for today'; **għal xejn** 'for no good reason', 'for nothing'; **għal sena** 'for one year; **għal xejn b'xejn** 'for no reason'; **mar għal oħtu** 'he went for his sister'; **għamel għalih** 'he attacked him'; **minn għalih** 'it seems, (seemed) to him'; **għal + iex** 'what' = **għaliex** meaning 'why?' or 'because', also + **fejn** 'why?' also 'whereto?'.

Exx. **Għaliex (għalfejn) siefer ħuk? Għaliex ma sabx xoghol Malta** 'why did your brother emigrate? Because he did not find work in Malta'; **għalfejn int illum?** 'where are you off to today?'.

17. **Quddiem**: Exx. **ghadda minn quddiemi** 'he passed in front of me'; **ħlas (kera) bil-quddiem** 'payment (rent) in advance'; **'il quddiem** 'later on'; **minn ta' quddiem** 'of the very first'; **quddiem in-nies** 'publicly'; **quddiem kulhadd** 'in everybody's presence'.

(Note that when prepositions which end in l combine with the definite article and the noun begins with an l, these prepositions are written with one l. Exx. **bħallupu** 'like the wolf'; **mil-lista** 'from the list' not **bħalllupu**, **mill-lista**. Similarly we write **min-nies**, 'from the people' for **minn + in-nies**).

The word **ta'** 'of', which becomes **tal-** in combination with the definite article **l-** or its assimilated forms, when followed by a noun is equivalent to an adjective or adjectival phrase in English indicating:

(i) *A moral or physical quality*: Exx. **raġel ta' ġieh** 'a man of honour' for 'an honourable man'; **mara ta' dixxiplina** 'a disciplinary woman'; **bniedem ta' saħħa** 'a strong person'; **jum ta' ferħ** 'a day of joy' for 'a joyful day'.

(ii) *The material of which something is made*: Exx. **gandlier tal-fidda** 'a silver candlestick'; **pinna tad-deheb** 'a golden pen'.

(iii) *trade or craft*: Exx. **tal-ħalib** 'milkman'; **tal-ħaxix** 'greengrocer'; **tal-laħam** 'butcher'; **tal-kappar** 'caper-seller' (generally a woman). In these and other similar phrases, the word **mara** or **raġel** is understood.

(iv) *function or use*: Exx. **ħwejjeġ ta' taħt** 'underwear'; **libsa ta' fuq** 'the dress'; **ilma tax-xorb** (ħasil) 'drinking (washing) water'.

Note on Particle 'il or 'l

Not to be confused with the definite article is particle **'il** which precedes a few adverbs of place. This particle is a shortened form of the Arabic adverbial particle **ʔilaa** meaning *to, till, towards*.

Exx. **'l isfel** (not l-isfel) 'downwards'; **'il fuq** 'upwards'; **'il ġewwa** 'inside'; **'il barra** 'outside'; **'l hemm** 'there'; **'l hawn** 'here' as in **jiġri 'l hawn u 'l hemm** 'he runs here and there'.

'il or **'l** is also to be distinguished from the definite article when it occurs before words which being already defined, do not take the definite article (See Lesson 1, p. 37).

EXERCISE 13

Translate:

(a) **Kemm fiha nies Malta? Fiha fuq** (over) **tliet mitt elf. Kemm kienet ilha kolonja Ingliża** (British Colony) **Malta qabel saret** (became) **indipendenti? Bil-għatx? Hawn l-ilma. Bil-ġuħ? Hawn il-ħobż. Ma' min mar** (went) **missierek? Mal-ħbieb** (friends). **Dil-mara għandha ċurkett** (ring) **tad-deheb. Raġel bla qalb** (heart) **u mara bla moħħ** (brain). **Hdejn Malta hemm tliet gżejjer** (islands) — **Ghawdex, Kemmuna u Filfla. Filfla hi blata** (rock) **għat-taħriġ ta' sparar** (firing exercises). **Vapur** (ship) **bejn sema u ilma. Dur** (turn) **fuq ix-xellug; fuq il-lemin. Hu ħares** (he looked) **'il fuq u 'l isfel u ma ra** (saw) **'l ħadd** (nobody).

(b) This (f.) is not like that (m.). The son is like his father, but the girl is like her mother. A silver (**fidda**) watch (**arloġġ**). He came (**ġie**) an hour and a half (**nofs**) behind time. For today it is enough (**biżżejjed**). Near his shop (**ħanut**) there is a house opposite the palace (**palazz**) of the governor (**gvernatur**). This is the fee (**ħlas**) for the month. This is a prize (**premju**) for a girl. Give it (**agħtih**) to the girl from Gżira (a place-name in Malta). He first (**l-ewwel**) went (**mar**) by sea then (**imbagħad**) by land.

Lesson 14

THE NUMERALS

CARDINAL NUMBERS

Of all cardinal numbers which are the simple ones as one, two, etc. (a) only number one has a masculine (**wieħed**) and feminine (**waħda**) gender; (b) numbers 2-10 have two different numerical forms, one used without the counted object (ex. **sitta** 'six') and another (the adjectival form) used with the counted object (ex. **sitt**

soldi 'six pence'). The adjectival forms are shown in brackets in the list below; (c) the 'tens' have the plural suffix **in** ('iin') added to the last consonant of the singular form (ex. **tlieta** 3, **tletin** 30); (d) the hundreds are formed by the cardinal adjectives plus **mija** (sing.) (ex. **tliet mija**, 300); (e) the thousands and the millions are formed by the cardinal adjective + **elef** (plural) or **miljuni** (ex. **tlitt elef** 3,000; **tliet miljuni**, 3,000,000); (f.) **mija** (**mitt** adjectival form) 'a hundred' and **elf** 'a thousand' have their plural forms **mijiet** 'hundreds' used indefinitely as in **mijiet ta' liri** 'hundreds of pounds'; **eluf** 'thousands', and their dual **mitejn** 'two hundred' and **elfejn** 'two thousand'; (g) **għ** is omitted in the adjectival numbers 4, 7 and 9 (exx. **erbat, sebat, disat irġiel** not **erbagħt, sebagħt, disagħt irġiel** '4, 7, 9 men'; (h) Similarly **għ** is omitted in numbers 11-19. We write **erbatax, sbatax**, etc. not **erbagħtax, sbagħtax**, etc.

With reference to section (b) for numbers 2-10, of the two adjectival forms, the one which ends in **t**, known as the **t marbuta**, is used (i) before words which begin with a vowel (ex. **ħamest elef** 5,000) (ii) before plural monosyllabic words which, in this case, take initial euphonic vowel **i** (ex. **ħamest iħmir** 'five asses') and sometimes, though less commonly also (iii) before dissyllabic words beginning with two consonants or with a consonant plus semi-vowel and initial euphonic vowel **i** (ex. **ħamest ikmamar** 'five rooms', **ħamest iżwiemel** 'five horses'). The other form is used more commonly with plural dissyllabic nouns which begin with more than one consonant or a consonant plus a semi-vowel. Exx. **ħames skieken** 'five knives', **ħames żwiemel** 'five horses'.

Initial **i** prefixed to a two-consonant group in some of the foregoing examples is purely euphonic and therefore does not form an integral part of the plural word. Thus the plural of **żiemel** is **żwiemel** not **iżwiemel**; of **kamra, kmamar** and not **ikmamar**. This euphonic **i** is required only when the numerical form used is that which ends in **t-marbuta**.

The Cardinal numbers are: **wieħed** (m.) 'one'; **waħda** (f.) 'one'; **waħdiet** (pl.) 'single ones'; **uħud** (common plural) 'ones'; **tnejn** (żewġ or żewġt, sometimes ġiex or ġiext 'a couple of') 2; **tlieta** (tliet or tlitt) 3; **erbgħa** (erba' or erbat) 4; **ħamsa** (ħames or ħamest) 5; **sitta** (sitt) 6; **sebgħa** (seba' or sebat for sebagħt) 7; **tmienja** (tmien or tmint) 8; **disgħa** (disa' or disat for disagħt) 9; **għaxra** (għaxar or għaxart) 10; **ħdax** (ħdax-il) 11; **tnax** (tnax-il) 12; **tlettax** (tlettax-il) 13; **erbatax** (erbatax-il) 14; **ħmistax** (ħmistax-il) 15; **sittax** (sittax-il) 16; **sbatax** (sbatax-il) 17; **tmintax** (tmintax-il) 18; **dsatax** (dsatax-il) 19; **għoxrin** 20.

Remark 1: Note that **tlitt** = **tliet** (three) + **t-marbuta**. So we write **tliet suldati** 'three soldiers' but **tlitt iswieq** 'three markets'; **tmien siġġijiet** 'eight chairs' but **tmint ijiem** 'eight days'.

Compound numbers: **wieħed u għoxrin**, (lit. one and twenty) 21; and so on till twenty nine; **tletin** 30; **wieħed u tletin** (lit. one and thirty) 31; and so on till thirty nine; **erbgħin** 40; and so on for the following tens: **ħamsin** 50; **sittin** 60; **sebgħin** 70; **tmenin**, 80; **disgħin** 90; **mija** 100; but **mija u wieħed** a hundred and one (101) and not **wieħed u mija** (lit. one and hundred). Similarly **mija u tnejn**, 102; **mija u tlieta**, 103; **mija u wieħed u għoxrin** 121, as in English a hundred and twenty one; **mitejn**, 200; **mitejn u tlieta u sebgħin** 273; **tliet mija** (sing.) 300; **erba' mija**, 400; **ħames mija**, 500; **disa' mija**, 900; **elf**, 1,000; **elf disa' mija u ħamsa u sittin**, 1,965; **elfejn**, 2,000; **elfejn u sitt mija u ħamsin**, 2,650; **ħamest elef**, 5,000; **sitt elef**, 6,000; **ħdax-il elf**, 11,00; **sbatax-il elf**, 17,000; **wieħed u għoxrin elf**, 21,000; etc. **miljun**, a million, 1,000,000; **żewġ miljuni**, two million, 2,000,000 **ħames miljuni u ħames mitt elf** 5,500,000.

NUMBERS 11 - 19

The hyphenated -il of **ħdax-il**, **tnax-il**, etc. which some Maltese grammarians mistook for the definite article is etymologically an integral part of the number. In

Arabic this is final **ar** in numerals from 11-19 as in **hi'daaṣar** 'eleven', **it'naaṣar** 'twelve', etc. which are composed of a shortened form of the cardinal number + adjectival numeral **għaxar**; thus **ħdax = wieħed** (one) + **għaxar** (ten); **tnax = tnejn** (two); + **għaxar** (ten).

The -il in **kemm-il** 'how many', 'many a' before a sing. noun is formed by analogy with the formation of this group of numbers.

Contrary to English, the smaller number comes before the greater, except in the case of **mija** 'a hundred' and **elf** 'a thousand'.

Exx. **sebgħa u tletin** (lit. seven and thirty) 37; but **mija u sebgħin** 170; and **elf u disa' mija** 1,900 in which the larger number precedes the smaller one as in English.

The conjunction **u** 'and' is used in an additional sense before the last single or composite number.

Exx. **elf, ħames mija u sitta** (single number) 1,506; **elf, ħames mija u sitta u għoxrin** (composite number) 1,526

THE NUMBER OF THE COUNTED OBJECTS

(a) *From numbers 2 - 10*. The counted nouns are in the plural: **żewġt, tlitt irġiel** 'two, three men'; **għaxar nisa** 'ten women'.

(b) *From numbers 11 - 101*. The counted nouns and their adjectives are in the singular. e.g. **ħdax-il fenek** 'eleven rabbits' (not pl. **fniek**); **għoxrin pinna** 'twenty pens' (not pl. **pinen**); **mitt student u wieħed** '101 students'; **ħdax-il suldat għajjien** 'eleven tired soldiers'. But note that while the single adjective is in the sing., the descriptive phrase or clause qualifying the noun is in the plural. Exx. **tlettax-il xebba lebsin** (not **liebsa** fem. sing.) **libsa bajda** 'thirteen maids wearing a white dress'; **sittax-il suldat ta' min ifaħħarhom** (**hom** = them) or **li mietu** (not **miet** 'he died') **għal pajjiżhom** (not **pajjiżu** 'his country') 'sixteen soldiers who are worthy of praise' or 'who died for their country'.

(c) *From 102 - 110.* The counted nouns are in the plural. Exx. **mija u seba' studenti** 'one hundred and seven students'.

(d) When one of the first ten numbers is added to a hundred, thousand, million or more etc. this smaller number appears after the noun.

Exx. **tmien mitt student** 'eight hundred students' but **tmiem mitt student u wiehed** 'eight hundred and one student(s)'; **elf (miljun) vapur u għaxra** 'a thousand, (million) and ten ships'.

(e) When **wiehed** (m.) **wahda** (f.) take the pronominal suffixes they mean 'alone', 'by one's self'.
Exx. **wahdi,** I alone; **wahdek,** you (one person) alone; etc.

(f) **Għaxra** 'ten', has the determinate plural **għaxriet** 'tens' and the indeterminate, but little used, plural **għexieri** 'tens'. **Egħxur,** now replaced by more common **dieċmi,** means 'tithes'.

(g) **Elf** 'thousand', has two plurals, (i) the counted or numbered plural **elef,** as in **sitt elef** 6,000; **sebat elef** 7,000; and (ii) the uncounted or unnumbered plural **eluf,** 'thousands'. Another plural form is **elufijiet,** 'many thousands', a double plural form because it is made up of pl. **eluf,** thousands + pl. suffix **ijiet.**

The cardinal plurals can be pluralised by adding stress-attracting suffixes, **-iet, ijiet,** and, less frequently, **at.** Those marked with an * are the less common forms:

Exx. **tnejn** (two)/**tnejnijiet** (twos); **tlieta** (three)/**tlitiet** or * **tlitijiet** (threes); **erbgħa** (four)/**erbgħat** or * **erbgħi‑jiet** (fours); **hamsa** (five)/**hamsiet** or * **hamsijiet** (fives); **sitta** (six)/**sittiet** or * **sittijiet** (sixes); **sebgħa** (seven); **sebgħat** (sevens); **tmienja** (eight/**tminjiet** (eights); **disgħa** (nine)/**disgħat** (nines); **għaxra** (ten)/**għaxriet** (tens); **hdax** (eleven)/**hdaxijiet** (elevens); **tnax** (twelve)/**tnaxijiet** (twelves); etc. **għoxrin** (twenty)/**għoxrinijiet** (twenties); **tletin** (thirty)/**tletinijiet** (thirties); **erbgħin** (forty)/**erbgħinijiet** (forties) etc.; **mija** (a hundred)/ **mijiet** (hundreds).

THE ORDINAL NUMBERS

These numbers which show rank or position in a series are used with the definite article and are invariable for both genders and numbers: **L-ewwel** 'whence' **ewlieni** (m. adj.) **ewlenija** (f. adj.) 'first'; **it-tieni** 'second'; **it-tielet** 'third'; **ir-raba'** 'fourth'; **il-ħames** 'fifth'; **is-sitt** 'sixth'; **is-seba'** 'seventh'; **it-tmien** 'eighth'; **id-disa'** 'the ninth'; **l-għaxar** 'the tenth'. The rest are as the cardinal numbers up to 99 + def. art. **il-** except **mitt** for the hundreth, e.g. **il-mitt tifel**, 'the hundreth boy'.

The. Cardinal Numbers except numbers 1 and 2 for *first* and *second*, do duty for ordinal numbers when these (i) follow proper names of kings, popes etc. Exx. **Ir-Re Ġorġ Sebgħa** 'King George VII'; **il-Papa Pawlu Sitta** 'Pope Paul VI' (ii) follow a verb except for numbers 1 - 5. Exx. **Ġie l-ewwel, (it-tieni, it-tielet, ir-raba', il-ħames) fl-eżami** 'he was first (second, third, fourth, fifth) in the examination'; but **ġie s-sitta** (sixth), **is-sebgħa** (seventh), **l-għaxra** (tenth). But the Ordinal numbers are used instead of the Cardinal before **wieħed** (m.) or **waħda** (f.) 'one'. So we say **ġie** (m.) or **ġiet** (f.) **is-sitt, is-seba'** or **l-għaxar + wieħed** (m.) or **waħda** (f.) 'one'.

(a) *Some numerical adverbs:* **Darba**, once; **darbtejn**, twice; **tliet darbiet**, thrice; **drabi** or **xi drabi**, sometimes.

(b) *Distributive adverbs:* These are expressed by repeating the number.

Exx. **wieħed wieħed**, 'one by one', or 'one at a time'; **tnejn tnejn**, 'two by two' or 'two at a time'; etc. **tnejn, tlieta, erbgħa, ħamsin, kull wieħed**, 'two three, four, fifty, each'.

(c) *Divisional numbers:* These are obtained by inserting the preposition **fi**, 'in', between the same, or different, two numbers.

Exx. **tnejn, f'sitta tlieta;** 'six divided by two equals three';

and more fully **tlieta f'sitta jidħlu tnejn**, 'two into six goes (lit. enter) three'.

(d) *Multiplicative numbers*: These are obtained by inserting the preposition **għal** between the same two, or different, numbers.

Exx. **tnejn għal tnejn erbgħa**, 'two times two four'; **sitta għal ħamsa tletin**, 'six times five thirty'.

(e) *Fractional numbers*: The fractional words are **nofs**, 'half' (plural **infas**, 'a measure of liquids'); **kwart**, 'one fourth' 1/4; **terz**, 'one third' 1/3; **kwint**, 'one fifth' 1/5. The other fractional words **robu**, **rbiegħ**, one fourth, are used only in the meat industry. An alternative method to the use of **kwart** 1/4; **terz** 1/3; and **kwint** 1/5 is obtained periphrastically thus: **Mit-tlieta waħda** (lit. one from three) **mill-erbgħa waħda** = 1/4; **mill-ħamsa waħda** = 1/5; **mis-sitta tnejn** = 2/6; **mill-għaxra seba'** 7/10 etc.

TIME-WORDS

The Days of the Week are: **It-Tnejn**, Monday; **it-Tlieta**, Tuesday; **l-Erbgħa**, Wednesday; **il-Ħamis**, Thursday; **il-Ġimgħa**, Friday; **is-Sibt**, Saturday, **il-Ħadd**, Sunday.

Clock or Watch Time: **Nofsinhar** (lit. mid-day) 'noon'; **is-siegħa** 'one o'clock'; **is-sagħtejn** 'two o'clock'; **it-tlieta** 'three o'clock'; **l-erbgħa** 'four o'clock'; **il-ħamsa** 'five o'clock'; **is-sitta** 'six o'clock'; **is-sebgħa** 'seven o'clock'; **it-tmienja** 'eight o'clock'; **id-disgħa** 'nine o'clock'; **l-għaxra** 'ten o'clock'; **il-ħdax** 'eleven o'clock'; **nofs il-lejl** 'midnight'. **Kwarta** 'quarter of an hour'; **nofs siegħa** 'half an hour'; **il-kwarta** 'quarter past twelve'; **in-nofs siegħa** 'half past twelve'; **minuta** 'minute'; **sekonda** 'a second'. **Nieqes** (lit. less) 'to'; **u** (lit. and) 'past'.

Exx. **Is-sebgħa nieqes** (sing.) or **neqsin** (pl.) **kwart** (or **ħames minuti**) 'it is quarter (or five) to seven'; **is-sebgħa u kwart** (or **u ħames minuti**) 'it is a quarter past seven (or five past seven)'.

a.m. = **ta' fil-għodu**. Ex. at 6 a.m. = **fis-sitta ta' fil-għodu**.

p.m. = **ta' fil-għaxija**. Ex. at 7 p.m. = **fis-seba' ta' fil-għaxija** (for later hours, **ta' bil-lejl**).

Time Verbs: **Daqq** (m. sing.) 'it struck'. Ex. **Daqq nofs inhar** 'it is twelve o'clock'. **Daqqet** (f. sing.). Ex. **Daqqet is-siegħa** 'it is one o'clock'. **Daqqu** (pl.) Ex. **Daqqu s-sagħtejn** 'it is two o'clock' **is-siegħa (is-sagħtejn) qed idoqqu** 'one (two) o'clock on the stroke'. **Huma** or **saru** (m.) **saret** (f.) **it-tmienja** 'it is eight o'clock'; **għoddu sar nofs il-lejl** 'it is almost midnight'; **għoddhom saru s-sagħtejn** 'it is nearly two o'clock'; **kull siegħa** 'every hour'; **kull sagħtejn** 'every two hours'; **fis-sebgħa** 'at seven (o'clock)'; **fil-ħamsa** 'at five (o'clock)' etc.

Ħin: (i) time, (ii) when. **X'ħin hu?** 'what time is it?'; **x'ħin ġej?** 'when is he (or are you) coming?'; **dal-ħin** 'at the present moment'; **dan mhux ħin** 'this is not the right time'; **kull x'ħin** or **kull meta** 'whenever'.

Particular Week Days: **l-Erbgħa tar-Rmied** 'Ash Wednesday'; **Ħamis ix-Xirka** 'Maundy Thursday'; **il-Ġimgħa l-Kbira** 'Good Friday'; **Sibt il-Għid** 'Holy Saturday'.

Names of the Months: **Jannar** 'January'; **Frar** 'February'; **Marzu** 'March'; **April** 'April'; **Mejju** 'May'; **Ġunju** 'June'; **Lulju** 'July'; **Awwissu** 'August'; **Settembru** 'September'; **Ottubru** 'October'; **Novembru** 'November' **Diċembru** 'December'.

The Seasons: **Ir-rebbiegħa** 'Spring'; **is-sajf** 'Summer'; **il-ħarifa** 'Autumn'; **ix-xitwa** 'Winter'.

Dates: The dates are indicated by the Ordinal Number for the first day only, and by the Cardinal Numbers + the definite article for the rest.

Exx. **L-ewwel ta' Mejju** 'the first day of May'; **it-tlieta ta' Frar** 'the third of February'; **fis-sebgħa ta' Ġunju** 'on the seventh of June'; **għandna ħamsa mix-xahar** 'this is the fifth day of the month' lit. we have five (days) of the month'; **kemm għandna mix-xahar?** what is the date?'.

Q. K. (short for **Qabel Kristu**) = B.C. and **W.K.** (short for **Wara Kristu**) = A.D.

Age: **Kemm-il sena għandha oħtok?** 'how old is your sister?'; **għandha għoxrin (sena)** 'she is twenty'; **għalqet għoxrin sena** 'she is (lit. she shut, i.e. completed) twenty years'; **meta tagħlaq sninha?** 'when is her birthday?'; **għandu ħafna żmien** (or **għomor**) 'he is very old'.

Other time-usages:

English "next" is expressed by (i) participial form **dieħel** 'entering' (ii) **li ġej** 'coming' for masc. time-words and **dieħla** or **li ġejja** for fem. time-words when the time-word is defined by the article or by (iii) **ieħor** (m.) **oħra** (f.) 'another' when it is not defined by the article. Exx. (i) **Ix-xahar id-dieħel** or (ii) **li ġej** or (iii) **xahar ieħor** 'next month'; (i) **il-ġimgħa d-dieħla** or (ii) **li ġejja** or (iii) **ġimgħa oħra** 'next week'. Eng. 'today week' is translated **bħal-lum u ġimgħa**, also without conjunction **u** as in **bħal għada ħmistax** 'tomorrow fortnight'.

Greetings: **Saħħa** 'good-bye'; **l-għodwa t-tajba** (colloquial **bonġu** or **bonġornu**) 'good morning'; **il-lejl it-tajjeb** (colloquial **bonasira** or **bonswa**) 'good night'; **arrivederċi** (au revoir!) 'see you again'; **bis-saħħa!** 'your health'; **nifraħlek** (also **għandi pjaċir**) 'congratulations'. **merħba** (+ **bik, bikom** 'with you' sing. & pl.) 'welcome'.

Currency: **tliet ħabbiet** ¼d.; **sitt ħabbiet** ½d; **sold** 1d; **sold u nofs** 1½; **żewġ soldi** 2d.; **tliet karnijiet** 2½; **tliet soldi** 3d; **sikspenz** 6d; **xelin** 1s; **disa' rbajja'** 1s 3d; **xelin u nofs** 1s. 6d.; **skud** 1s. 8d.; **żewġ xelini** 2s; **tmintax irbiegħi** 2s.6d; **nofs lira** 10s; **lira** £1; **lira u nofs** £1 10s; **żewġ liri** £2.

Weights and Measures with the British Equivalent:

(a) *Length*: **1 pulzier** = 0.859 ins; **1 xiber** 'span' (=12-il **pulzier**) 10.312 ins; **qasba** (= 8 **xbar** = 96 **pulzier**) 2.292 yds; **jarda** (= 36 **pulzier**) 1 yd.

(b) *Area*: **qasba kwadra** = 5.252 sq yd; **kejla** = 22.41 sq yd. **siegħ** (= **10 kejliet**) 224.1 sq. yd; **tomna** (= **6 sigħan**) 0.278 acres; **wejba** (= **4 tomniet**) 1.111 acres; **modd** (= 16-il **tomna**) 4.444 acres.

c) *Volume*: **xiber kubu** = 0.635 cu. ft.; **qasba kubu** = 12.04 cu. yd.

(d) *Weight*: **uqija** 0.933 oz; **ratal** (= **30 uqija**) 1.750 lb; **wiżna** (= **5 rtal**) 8.750 lb; **qantar** (= **20 wiżna**) 175.000 lb; **12.8 qantar** (= 1 ton **tunnellata**) 2240 lbs.

(e) *Capacity*: (a) *Dry Goods*: **tomna** = 0.0625 qrs. **modd** (= 16-il **tomna**) 1.000 qr. (b) *Oil and Milk*: **terz** = 0.281 qt; **nofs** (= **2 terzi**) 0.562 qt; **kartoċċ** (= **2 nfas**) 1.126 qt; **kwarta** (= **4 krataċ**) 1.125 gall.

EXERCISE 14

Translate:

(a) **Qoffa fiha mitejn bettieħa** (melons). **Is-sena elf disa' mija u tlieta u sittin, sena ta' ġrajjiet** (events) **kbar. Kemm-il elf suldat miet** (died) **fil-Gwerra l-Kbira** (great) **tal-elf disa' mija u erbatax, elf disa' mija u tmintax? Ħamsin raġel u tlettax-il mara flimkien ma'** (together with) **mitt suldat strajkjaw** (went on strike). **Il-Papa Pawlu Sitta laħaq wara** (succeeded) **l-Papa Ġwanni Tlieta u Għoxrin. Ġie l-għaxar wieħed fil-klassi; oħtu ġiet ir-raba' u ħuhom iż-żgħir ġie l-ħames. Ħamsa għal għaxra ħamsin; naqqas** (take off) **ħamsa jibqa'** (remain) **ħamsa u erbgħin. Robu hu l-kwart ta' baqra. Laħam il-baqra jgħidulu** (is called lit. 'they call it') **ċanga.**

(b) (N.B. Numbers to be given in words).

These are memorable dates (**dati ta' min jiftakarhom**) in the history (**storja**) of Malta:

2,300 — 2,200 B.C. (=**Q.B.** i.e. **Qabel Kristu**): Coming of man to Malta: 1,400 B.C.: Bronze age (**żmien il-Bronż**): 900 B.C.: Iron (**Ħadid**) age: 218 B.C.: Malta under the Romans: 60 A.D. (= **W.K.** i.e. **Wara Kristu**): Shipwreck (**l-għarqa**) of St. (**San**) Paul (**Pawl**); 533: Malta under

the Eastern (**tal-Lvant**) Emperors (**imperaturi**); 870:
Malta under the Arabs; 1091: The beginning of Norman
(**Normanna**) rule (**ħakma**) in Malta; 1283: Aragonese
(**Aragoniżi**) rule in Malta; 1530: Coming (**il-miġja**) of the
Knights (**kavallieri**); 1565: The great Siege (**Assedju**);
1768: Foundation (**fondazzjoni**) of a University; 1798:
Napoleon in Malta; 1800: French garrison (**il-forzi**) sur-
renders (**iċiedu**) to the English; 1814: Malta joins (**tidħol**
fl-) the British Empire; 1921: First Self-Governing
(**gvern responsabbli**) Constitution (**kostituzzjoni**); 1940:
Second Great Siege; 1942: Award (**l-għoti**) of the George
Cross; 1947: Restoration (**ir-radd**) of self government;
1959: Entering into force (**is-seħħ**) of a new constitution
instead of (**flok** or **minflok**) another which was repealed
(**imneħħija**); 1960: St. Paul's Centenary (**ċentinarju**);
1961: Malta known as the State (**Stat**) of Malta; 1962:
General Election (**elezzjoni ġenerali**) won by the Nation-
alist Party (**partit Nazzjonalista**); 1963: The Colonial Sec-
retary (**segretarju tal-Kolonji**) promised Independence
(**wiegħed l-Indipendenza**) to Malta from May of 1964.
Malta became Independent on 21st September 1964.

PART III

Lesson 15

THE VERB

Maltese has no infinitive verb. It has instead, like Arabic and the other Semitic languages, a verbal STEM-WORD *which consists of the verb in the form of the third person singular, masculine, Perfect Tense.* Thus, for the purpose of our grammar, the equivalent of Engglish "to think' is **ħaseb** 'he thought'; "to work" is **ħadem** 'he worked'. It is important to note even at this stage that the English infinitive as the object of a verb in Maltese is conjugated and agrees with the finite verb in gender and in number. Thus the Maltese say 'I want + I eat' for 'I want to eat'; 'they promised + they give' for 'they promised to give'.

As already explained in Lesson 2 this verbal stem can consist (i) of three consonants called radicals (triliteral verbs) with the medial radical between one of six vocalic sequences; (ii) of four consonants (quadriliteral verbs), some of which can consist of two repeated biradical bases; (iii) of two consonants or a consonant + a semi-vowel because one of the three radicals is dropped.

Verbs, the 3rd radical of which is **għ** or **j** preceded by **a**, show only the first two radicals in the Stem-Word, which ends in **a'** in open syllable.

(1) Verbs having three consonants, none of which is one of the two semi-vowels, are called *Sound* or *Strong*, that is complete verbs. (2) Other triliteral verbs, the third radical of which is silent **għ** represented by ' or (3) semi-vowel **j**, are called *Defective* or *Weak* Verbs respectively. (4) Triliteral verbs with long **a** or **ie** between the 1st and 3rd radicals are called *Hollow Verbs.* Long **a** or **ie** stands for original hypothetical **aWa** or **aJa**, with medial **W** and **J** absorbed into the long vowel or its mutation **ie**. (5) Tri-

literal verbs of which the second and third radicals are identical are called *Doubled* or *Geminated* Verbs.

Examples of these five types of conjugations are:

(1) **HaReĠ** (Sound verb) 'he went out' (triliteral); **HaRBex** 'he scribbled' (quadriliteral).

(2) **QaTa'** for **QaTaGH** (Defective verb) 'he cut'.

(3) **MeXa** for **MeXaJ** (Weak verb) 'he walked'.

(4) **QaL** for **QaWaL** 'he said'; **SaB** for **SaJaB** 'he found', (Hollow verbs).

(5) **HaBB** for **HaBaB** (Doubled or Geminated verb) 'he loved'.

THE TENSES AND VOWEL TYPES OF THE STRONG VERB

The Maltese verb has the following two tenses:

(1) The *Perfect*, which indicates an action done corresponding to the Past Tense or the Perfect of English. Ex. **seraq** 'he robbed' or 'he has robbed'.

(2) The *Imperfect*, which corresponds to the Present and frequently to the Future. Ex. **Jisraq** 'he steals' or 'he will steal'.

Besides these two tenses every verb has:

(3) The *Imperative Mood*. Ex. **israq** (sing.)/**isirqu** (pl.) 'rob'.

(4) The *Present Participle* feminine and masculine, with both a verbal and adjectival function, which, unlike Arabic, is taken by intransitive verbs only and a few other verbs indicating 'motion'. Exx. **nieżel** (m.)/**nieżla** (f.) **neżlin** (pl.) 'descending'; but not **kieteb/kietba** 'writing' or **ġiebed/ġiebda** 'pulling' from transitive verbs **kiteb** and **ġibed**.

(5) The *Past Participle* masculine and feminine with both a verbal and adjectival function. Exx. **misruq** (m.) **misruqa** (f.) **misruqin** (pl.) 'robbed'.

(6)   The *Verbal Noun*. Ex. **serq** 'robbing' or 'theft'.
      The stem or basal form of a verb can take one of
      the following six vowel sequences shown in bold in
      the pattern.

Patterns	*Vocabulary*
1. KaTaB:	Exx. (i) **qasam** 'he broke' (ii) **waqaf** 'he stopped' (iii) **qara** 'he read' (iv) **ġara** 'it happened'. In the last two, the third radical j is quiescent and unwritten.
2. KaTeB:	Exx. (i) **qabeż** 'he jumped' (ii) **ħareġ** 'he went out'.
3. KeTeB:	Exx. (i) **xegħel** 'he lighted' (ii) **fehem** 'he understood' (iii) **qered** 'he destroyed'.
4. KeTaB:	Exx. (i) **seraq** 'he stole' (ii) **wera** 'he showed' (iii) **ġema'** also **ġama'** 'he gathered'. In the last two, the third radical j and għ (') are quiescent and unwritten, as in No. 1 (iii) & (iv).
5. KiTeB:	Exx. (i) **kiser** 'he broke' (ii) **wiżen** 'he weighed'.
6. KoToB:	Exx. (i) **qorob** 'he got near' (ii) **għolob** 'he grew thin'.

There are only three verbs with vocalic sequence o-a.   These three verbs have j for their third radical.   They are **għola** 'he went up high'; **għoxa** 'he swooned' and **ħola** (also **ħela**) 'it (he) grew sweet'.

THE PARADIGM OF THE STRONG VERB

The Perfect Tense, the 1st and 2nd pers. sing. of which are identical, is formed by the following suffixes attached to the third radical of the Stem-Verb.

(a) *Singular*	(b) *Plural*
3rd pers. masc. Stem-Word	3rd pers. **u**
3r. pers. fem. **et**	
2nd pers. **t**	2nd pers. **tu**
1st pers. **t**	1st pers. **na**

(In this and other verbal paradigms, first memorise the conjugations and only after you have done so, refer to the explanatory remarks for further information. If you find it difficult to remember the conjugations starting from the Stem-Word (3rd pers, masc. sing.) start from the 1st pers. sing. and pl.).

(a) *Singular*

Verbal Stem-Words with their six different vocalic sequences:

3rd pers. masc.	(i) talab 'he asked' (ii) qatel 'he killed' (iii) fehem 'he understood' (iv) seraq 'he stole' (v) ġibed 'he pulled' (vi) ḥolom 'he dreamt'.
3rd pers. fem. (See Rem. 1 below)	(i) talbet (ii) qatlet (iii) fehmet (iv) serqet (v) ġibdet (vi) ḥolmot.
2nd & 1st pers. (See Rem. 2 below)	(i) tlabt (ii) qtilt (iii) fhimt (iv) sraqt (v) ġbidt (vi) ḥlomt.

Remark 1: This form is obtained by (i) the elision of the *second* vowel of the sequence in the Stem-Word. This brings the second and third radicals together + suffix **et** ('**talbet**, '**qatlet** etc. instead of '**talabet**, '**qatalet** etc.).

Remark 2: This form is obtained by the omission of the *first* vowel of the vocalic sequence in the Stem-Word. This brings the first two radicals together with vowel **e** shaded into vowel **i** + suffix **t** (i.e. **tlabt**, **qtilt** etc. for **ta'labt**, **qa'tilt** etc). As the form is common to both first and second persons singular, the person meant is known by the context.

(b) *Plural*

3rd pers. (See Rem. 3)	(i) talbu 'they asked' (ii) qatlu 'they killed' (iii) fehmu 'they understood' (iv) serqu 'they stole' (v) ġibdu 'they pulled' (vi) ħolmu 'they dreamt'.
2nd pers. (See Rem. 4)	(i) tlabtu (ii) qtiltu (iii) fhimtu (iv) sraqtu (v) ġibdtu (vi) ħlomtu.
1st pers. (See Rem. 5)	(i) tlabna (ii) qtilna (iii) fhimna (iv) sraqna (v) ġibdna (vi) ħlomna.

Remark 3: This form is obtained by the omission of the *second* vowel in the sequence of the Stem-Word. This brings the third and second radicals together + suffix u ('talbu, 'qatlu etc. for 'talabu 'qatalu etc.). As a verbal form, independently of its present conjugation, talbu, qatlu etc. can also be compound formations for talb + pron. suffix u; qatl + pron. suffix u etc., meaning 'he asked him' and 'he killed him' respectively.

Remark 4: This form is obtained by the omission of the *first* vowel in the vocalic sequence of the Stem-Word. This brings the first two radicals together + suffix tu, (i.e. 'tlabtu, 'qtiltu etc. for ta'labtu qa'tiltu etc.). As in the previous case, this form, apart from the present conjugation, can also stand for tlabt + pron. suffix u; qtilt + pron. suffix u (See first and second persons sing. above) meaning 'I (or you) have asked him', 'have killed him'.

Remark 5: This form is obtained by the omission of the *first* vowel in the vocalic sequence; this brings the first two radicals together + suffix na. (i.e. 'tlabna 'qtilna etc. for ta'labna, qa'tilna etc.).

Note that all the foregoing conjugations, other than that of the Stem-Word which serves as a sort of term of reference, are formed by a number of short unstressed suffixes which affect the position of the original stress, according to the general rule explained on p. 32 (ii), namely *that one stressed syllable cannot be followed by more than one unstressed syllable, so that the addition of a syllabic suffix or a stress-attracting 't' causes the elision of the unstressed vowel in the vocalic sequence of the Stem-Word.* As an example take the addition of suffix **u** in the third person plural to Stem-Word TaLaB. Without the omission of the second unstressed vowel we would have the non-Maltese forms 'TaLaBu. In the case of the monosyllabic forms common to the first and second person singular, the omitted vowel is the first stressed one of the sequence because in this particular case, Maltese has developed a monosyllabic form. We say **qtilt** instead of **qa'tilt** and **tlabt** instead of **ta'labt**. But if the first radical is **għ** or **w** then we have the full dissyllabic form. Thus we say **għamilt** 'I (you) did'; **wasalt** 'I (you) arrived' not **għmilt, wsalt**.

Kien/ikun — *(he, it) was/will be*

This is a Hollow Verb, the subject-matter of Lesson 23. But as the verb can be used both independently as a main verb like English *to be*, and as an auxiliary verb like English *to have*, in order to express the time when an action has been performed, the student is advised to memorise its conjugation which is as follows:

Perfect

(hu) **kien**; (hi) **kienet**; (int, jien) **kont**; — (huma) **kienu**; (intom) **kontu**; (aħna) **konna**.

Imperfect

(hu) **ikun**; (hi, int) **tkun**; (jien) **inkun**; — (huma) **ikunu**; (intom) **tkunu**; (aħna) **nkunu**.

Examples illustrating the usages of **kien/ikun** *as an auxiliary verb:*

(i) **kien** etc. + Perfect tense = English auxiliary verb *had* + past participle.

Ex. **Kienu ħarġu xħin wasal missierek** or **xħin missierek wasal** 'they had gone out when your father arrived'.

(ii) **kien** etc. + Imperfect tense = English auxiliary verb *was, were* + present participle.

Ex. **Kien jiekol xħin wasal missierek** 'he was eating when your father arrived'.

(iii) **ikun** etc. + Perfect tense = English *shall* or *will have* + past participle.

Ex. **Ġanni jkun kiel meta jasal tal-posta** 'John will have eaten (finished eating) when the postman will arrive'.

(iv) **ikun** etc. + Imperfect tense = English *shall* or *will be* + present participle.

Ex. **Aħna nkunu nieklu xħin jasal tal-posta** 'we shall be eating when the postman arrives' (or will arrive).

Kien/ikun as auxiliary verbs can precede also a present participle (Lesson 15).

Ex. **Ħuk kien dieħel** 'your brother was entering'; **ħutek ikunu deħlin** 'your brothers will be entering'.

The Passive

There is no special form for the passive voice as in Classical Arabic. In Maltese, this is expressed by (i) the fifth (ii) the sixth (iii) the seventh or (iv) the eight derived form of the verb explained in Lesson 19, or by **kien** etc. 'it or he was'; **ikun** etc. 'it or he will be'; and sometimes by **safa'** 'he was reduced to the state or condition of'; and in colloquial Maltese also by **ġie** etc. 'it or he came' or **jiġi** 'comes' etc. (Lesson 27 p. 197) + past. participle.

Exx. **Il-bieb tkisser** (5th form) 'the door was broken'; **Dak li twiegħed** (6th form) **irid jingħata** 'what was promised must be given'; **il-ktieb inkiteb** (7th form) 'the book was written'; **Ġanni ftaqar** (8th form) 'John was impoverished'; **il-bieb kien miksur** 'the door was broken'; **il-ktieb kien** (or **ġie**) **miktub mitt sena ilu** 'the book was written a hundred years ago'; **ir-raġel ikun** (or **jiġi**) **maqtul** 'the man will be killed'; **safa' maqtul fil-gwerra** 'he was killed in the war'; sfaw (also sefgħu) midrubin mill-ghadu 'they were wounded by the enemy'.

The widespread use of ġie, Italian *venne*, as in *venne ucciso* 'he was killed', is often discarded in the literary language.

EXERCISE 15

Translate:

(a) Holmot holma kerha tassew (indeed). Il-halliel xegħel il-lampa u seraq it-teżor (treasure). Tlabna l-għajnuna (help) t'Alla. L-istudent (the student) qara r-rumanzi (novels) ta' Walter Scott. Il-marid għolob ħafna. Meta qorbot lejja għaraft min kienet. Tlabna u għa-żilna l-aħjar dar Marsaxlokk (bay in Malta). Ma kontx għaraftek għax ma kontx qrobt lejja biżżejjed (enough). X'kien għamel ħuk għalija? Hija kien talab l-għajnuna meħtieġa.

(b) He went out, walked and found a new street to (għal) an old village. When he got near she recognised (għarfet) the thief. She stole a pound's worth of butter (butir) and cheese. We understood the lesson (lezzjoni). He broke his leg (riġel) and she broke her arm (driegħ). They killed the thief who had stolen the jewels (ġawhar). We pulled the string (spaga) and they pulled the rope (ħabel). You have chosen a beautiful house near the sunniest bay in Gozo. The murderer had killed the old woman when the police (pulizija) arrived. They asked £23 (£ = lira after the number) for the radio (radju).

Lesson 16

THE IMPERFECT
AND THE IMPERATIVE

1. The Imperfect Tense is formed by (i) a set of prefixes for the three persons of the singular; and (ii) prefixes + suffix u for the three persons of the plural.

These prefixes are tacked onto a vowel which, in many instances, is the first vowel in the vocalic sequence of the Stem-Word itself placed before the 1st radical, so that the 1st radical and the 2nd radical come in immediate contact with each other. Thus in the verb KiTeB, these affixes are added to iKTeB, displaced vowel i of the Perfect being moved back and placed before the 1st radical with **K** and **T**, the 2nd and 3rd radicals, brought in immediate contact with each other. Note that the verbal forms of the 2nd and 3rd pers. fem. sing. are identical.

2. The resultant form before the addition of the prefixes of the Imperfect Tense Singular, whichever the 1st vowel before the 1st radical, is that of the Imperative Singular, the plural of which is obtained by the addition of suffix **u** after the omission of the 2nd unstressed vowel in accordance with the principle of Maltese stress.

THE AFFIXES OF THE IMPERFECT

(1) *Singular*	(11) *Plural*
(by prefixes only)	(by prefixes + suffix **u**)

j (he)
(before a vowel)
i
(before a consonant)

t (she or you)

n (I)
(before a vowel)
in
(before a consonant)

j (they)
(before a vowel)
i
(before a consonant)

t (you)

n (we)
(before a vowel)
in
(before a consonant)

FORMS OF THE IMPERATIVE

The foregoing rule that the forms of the Imperative, like those of the Imperfect with the addition of the affixes, are obtained by making the 1st vowel of the Perfect tense precede the 1st radical of the Stem-Verb is applicable only when the vocalic sequence of this Stem-Verb is one of the following:

(i) a - a, but only when the first radical is għ, q, or ħ except ħanaq/joħnoq (not jaħnaq) 'he strangled/ strangles'.

Exx. *Perfect*: ħabat 'he struck'; *Imperative*: aħbat/aħbtu 'strike'; *Imperfect*: jaħbat jaħbtu 'he strikes/they strike' etc.; but rabat 'he tied' gives orbot/orbtu 'tie' whence jorbot/jorbtu.

(ii) e - e, only in the case of some verbs.

Exx. ħeles 'he freed'; eħles/eħilsu 'free'; jeħles/jeħilsu 'he frees/they free'; but several other verbs with this vocalic sequence take the combination i - e in the Imperfect.

Exx. fehem 'he understood'; ifhem/ifħmu 'understand'; jifhem/jifħmu 'he understands/they understand'; xeħet 'he threw'; ixħet/ixħtu 'throw'; jixħet/jixħtu 'he throws/they throw'.

(iii) e - a in resaq 'he approached'; ersaq/ersqu 'approach'; jersaq/jersqu 'he approaches/they approach'. In other verbs it often becomes i - a in the Imperative and the Imperfect.

Exx. fetaħ 'he opened'; iftaħ/iftħu 'open'; jiftaħ/jiftħu 'he opens/they open'. Verbs in this class form other vowel-combinations as will be shown on p. 143.

(iv) i - e. Exx. kiteb 'he wrote'; ikteb/iktbu 'write'; jikteb/jikbtu 'he writes/they write'. The only exception in use is siket 'he kept silent'; iskot/isktu 'keep silent'; jiskot/jisktu 'he keeps silent/they keep silent'.

The Conjugation of the Imperfect of KiTeB *'he wrote'*

Sing.: hu jikteb 'he writes'; int (hi) tikteb 'you (she) write(s)'; jien nikteb 'I write'.

Pl.: huma jiktbu 'they write'; intom tiktbu 'you write'; aħna niktbu 'we write'.

INTERROGATION AND NEGATION

As already explained on p. 96 in Lesson 11, interrogation is a matter of intonation generally on a rising tone. The phrasal and sentence structure remains unaltered. In the negative forms the stress falls on the final syllable ending in **x**.

Exx. **Ħuk jiekol/ma jikolx** could mean (i) 'Your brother eats/does not eat'; (ii) 'Does your brother eat?/Does not your brother eat?'; **għandek il-ġuħ (l-għatx)** could mean (i) 'You are hungry (thirsty)'; (ii) 'Are you hungry (thirsty)?'.

The negation of the Perfect and the Imperfect tense is expressed by **ma** (**m'** before a vowel, silent **h** or **għ**) + the verb + stress-bearing suffix **x**. Neither . . . nor is expressed by **la** . . . **la** placed before the negatived verbs as in English, but without the negative suffix **x**.

Exx. **hu jiekol** 'he eats'; **hu ma jikolx** 'he does not eat'; **La jiekol u la jixrob**, (note omission of negative suffix **x**), 'he neither eats nor drinks'.

In the Imperative the prohibition is expressed by **la** + the verb (Impf. 2nd pers. sing. or pl.) + suffix **x**.

Exx. sing. **la tikolx**/pl. **la tiklux** 'do not eat'; sing. **la toqtolx**/pl. **la toqtlux** 'do not kill'.

Particles ser, sa, ħa, għad + Imperfect

The Imperfect Tense in Maltese indicates not only the present but, as a rule, also the future. There are four particles which modify the idea of the time when the action takes place. These particles are:

(i) **Ser**, short for **sejjer** (m.) **sejra** (f.) **sejrin** (pl.) 'going', indicating an action that is going to take place. Ex. **Ser nikteb ittra lil ħija** 'I am going to write a letter to my brother'.

(ii) **Sa** indicating a very near future.

Exx. **Meta sa jiġi Malta ħuk?** 'When will your brother

come to Malta?'; **jiena sa mmur l-Ingilterra sena oħra** 'I shall go to England next year'.

(iii) **Ħa** expressing the intention of doing something can also be used as a separate prefix of the Imperative.

Exx. **Ħa niktiblu ittra u ngħidlu kollox** 'I'll write him a letter and tell him everything' or 'I intend to write him a letter and tell him everything'; **x'ħa (or x'sa) tagħmel waħdek?** 'what will you do alone?'; **issa ħa nitkellem jien** 'now let me speak.'

(iv) **Għad** indicating a future event of a certain importance, or an event which may take place sometime.

Exx. **Dan it-tifel għad jirnexxi ħafna** 'this boy will one day be very successful'; **għad jiġi żmien meta . . .** 'a day will come when . . .'.

The idea of futurity and imminent action in the past can be expressed by the verb **kien/kienet** etc. preceding the particle **ħa, sa** or **ser** and the verb in the Imperfect.

Exx. **Konna sa (or ser) niktbu meta waslitilna l-ittra tiegħek** 'we were going to write when your letter reached us'; **kienet sa (or ser) toħroġ meta wasal żewġha** 'she was going out when her husband arrived'; **kont ħa ngħidlu imma kien hemm in-nies** 'I was going to tell him but there were people about'.

Ikun etc. + particle **ħa, sa** or **ser** + Imperfect indicates an action expected to take place in the future or imminently (**ser**) when another action will also be taking place at more or less the same time.

Ex. **Inkunu sa (ħa or ser) nerġgħu lura lejn Malta xħin inti tasal l-Italja** 'we shall be returning to Malta when you arrive in Italy'.

THE PERFECTS AND THEIR CORRESPONDING IMPERFECTS

Before we proceed further remember (i) that the form of the Imperative for the 2nd person sing. and pl.

is obtained by making a vowel precede the first two radicals which may or may not be the first vowel of the Stem-
Verb + addition of suffix **u** for the plural with the omission of the 2nd unstressed vowel of the sing.; (ii) that
the third person sing. masc. and fem. and the first and
third person plural, with or without particle **ħa**, can also
be used as Imperatives corresponding to the use of
English let+him, her, us, them (Exx. [ħa] igħid (he says)
li **jrid** 'let him say what he wants (to say)'; (ħa) **naħ-
dmu** (we work) għal **pajjiżna** 'let us work for our
country'); (iii) that when the second radical of the verb
is **l**, **m**. **n** and, by analogy **għ**, a euphonic vowel must be
inserted before one of these consonants, whichever it
may be, in order to break up the triconsonantal group
and (iv) that the main stress falls on the penultimate
syllable, except in the sing. masc. form of the past participle, its plural form and when stress-bearing pron. suffix
-uk -h or **-uh** or negative particle **x** are attached to the
verb.

The various forms of the Perfect Tense with their
various vocalic sequences are related to variable vocalic
sequences in the corresponding forms of their Imperfect.

STEM-WORD 1. KaTaB: forms of its Imperfects are (i)

jaKTaB (ii) jiKTaB (iii) jiKToB (iv) joKToB.

Patterns	*Vocabulary*
KaTaB (Perf.) (i) /jaKTaB (Impf.)	Exx. **ħabat** (*Perfect*) 'he struck'; **jaħ-** **bat** (*Imperfect*) 'he strikes'; **aħbat/** **aħbtu** (*Impv. sing. & pl.*) 'strike'; **ħaqar** 'he oppressed'; **jaħqar** 'he op- presses'; **aħqar/aħqru** 'oppress'. Other verbs conforming to this pat- tern: **ħalaq** 'he created'; **ħaraq** 'he burnt'; **ħataf** 'he snatched'; **qasam** 'he divided'; **għalaq** 'he shut'; **għasar** 'he squeezed'; **għażaq** 'he dug'.

KaTaB/
jiKTaB

(ii) **Exx. bagḥat** 'he sent'; **jibgḥat** 'he sends'; **ibgḥat/ibagḥtu** 'send'; **ċaḥad** 'he denied'; **jiċḥad** 'he denies'; **iċḥad/ iċḥdu** 'deny'.

Other verbs falling under this category are: **daḥak** 'he laughed'; **dalam** 'it grew dark'; **fadal** 'it was left over'; **fasad** 'he bled'; **laḥaq** 'he reached'; **lagḥab** 'he played'; **lagḥaq** 'he licked'; **marad** 'he fell sick'; **sahar** 'he worked overtime'; **taḥan** 'he ground'.

KaTaB
jiKToB

(iii) **Exx. daḥal** 'he entered'; **jidḥol** 'he enters'; **idḥol/idḥlu** 'enter'; **ġabar** 'he collected'; **jiġbor** 'he collects'; **iġbor/ iġbru** 'collect'.

Other verbs: **saḥan** 'it became warm'; **talab** 'he prayed'.

KaTaB/
joKToB

(iv) **Exx. maxat** 'he combed'; **jomxot** 'he combs'; **omxot/omxtu** 'comb'; **qagḥad** 'he stood'; **joqgḥod** 'he stays'; **oqgḥod /oqogḥdu** 'stay'; **bagḥad** 'he hated'; **jobgḥod** 'he hates'; **obgḥod/obogḥdu** 'hate'.

Other verbs: **baram** 'he twisted'; **barax** 'he scratched'; **ḥanaq** 'he made hoarse'; **laqat** 'he hit'; **qaras** 'he pinched'; **rabat** 'he tied'; **raqad** 'he slept'.

STEM-WORD 2. KaTeB: forms of its Imperfects are (i)

jaKTeB (ii) joKToB.

Patterns	*Vocabulary*
KaTeB/ jaKTeB	(i) **Exx. ḥadem** 'he worked'; **jaḥdem** 'he works'; **aḥdem/aḥdmu** 'work'; **ḥafer** 'he forgave'; **jaḥfer** 'he forgives'; **aḥfer/aḥfru** 'forgive'.

Other verbs: ħaleb 'he milked'; ħalef
'he swore'; ħaseb 'he thought'; ħasel
'he washed'; għalef 'he fed animals';
għamel 'he did'; għażel 'he chose';
qabel 'he agreed'; qabeż 'he jumped'.

KaTeB/
joKToB

(ii) Exx. ħareġ 'he went out'; joħroġ 'he
goes out'; oħroġ/oħorġu 'go out'; qatel
'he killed'; joqtol 'he kills'; oqtol/oqtlu
'kill'. No other examples.

STEM-WORD 3. KeTeB: forms of its Imperfects are (i)
jeKTeB (ii) jiKTeB.

KeTeB/
jeKTeB

(i) Exx. ħeles 'he delivered'; jeħles 'he
delivers'; eħles/eħilsu 'deliver'; għe-
req 'he sank'; jegħreq 'he sinks';
egħreq/egħirqu 'sink'.
Other verbs: ħemeż 'he fastened
with a pin'; and a few others used
mainly in the written language:
ħeġem 'he devoured'; ħebeż 'he reced-
ed'; ħeres 'he pounded with a pestle';
ħebel 'he raved'; ħemer 'it fermented';
ħerek 'he rose early'.

KeTeB/
jiKTeB/

(ii) Exx. deher 'he appeared'; jidher 'he
appears'; idher/idhru 'appear'; fehem
'he understood'; jifhem 'he under-
stands'; ifhem/ifhmu 'understand';
xeher 'he wailed'; jixher 'he wails';
ixher/ixhru 'wail'.

STEM-WORD 4. KeTaB: forms of its Imperfects are (i)
jeKTaB (ii) jiKTaB (iii) jiKToB (iv) joKToB.

Patterns   *Vocabulary*

KeTaB/
jeKTaB

(i) Exx. resaq 'he approached'; jersaq 'he
approaches'; ersaq/ersqu 'approach';
(the only example).

KeTaB/
jiKTaB

(ii) **Exx. feraħ** 'he rejoiced'; **jifraħ** 'he rejoices'; **ifraħ/ifirħu** 'rejoice'; **fetaħ** 'he opened'; **jiftaħ** 'he opens'; **iftaħ/iftħu** 'open'.

Other verbs: **felaħ** 'he was strong'; **kesaħ** 'he was cold'; **lemaħ** 'he perceived'; **mesaħ** 'he wiped'; **rebaħ** 'he won'; **reżaħ** 'he shivered'; **sebaħ** 'it dawned'; **seraq** 'he stole'; **telaq** 'he departed'.

KeTaB/
jiKToB

(i) **Exx. selaħ** 'he skinned'; **jisloħ** 'he skins'; **isloħ/isolħu** 'skin'; **żebagħ** 'he painted'; **jiżbogħ** 'he paints'; **iżbogħ iżbgħu** 'paint'.

Other verbs: **sebaq** 'he outstripped'; **żelaq** 'he slipped'.

KeTaB/
joKToB

(ii) **Exx. nefaħ** 'he blew'; **jonfoħ** 'he blows'; **onfoħ/onfħu** 'blow'; **nefaq** 'he spent'; **jonfoq** 'he spends'; **onfoq/ onfqu** 'spend'.

Other verbs: **beżaq** 'he spat'; **fetaq** 'he unstitched'.

STEM-WORD: 5. KiTeB: forms of its Imperfects are (i) jiKTeB (ii) jiKToB.

Patterns   *Vocabulary*

KiTeB/
jiKTeB

(1) **Exx. niżel** 'he descended'; **jinżel** 'he descends'; **inżel/inżlu** 'descend'; **bidel** 'he changed'; **jibdel** 'he changes'; **ibdel/ibdlu** 'change'.

Other verbs: **difen** 'he buried'; **dilek** 'he smeared'; **fired** 'he separated'; **firex** 'he spread'; **ġibed** 'he pulled'; **ġideb** 'he lied'; **ġidem** 'he bit'; **ġiref** 'he scratched'; **kiber** 'he grew'; **kines** 'he swept'; **kiser** 'he broke'; **nidem** 'he

repented'; **kixef** 'he unveiled'; **siker**
'he got drunk'; **silef** 'he lent'; **tilef** 'he
lost'; **żifen** 'he danced'.

KiTeB/
jiKToB

(ii) Exx. siket 'he was silent'; **jiskot** 'he is
silent'; **iskot/isktu** 'silent' — the only
other verb **tines/jotnos** 'he wept' is
obsolete.

STEM-WORD: 6. KoToB: forms of its Imperfects are (i)
jiKToB (ii) joKToB.

KoToB/
jiKToB

(i) Exx. sogħol 'he coughed'; **jisgħol** 'he
coughs'; **isgħol/isogħlu** 'cough'; **xorob** 'he drank'; **jixrob** 'he drinks'; **ix-
rob/ixorbu** 'drink'.

The only other example is **sogħob/
jisgħob** occurring in the Act of Contri-
tion: **jisgħob** (+ **bija**) 'I am sorry'; lit.
it is heavy (painful) to me.

KoToB/
joKToB

(ii) Exx. ħolom 'he dreamt'; **joħlom** 'he
dreams'; **oħlom/oħolmu** 'dream'; **korob**
'he groaned'; **jokrob** 'he groans';
okrob/okorbu 'groan'.

Other verbs: **ħoloq** 'he created'; **forogħ** 'it (the sea) ebbed'; **kotor** 'it
abounded'; **għodos** 'he dived'; **għokos**
'he decayed'; **għolob** 'he grew thin';
għorok 'he rubbed'; **qorob** 'he approached'.

EXERCISE 16

Translate:

(a) **Ħuk għalaq il-kexxun** (drawer). **Iftaħ il-bieb
u agħlaq it-tieqa** (window). **Għax ftaħtu t-tieqa? Agħal-
quha. La taħqarx il-fqar. Igbru l-flus mill-art. Aħdem
sewwa** (well) **imma** (but) **aħseb x'sa tagħmel qabel tibda**
(begin) **taħdem. Dar-raġel jiflaħ ħafna. It-temp** (the

weather) **beda** (began) **jiksaħ. Ir-riħ jonfoħ minn qalb** (amongst) **is-siġar. Aħna xrobna l-inbid;⁻ issa huma jixorbu l-birra.**

(b) The man struck the boy with a stick (**bastun**). Strike (sing. & pl.) the bad boy with the stick. The good father does not oppress his family (**famiija**). God created heaven and earth out of nothing (**xejn**). Man invents (**jivvinta**) but he does not create. Comb your hair properly (**sewwa**). She stayed with her uncle two weeks (**ġimagħtejn**). Sit on this chair and read today's (**tallum**) paper (**gazzetta**) She appeared before the judge (**imħallef**) but could not understand the indictment (**akkuża**). Let us free the world (**dinja**) from fear (**biża'**) and poverty (**faqar**).

Lesson 17

PARTICIPLES OF THE STRONG VERB

Maltese has two kinds of Participles: (i) the Present or Active Participle (ii) the Past or Passive Participle.

Present Participles all characterised by the long vowel **a** or its mutated form **ie** after the first radical. are used as adjectives and can be masculine or feminine, singular or plural. As already pointed out on p. 129 (4). unlike classical Arabic and other Arabic dialects, in Maltese, with few exceptions, only intransitive verbs and a few verbs indicating motion which can be followed by a noun, take the Present (Active) Participles.

Exx. (**raġel**) **riekeb iż-żiemel** '(a man) riding a horse'; **tiela'** (m.) **tielgħa** (f.) **telgħin** (pl.) **t-taraġ** 'going up the stairs'; **sejjer id-dar** 'going home' etc.

The following are the main forms of strong triradicál verbs with the roots in brackets.

PATTERN 1

KieTeB (m.) KieTBa (f.) KeTBin (pl.) Exx. ħieles (m.) ħielsa (f.) ħelsin (pl.) 'free' (ħeles int. v. 'he was free'; tr. v. 'he freed'); liebes (m.) liebsa (f.) lebsin (pl.) 'dressed' (libes 'he dressed'); rieqed (m.) rieqda (f.) reqdin (pl.) 'sleeping' (raqad 'he slept').

PATTERN 2

KieTaB (m.) KieTBa (f.) KeTBin (pl.) Exx. wieqaf (m.) wieqfa (f.) weqfin (pl.) 'standing', 'stopping' (waqaf 'he stopped'); tielaq (m.) tielqa (f.) telqin (pl.) 'departing' (telaq 'he departed').

Remark 1: There are no forms of the present participles of verbs having the 2nd and 3rd radicals alike and only a few examples of such participial forms of intransitive verbs the 3rd radical of which is għ. Such are tiela' (m.) tielgħa (f.) telgħin (pl.) from tela' 'he went up' or 'mounted'; fieragħ (m.) fiergħa (f.) fergħin (pl.) 'empty' from foroġ 'it ebbed (sea)'; wiesa' (m.) wiesgħa (f.) wesgħin (pl.) 'wide'. Waqa' 'he fell' and waġa' 'it ached' though intransitive verbs have no present participle.

Remark 2: Ħakem 'governor'; ħares 'haunting ghost'; ħatem 'signet-ring'; għażeb 'bachelor', originally participial forms with vocalic sequence a - e ('aa - e) are now used as nouns.

Qiegħed (m.) Qiegħda (f.) Qegħdin (pl.)

This participial form, often shortened into invariable qed, is used as an auxiliary before a verb in the Imperfect, to indicate (i) present or (ii) past progressive action.

Exx. (i) qiegħed (m.) qiegħda (f.) or qed nifhem 'I am understanding'; qegħdin (pl.) nifhmu or qed nifhmu 'we are understanding'.

Progressive action in the past is indicated by adding before **qieghed** etc., the verb **kien** (he or it was) etc.

Exx. (ii) **kont qieghed** (m.) or **qieghda** (f.) or **(qed) nifhem** 'I was understanding'; **konna qeghdin (qed) nifhmu** 'we were understanding'.

THE PAST PARTICIPLE

The Past Participle of Strong and Defective Verbs, which have **gh** as third radical, are formed by prefixes (i) **ma** (ii) **mi** (iii) **me** added to pattern KTuB (**ktuub**), consisting of the first and second radicals together followed by long u closed by the third radical. As every past participle has the function of an adjective, it can be masculine, feminine, singular and plural.

PATTERN 1 ma + KtuB

Exx. **mahsul** (m.) **mahsula** (f.) **mahsulin** (pl.) 'washed' (**hasel** 'he washed'); **maghluq** (m.) **maghluqa** (f.) **maghluqin** (pl.) 'shut' (**ghalaq** 'he shut'); **maqtul** (m.) **maqtula** (f.) **maqtulin** (pl.) 'killed' (**qatel** 'he killed'); **marbut** (m.) **marbuta** (f.) **marbutin** (pl.) 'bound' (**rabat** 'he bound').

PATTERN 2 mi + KTuB

Exx. **mikxuf** (m.) **mikxufa** (f.) **mikxufin** (pl.) 'uncovered' (**kixef** 'he uncovered'); **milqugh** (m.) **milqugha** ,f.) **milqughin** (pl.) 'welcomed' (**laqa'** 'he welcomed'); **misdud** (m.) **misduda** (f.) **misdudin** (pl.) 'plugged' (**sadd** 'he plugged'); **mizrugh** (m.) **mizrugha** (f.) **mizrughin** (pl.) 'sown' (**zara'** 'he sowed'); **mitmum** (m.) **mitmuma** (f.) **mitmumin** (pl.) 'finished' (**temm** 'he finished').

Remark 3: This form is generally favoured by verbs the first radical of which is not **gh**, **q**, **h**, or **ħ** and sometimes an **r**, and also by Stem-Verbs, the first radical of which is **w**. Exx. **mizun** (m.) **mizuna** (f.) **mizunin** (pl.)

'weighed' (wiżen 'he weighed'); miġugħ (m.) miġugħa
(f.) miġugħin (pl.) 'aching' (waġa' 'it ached').

PATTERN 3 me + KTuB

Exx. meħlus (m.)   meħlusa (f.)   meħlusin (pl.)   'freed'
(ħeles 'he freed'); merfugħ (m.) merfugħa (f.) merfu-
għin (pl.) 'raised' (refa' 'he raised').

Remark 4: This form is generally favoured by verbs
beginning with h or ħ.

Two Irregular Forms of the Past Participle

Exx. meħud (m.) meħuda (f.) meħudin (pl.) 'taken' from
ħa 'he took' which is a strong triradical verb in Arabic
(ʔaxað) and mekul (more commonly mikul) + a (f.) +
in (pl.) from kiel 'he ate' which is a strong triradical
verb in Arabic (ʔakal).

EXERCISE 17
Translate:

(a)   Rajt (I have seen) raġel riekeb fuq żiemel u
tfal rekbin fuq ħmar. Ilni wieqfa ħafna. Damu sagħtejn
weqfin. Karlu (Charles) għażeb rieqed waħdu fid-dar il-
qadima. Il-mara liebsa libsa ġdida u t-tfal lebsin ħażin.
(shabbily). F'din id-dar hawn il-ħares. Qed nifhem il-
gazzetta; ma jiniex nifhem il-ktieb għax tqil. Libsa maħ-
sula tidher (looks) ġdida. Dar mikrija fejn il-baħar.
Tieqa miftuħa: xemx u arja friska (fresh) fid-dar u
saħħa (health) kbira għall-familja.

(b)   They are writing a book. We are not understanding the lesson. They were welcomed by the people
(nies) of Malta and Gozo. The sown field (għalqa) belongs to (ta' = of) John. There is a ghost in the bachelor's
house. There were 6,200 soldiers killed in that war.
(gwerra). The books have been taken by your father.
Your sister was wearing an old dress. All (kollha, after
the noun) the boys were asleep. I saw him (rajtu) standing near the shop alone.

Lesson 18

VERBAL NOUNS OF STRONG UNDERIVED VERBS

There are two kinds of verbal nouns. One which (i) denotes the action or state indicated by the meaning of the verb, (ii) is of masculine gender singular in number, and, (iii) like any other noun, can be preceded by the definite article, but has no plural (Exx. **dfin** 'burial' from **difen/jidfen** 'he buried/buries', **id-dfin** 'the burial'), and another which (i) expresses a single occurrence of action or state indicated by the verb (ii) is of feminine gender singular in number; (iii) forms its plural by suffix **iet** and (iv) can be preceded by the definite article (Exx. **difna** 'a burial'; **id-difna** 'the burial'; **difniet** or **id-difniet** 'burials, the burials'). The following are the main patterns of the simple, i.e. underived first forms with the Stem-Verbs in brackets.

Patterns	*Vocabulary*
1. KTiB/ KaTBa (ktiib/'katba)	Exx. **ġbir** 'gathering'/**ġabra** 'a collection' (**ġabar**); **qtil** 'killing'/**qatla** 'a slaughter' (**qatel**).
2. KTiB/ KeTBa (ktiib/'ketba)	Exx. **nbiħ** 'barking'/**nebħa** 'a bark' (**nebaħ**); **nfiħ** 'blowing'/**nefħa** 'a blow' (**nefaħ**); **bligħ** (**bliəħ**) 'swallowing'/**belgħa** 'a gulp' (**bala'**); **ġmigħ** (**dʒmiəħ**) 'gathering'/**ġemgħa** 'a gathering' (**ġama'**).
3. KTiB/ KiTBa (ktiib/'kitba)	Exx. **bdil** 'changing'/**bidla** 'a change' (**bidel**); **żfin** 'dancing'/**żifna** 'a dance' (**żifen**).
	Note that the vowel of the verbal noun indicating one occurrence is the first vowel of the Stem-Word but lengthened. Exceptions to this rule are:

ħdim 'work'/ħidma 'activity' (ħadem);
sokor 'drunkenness'/sakra 'an intoxi-
cation' (siker); self 'lending'/selfa
'a loan' (silef); telf 'loss' telfa 'a loss'
(tilef); xorb 'drinking'/xarba 'a drink'
(xorob); logħob 'playing'/logħba 'a
game' (lagħab).

4. KTaB/   Exx. dlam 'darkness'/dalma 'a dark-
   KaTBa   ness' (dalma); rqad 'sleeping'/raqda
   (ktaab/   'a sleep' (raqad).
   'katba)

5. KTuB/   Exx. dħul 'entrance'/daħla 'an en-
   KaTBa   trance' (daħal); ħruġ 'exit'/ħarġa 'an
   (ktuub/'katba) outing' (ħareġ).

6. KTuB/   Exx. nżul 'descent'/niżla 'a slope'
   Ki[e]TBa   (niżel); tlugħ 'ascent'/telgħa 'an up-
   (ktuub/'ki[e]tba) hill' (tela').

7. KaTB/   Exx. daħk 'laughter'/daħka 'a laugh'
   KaTBa   (daħak); mard 'sickness'/marda 'an
               illness' (marad).

8. KeTB/   Exx. ferħ 'joy'/ferħa 'a joy' (feraħ);
   KeTBa   rebħ 'victory'/rebħa 'a victory' (rebaħ).

9. KoTB/   Ex. ħolm 'dreaming'/ħolma 'a dream'
   KoTBa   (ħolom).

10. KeTBien/   (N.B. KeTBien made up of patt. no. 8
    KeTBa   and suffix ien). Exx. ħelsien 'freedom',
    (ket'biən/ ħelsa 'a release' (ħeles); telfien 'loss',
    'ketba)   'damnation'/telfa 'a loss' (tilef).

EXERCISE 18

Translate:

(a) Il-mewt ta' missierha kienet telfa kbira. Xewqit-
na hija l-ħelsien tal-poplu (people) tagħna. Żfinna żifna
folkloristika, L-inbiħ tal-klieb bil-lejl. Raqda twila fid-

dlam bit-tieqa u l-bieb magħluqin. Dħul bil-flus u ħruġ b'xejn. Il-belt Valletta mimlija bi nżul u tlugħ. Poeżiji fuq (about) tlugħ u nżul ix-xemx. Ir-rebħa ta' Malta kontra (against) l-attakki (attacks) tan-Nażisti u l-Faxxisti flaħħar gwerra għall-ħelsien tal-Mediterran. Il-ġbir tal-qamħ f'Lulju.

(b) There is a collection of old books on the table. The gathering of the harvest (wiċċ tar-raba') takes place (isir) in June. In a long night (lejla) dancing pleases (jogħġob) the young. A life (ħajja) of great activity. Drunkenness is bad (ħażin) for health (saħħa). The barking of the dog awakened (qajjem) the sleeping children. A great darkness fell (waqgħet) on the city of Valletta. He awakened (qam) from a long sleep and an ugly dream. Laughter in the mouth (ħalq) of fools. There was great joy in the village (raħal).

Lesson 19

DERIVED VERBS

A characteristic feature of Maltese, like that of other Semitic languages, is that by means of a combination of, (i) prefixes (ii) infixes (iii) suffixes, it can vary the basic meaning of the Stem-Word adding a different signification or connotation to that indicated by the Stem-Word. Theoretically, including the Stem-Word, there are ten such verbal stems, namely, the original Stem-Word and nine derived stems. All these ten forms exist for one verb or another, but there is not one Maltese verb which has all the ten forms. Exx. ċaħad 'he denied' has derived forms 2, 5 and 7; gideb 'he lied' (2, 5 and 7); niten 'it stank' (2, and 5); qarr 'he confessed' (3, 6 and 10); ħarat 'he ploughed' (7).

It should also be noted that the root form (3rd. pers. masc. sing.) of every derived verb is also the sing. form of the Imperative which becomes plural by the addition of **u** and the omission of the second unstressed vowel in the Root or Stem-Verb. The derived forms form their Perfect and Imperfect by the use of the same suffixes and prefixes as shown in the paradigm of the Strong Verb in Lesson 15. The movements of the main stress or tonic accent follow the general rule governing the position of the Stress as explained on pp. 30-32.

A conjugated verb for every form illustrates the general manner of conjugation of all verbs belonging to the same class; but one must bear in mind that verbs have variable vocalic sequences which they retain in their conjugations.

No derived verb has a form for the Present Participle. Some grammarians consider the names of 'the doer' of an action obtained by reduplication of the medial radical between a vocalic sequence the 2nd vowel of which is long **a** or **ie** as participial forms or nearly so. Of these only **għaddej** (m.) (+**ja**, f. + **in** pl.) which may have originally been **għadi** (m.) **għadja** (f.) **għadjin** (pl.) has a verbal function. Ex. **Kien (kienet) għaddej (għaddejja)** 'he/she was passing' but **kien qattiel** which has an adjectival function means 'he was a killer' and not 'he was killing'. For other examples of names of "doers" see Lesson 3 pp. 48-50 nos. 3 & 4.

PATTERNS OF DERIVED FORMS WITH THEIR IMPERFECTS

In the following patterns affixes, variable vowels and vocalic sequences are shown in bold type.

PATTERN 1

Stem-Verb **KaTaB** (with the 6 variable voc. seq. shown on p. 131 retained in the derived forms).

PATTERN 2

KaTTaB (Perfect)/**iKaTTaB** (Imperfect) — obtained by doubling the second radical of the Stem-Word.

FUNCTION: — (i) *indicates intensity of action*:

Ex. kiser 'he broke' the second form of which **kisser** 'he broke to pieces' is obtained by doubling the second radical.

(ii) *gives a causal meaning to intransitive verbs*:

Exx. daħħak 'he made one laugh' (amused) from **dahak** 'he laughed'; **raqqad** 'he put to sleep' from **raqad** 'he slept'.

(iii) *derives verbs from nouns*:

Exx. baħħar 'he navigated' from **baħar** 'sea'; **xemmex** 'he exposed to the sun' from **xemx** 'sun'.

(iv) *from adjectives*:

Exx. ġedded 'he renewed' from **ġdid** 'new'; **qassar** 'he shortened' from **qasir** 'short'.

Conjugation of KiSSeR
Perfect:

(hu) **kisser** (1st form KiSeR 'he broke') 'he smashed'; (hi) **kissret**; (int, jien) **kissirt**; — (huma) **kissru**; (intom) **kissirtu**; (aħna) **kissirna**.

Imperfect

(hu) **ikisser**; (hi, int) **tkisser**; (jien) **inkisser** — (huma) **ikissru**; (intom) **tkissru**; (aħna) **inkissru**.

Imperative
kisser (sing.)/**kissru** (pl.).

Past Participle
imkisser (m.) **imkissra** (f.) **imkissrin** (pl.) 'smashed'. (Note that initial i being euphonic is omitted when preceded by a word ending in a vowel).

Verbal Noun
tiksir or **tkissir** 'smashing' (both + a when we want to indicate a single action; **tiksira, tkissira** 'a smashing').

N.B. Some other verbs take (i) prefix **ta** or (ii) **te** as a preformative. **Exx. tagħlim** 'instruction'/**tagħlima** 'a les-

son' (għallem);   taqsim or tqassim 'distribution'/taqsima
or tqassima 'a distribution' (qassam); (ii) tehdid or thed-
did 'threatening'/tehdida or theddida 'a threat' (hedded).

PATTERN 3

KieTeB or KaTaB/iKieTeB or iKaTeB formed by
lengthening the first vowel.

FUNCTION: — (i) *derives verbs from nouns*:

Exx. bierek 'he blessed' from barka 'a blessing'; siefer 'he
emigrated' from safar 'departure'.

(ii) *gives a causal force to verbs the second radical
of which is għ or h both of which are incapable of phonetic reduplication and therefore instead of going under
Pattern 2, as they should, go under Pattern 3 to express
the same idea*:

Exx. biegħed (for bagħghad) 'he put at a distance' from
bogħod 'distance'; ġiegħel (for ġagħghal) 'he compelled' (from ġagħal first form); fiehem (for fehhem) 'he
made one understand' from fehem 'he understood'.

Conjugation of GaGHaL *'he compelled' and*
SieFeR *'he went abroad'*

Perfect

(i) (hu) ġiegħel; (hi) ġiegħlet; (int, jien) ġe-
għilt; — (huma) ġiegħlu; (intom) ġegħiltu; (aħna) ġe-
għilna.

(ii) (hu) siefer; (hi) siefret; (int, jien) sifirt; —
(huma) siefru; (intom) sifirtu; (aħna) sifirna.

Imperfect

(i) (hu) iġiegħel; (hi, int) iġġiegħel; (jien) inġie-
għel; — (huma) iġiegħlu; (intom) iġġiegħlu; (aħna)
inġiegħlu.

(ii) (hu) siefer: (hi, int) issiefer; (jien) insiefer;
— (huma) isiefru; (intom) issiefru; (aħna) nsiefru.

Imperative

(i) ġiegħel (sing.)/ġiegħlu (pl.)

(ii) siefer (sing.)/siefru (pl.).

Past Participle

(i) mġiegħel (m.) mġiegħla (f.) mġegħlin (pl.) 'compelled'.

(ii) msiefer (m.) msiefra (f.) msifrin (pl.) 'gone abroad'.

Verbal Noun

(i) tiġġgħil (but more commonly ġegħil) 'compelling'.

(ii) siefer has no verbal noun, but the form is tKeTiB (tke'tiib). Exx. tberik 'blessing' + a, 'a blessing' (bierek); tbegħid 'removing' + a, 'a removal' (biegħed).

Maltese safar 'navigation', the verbal form in use, belongs to the first form of the verb which is used in Arabic but not in Maltese.

PATTERN 4

aKTaB: Formed by prefixing a and dropping the vowel after the first radical. This form does not exist in Maltese except in a few remnants and is added for the benefit of the student interested in the study of Arabic dialectology. This causative function of the Arabic fourth form has now passed to the second form.

PATTERN 5

tKaTTaB/jitKaTTaB: Formed by prefixing t to Stem 2. Remember that t assimilates with ċ, d, ġ, n, s, x, ż, z.

FUNCTION: — (i) *reflexive of the second form*:

Exx. tkabbar 'he grew proud' (lit. he made himself great) from kabbar 'he enlarged'; tgħallaq 'he hanged himself' from għallaq 'he hanged' or 'strangled'.

(ii) *indirect reflexive*:

Exx. **iċċaħħad** (for **t + ċaħħad**) 'he denied himself' from **ċaħad** 'he denied'; **issellef** 'he borrowed' (for **t + sellef**) from **sellef** 'he lent'.

(iii) *passive of the second form*:

Exx. **tgħammed** 'he was baptised' from **għammed** 'he baptised'; **tniżżel** 'he (or it) was brought down' from **niżżel** 'he brought down'.

Perfect

(i) (**hu**) **tkabbar**; (**hi**) **tkabbret**; (**int, jien**) **tkabbart**; — (**huma**) **tkabbru**; (**intom**) **tkabbartu**; (**aħna**) **tkabbarna**.

(ii) (**hu**) **iċċaħħad**; (**hi**) **iċċaħħdet**; (**int, jien**) **iċċaħħadt**; — (**huma**) **iċċaħħdu**; (**intom**) **iċċaħħadtu**; (**aħna**) **iċċaħħadna**.

Imperfect

(i) (**hu**) **jitkabbar**; (**hi, int**) **titkabbar**; (**jien**) **nitkabbar**; — (**huma**) **jitkabbru**; (**intom**) **titkabbru**; (**aħna**) **nitkabbru**.

(ii) (**hu**) **jiċċaħħad**; (**hi, int**) **tiċċaħħad**; (**jien**) **niċċaħħad**; — (**huma**) **jiċċaħħdu**; (**intom**) **tiċċaħħdu** (**aħna**) **niċċaħħdu**.

Imperative

(i) **tkabbar** (sing.)/**tkabbru** (pl.)

(ii) **iċċaħħad** (sing.)/**iċċaħħdu** (pl.).

Past Participle

None.

Verbal Noun

(i) **tkabbir** 'self-importance' or 'enlarging'.

(ii) **tiċħid** 'denial', but this is more properly the verbal noun of the second form. Other verbs follow a pattern with vocalic sequence (i) **e - i** or (ii) **i - i**, the first vowel being in every case the first vowel of the verbal pattern itself.

Exx. (i) **theġġiġ** 'stimulating'/**theġġiġa** 'an act of enthusiasm, stimulation' (**ħeġġeġ**); **tmellis** 'caressing'/**tmellisa** 'a caress' (**melles**); (ii) **tkissir** 'breaking'/**tkissira** 'a break' (**kisser**); **tfissir** 'explanation'/**tfissira** 'an explanation' (**fisser**).

Though the conjugated verbs have no Past Participles, there are a few verbs belonging to the same pattern which form their past participle by prefixing **mit** to the first radical of the second derived verb. These are: **mitkellem** 'spoken' (**t + kellem**); **mitkixxef** 'explored' (**t+kixxef**); **mitkisser** 'broken' (**t+kisser**) of which only **mitkellem** is in frequent use.

EXERCISE 19

(a) **It-tfal kissru s-siġar** (trees) **kollha li kien hemm fil-ġnien** (garden). **Ħeġġeġ lit-tfal jistudjaw** (study) **iżjed. L-omm tiċċaħħad minn ħafna ħwejjeġ** (things) **għal uliedha. Dat-tkabbir kollu għalfejn? Il-bieb** (door) **tkisser bir-riħ** (wind). **Hija msiefer l-Amerika u oħti msiefra l-Ingilterra. Alla jbierek lill-għani** (rich) **u lill-fqir. Tkabbret ħafna għax wirtet lil zijuha** (her uncle). **Issellift mitejn lira minn għand negozjant** (business man). **Il-qaddis** (saint) **jiċċaħħad mill-kumditajiet** (comforts) **tal-ħajja.**

(b) Who broke the new glass (**tazza**)? Which glass was broken yesterday? She put the baby (**tarbija**) to sleep. I enjoy (**inħobb**) sunning myself on the beach (**xtajta**) of Għadira (name of a bay in Malta). We borrowed £200 from the bank (**bank**). He has become very (**ħafna** after verb) proud. I was baptised at Sannat (village name) in Gozo. I did not go abroad this year. The smashing of window panes (**ħġieġ tat-tieqa**). Pride destroys (**jeqred**) man (**bniedem**).

Lesson 20

MORE DERIVED FORMS

PATTERN 6

tKieTeB/jitKieTeB or tKaTaB/jitKaTaB: Formed by prefixing t to the third derived pattern, with the assimilation of t before ċ, d, ġ, s, ż, z.

FUNCTION:— (i) *reflexive*:

Exx. tbiegħed 'he went (lit. put himself) far away' from biegħed 'he placed far off'; tmiegħek 'he wallowed' from miegħek 'he rolled about' or 'wallowed'.

(ii) *passive*:

Exx. tbierek 'he was blessed' from bierek 'he blessed'; tqiegħed 'he (or it) was placed' from qiegħed 'he placed'.

(iii) *reciprocal of the third form*:

Exx. issieħeb 'he associated himself', from sieħeb 'he associated'; iġġieled 'he quarrelled' from ġieled (obsolete) 'he provoked quarrels'; tqabad 'he opposed' (mutual opposition) from qabad 'he seized'.

Conjugation of (i) **Tmiegħek** 'he wallowed'

(ii) **Tqabad** 'he struggled'

Perfect

(i) (hu) tmiegħek; (hi) tmiegħket; (int, jien) tmegħikt: — (huma) tmiegħku; (intom) tmegħiktu; (aħna) tmegħikna.

(ii) (hu) tqabad; (hi) tqabdet; (int, jien) tqabadt; — (huma) tqabdu; (intom) tqabadtu; (aħna) tqabadna.

Imperfect

(i) (hu) jitmiegħek; (hi, int) titmiegħek; (jien) nitmiegħek; — (huma) jitmiegħku; (intom) titmiegħku; (aħna) nitmiegħku.

Imperative

  (i) **tmieġhek** (sing.)/**tmieġhku** (pl.)

  (ii) **tqabad** (sing.)/**tqabdu** (pl.).

Past Participle

  (i) **mitmieġhek** (unusual) (ii) none. The only forms in common use are: **mitbieġhed** 'placed at a distance'; **miġġieled** 'not on speaking terms'. (Note assimilation of **t + ġ**).

Verbal Noun

  (i) **tmeġhik** 'wallowing'/**tmeġhika** 'a wallowing'.

  (ii) **tqabid** 'fighting'/**tqabida** 'an opposition'. Other verbal nouns in use are **tneħid/a** 'sighing' (**tnieħed**); **treġhid/a** 'trembling' (**trieġhed**); **tberik/a** 'blessing' (**bierek**).

PATTERN 7

inKaTaB/jinKaTaB: Formed by prefixing **n** to the Stem-Word (first form with variable voc. seq.). Note that initial **n** followed by a consonant takes the euphonic vowel **i**.

FUNCTION:— (i) *reflexive*:

Exx. **indaħal** 'he interfered' from **daħal** 'he entered'; **intelaq** 'he abandoned himself' from **telaq** 'he left'; **infirex** 'it was spread' from **firex** 'he spread'.

(ii) *passive of the first form*:

Exx. **inqabad** 'he was caught' from **qabad** 'he caught'; **inseraq** 'it was stolen' from **seraq** 'he stole'.

Another variant of Pattern 7 is obtained by prefixing **in** as for the seventh form and infixing **t** after the first radical as for the eighth form.

Exx. **instab** or **insab** 'he (or it) was found' from **sab** 'he found'; **instama'** or **insama'** 'he (it) was heard' from **sama'** 'he heard'; **insteraq** or **inseraq** 'he (it) was stolen' from **seraq** 'he stole'; **inxtamm** or **inxamm** 'it was smelt' from **xamm** 'he smelt'; **inħtieġ** 'it was necessary' from unused Stem-Word **ħieġ**.

Remark 1: This form generally occurs with a few verbs the first radical of which is **s** or **x** and, in one instance only, **ħ**.

Perfect

(i) (hu) **insteraq**; (hi) **insterqet**; (int, jien) **instraqt**; — (huma) **insterqu**; (intom) **instraqtu**; (aħna) **instraqna**.

(ii) (hu) **indaħal**; (hi) **indaħlet**; (int, jien) **indħalt**; — (huma) **indaħlu**; (intom) **indħaltu** (aħna) **indħalna**.

Imperfect

(i) (hu) **jinsteraq**; (hi, int) **tinsteraq**; (jien) **ninsteraq**; — (huma) **jinsterqu**; (intom) **tinsterqu**; (aħna) **ninsterqu**.

(ii) (hu) **jindaħal**; (hi, int) **tindaħal**; (jien) **nindaħal**; — (huma) **jindaħlu**; (intom) **tindaħlu**; (aħna) **nindaħlu**.

Imperative

(i) **insteraq** (sing.)/**insterqu** (pl.).

(ii) **indaħal** (sing.)/**indaħlu** (pl.).

No *Past Participle* and no *Verbal Noun*.

PATTERN 8

KtaTaB/jitKaTaB: Formed by infixing **t** after the first radical of a verb or a noun, with its variable vocalic sequence.

FUNCTION:— (i) *reflexive*:

Exx. **ftaqar** 'he became poor' from **faqar** 'poverty'; **xteħet** 'he threw himself' from **xeħet** 'he threw'.

(ii) *passive* (*euphonic* i + first radical ṅ or r).

Exx. **intefaq** 'it was spent' from **nefaq** 'he spent'; **intra-bat** 'he (it) was bound' from **rabat** 'he bound'; **intesa** 'he (it) was forgotten' from **nesa** 'he forgot'; **ftehem** 'he (it) was understood' from **fehem** 'he understood'.

(iii) *reciprocal of the third form*:

Exx. **ftiehem** 'he was in agreement' from **fiehem** 'he made one understand' (only example).

Perfect

(i) (hu) **ftaqar** (hi) **ftaqret**; (int, jien) **ftaqart**; — (huma) **ftaqru**; (intom) **ftaqartu**; (aħna) **ftaqarna**.

(ii) (hu) **intesa**; (hi) **intesiet**; (int, jien) **inte-sejt**; — (huma) **intesew**; (intom) **intesejtu**; (aħna) **inte-sejna**.

Imperfect

(i) (hu) **jiftaqar**; (hi, int) **tiftaqar**; (jien) **nifta-qar**; — (huma) **jiftaqru**; (intom) **tiftaqru**; (aħna) **nif-taqru**.

(ii) (hu) **jintesa**; (hi, int) **tintesa**; (jien) **nin-tesa**; — (huma) **jintesew**; (intom) **tintesew**; (aħna) **nintesew**.

Imperative

(i) **ftaqar** (sing.)/**ftaqru** (pl.).

(ii) **intesa** (sing.)/**intesew** (pl.).

(i) & (ii) no *Past Participle* and no *Verbal Noun*.

The only participial form in use is **miftakar** (+ a, f. + in, pl.) 'remembered' (**ftakar** 'he remembered') and the only example of a verbal noun in use is **ftehim** 'agreement'/**ftehima** 'an agreement' (**ftehem**).

PATTERN 9

KTaB/jiKTaB or **jiKTieB**: Formed by inserting a long a or its mutated form **ie** between the second and third

radical of the adjective from which they are formed with
no vowel between the first and second radical.

FUNCTION:— (i) *Acquisition of a colour*:

Exx. **ħdar** 'it grew green' from **aħdar** (m.) **ħadra** (f.)
'green'; **ħmar** 'it grew red' from **aħmar** (m.) **ħamra** (f.)
'red'; **sfar** 'it, he grew yellow or pale' from **isfar** (m.)
safra (f.) 'yellow'; **swied** 'it, he grew black' from **iswed**
(m.) **sewda** (f.) 'black'.

(ii) *physical qualities*:

Exx. **sbieħ** 'he became beautiful' from **sabiħ** (m.) **sabiħa**
(f.) 'beautiful'; **blieh** 'he grew foolish' from **iblah** (m.)
belha (f.) 'foolish'; **ċkien** 'he grew small' from **ċkejken**
(m.) **ċkejkna** (f.) 'small'.

Conjugation of (i) **ħmar** (ii) **ċkien**, *with the stress
(main accent) falling on* **ar** & **ien**

Perfect

(i) (**hu**) **ħmar**; (**hi**) **ħmaret**; (**int, jien**) **ħmart**
— (**huma**) **ħmaru**; (**intom**) **ħmartu**; (**aħna**) **ħmarna**.

(ii) (**hu**) **ċkien**; (**hi**) **ċkienet**; (**int, jien**) **ċkint**; —
(**huma**) **ċkienu**; (**intom**) **ċkintu**; (**aħna**) **ċkinna**.

Imperfect

(i) (**hu**) **jiħmar**; (**hi, int**) **tiħmar**; (**jien**) **niħ-
mar**; — (**huma**) **jiħmaru**; (**intom**) **tiħmaru**; (**aħna**) **niħ-
maru**.

(ii) (**hu**) **jiċkien**; (**hi, int**) **tiċkien**; (**jien**) **niċ-
kien**; — (**huma**) **jiċkienu**; (**intom**) **tiċkienu**; (**aħna**)
niċkienu.

Imperative

(i) **iħmar** (sing.)/**iħmaru** (pl.)

(ii) **iċkien** (sing.)/**iċkienu** (pl.).

No Past Participle

Remark 2: Though these two verbs have no present

participles, there are a few which belong to this category and have a descriptive participial form. These are: **midbiel** 'withered' (**dbiel**); **misnieħ** 'rancid' (oil) (**snieħ**); **musfar** 'yellowish' (**sfar**); **moqżież** 'filthy' (**qżież**); **mus-ħab** 'cloudy' (**sħab**). The following are archaic forms which one comes across in the written language: **muħġar** 'stony' (**ħaġar**); **muħrar** 'dry and barren' (**ħrar**); **mus-ħaħ** 'sturdy' (**sħaħ**); **mutrab** 'dusty' (**trab**).

No Verbal Noun

Remark 3: Verbal forms **tiċkin** 'belittling'; **taqżiż** 'affectedness'; **taqsir** 'shortening'; **tisbiħ** 'beautifying'; **tirtib** 'softening' presuppose Stem-Verbs belonging to pattern No. 2.

PATTERN 10

staKTaB / jistaKTeB or **stKaTTaB / jistKaTTaB**, Formed by (i) prefixing **st** to the first vowel of the vocalic sequence of the Stem-Word, which can also be a noun or an adjective, moved out of its place and put before the first radical as in pattern No. 4 (ii) to the second form.

FUNCTION:— *The expression of a generally unfavourable opinion or reaction.*

Exx. (i) **stagħġeb** 'he was amazed' from **għaġeb** 'a marvel'; **stkerraħ** 'he loathed' from **ikrah** (m.) **kerha** (f.) 'ugly'; (ii) **stħarreġ** 'he inquired' from **ħareġ/joħroġ** 'he went/goes out', also **staħreġ** which like **stagħġeb** is made up of prefix **st** + obsolete verbal pattern No. 4.

Perfect

(hu) **stagħġeb**; (hi) **staħġbet**; (int, jien) **staħ-ġibt** — (huma) **staħġbu**; (intom) **stagħġibtu**; (aħna) **staħġibna**.

Imperfect

(hu) **jistagħġeb**; (hi, int) **tistagħġeb**; (jien) **nis-tagħġeb**; — (huma) **jistaħġbu**; (intom) **tistaħġbu**; (aħna) **nistaħġbu**.

Imperative

stagħġeb (sing.)/**stagħġbu** (pl.).

Past Participle

mistagħġeb (m.) **mistagħġba** (f.) **mistagħġbin** (pl.)
'amazed'.

Verbal Noun

stagħġib 'amazement'/**stagħġiba** 'an exclamation'.
Other examples in use are **stenbiħ** 'awakening'/**stenbiħa**
'an awakening' (**stenbaħ**); **stkerriħ** 'loathing'/**stkerriħa**
'a loathing' (**stkerrah**).

EXERCISE 20

Translate:

(a) Ftaqar u kellu jissellef il-flus. L-ismijiet (the
names) tal-qalbiena (the brave) ma jintesew qatt. Xjieħ,
krieh u blieh. Fit-22 ta' Ġunju l-ġurnata tibda tiqsar.
M'hemmx għalfejn dan l-istagħġib kollu. Hija stkerrhet
ir-raġel tagħha xiħ u ikrah. Il-flus (pl.) insterqu minn
ġol-kexxun. Tindaħalx bejn raġel u mara miżżewġin.
Kollox (everything) jintesa f'din id-dinja barra l-miktub.
Ward midbiel ġo vażun (vase) qadim.

(b) The thief was caught by the police (**pulizija**).
The money (**flus**) was stolen from the bank (**bank**). She
was blessed by a holy (**qaddis**) man. They quarelled
and opposed one another because they had no money.
They were found dead (**mejta**) in the street. This book
was written a hundred years ago. They spent all (**kollha**
after noun) their money and became very (**wisq** after
adj.) poor. He was soon (**malajr**) forgotten after his
death. They agreed about (**fuq**) the contract (**kuntratt**).
Her face (**wiċċ**) grew red with shame (**mistħija**).

Lesson 21

STEM-VERBS ENDING IN a
IN OPEN SYLLABLE

Verbs ending in **a** in open syllable can present some difficulty to the non-Maltese, because one cannot tell from the Stem-Word itself whether the third quiescent radical is **għ** or **j**. Thus **tefa'** 'he threw' and **tefa** 'he extinguished' (a lamp) sound alike. The following two criteria help to distinguish one final radical from another:

1. If after the addition of **ha** and **hom**, the pronominal suffixes of the third person sing. feminine and pl., the first vowel of the Stem-Verb is dropped and the first two radicals come in immediate contact with each other, then the final radical is **j**. If, on the other hand, the first vowel of the vocalic sequence is retained, then the final radical is **għ**.

Exx. **tefa** 'he extinguished (a lamp)', **tfiet** (for **tefiet**) 'she extinguished'. (Note omission of the first unstressed vowel). The third radical of **tefa** is **j**; but **tefa'** 'he threw', **tefgħet** 'she threw' (Note retention of the first stressed vowel). The third radical is **għ**.

2. If the addition of pronominal suffixes **ha** and **hom** to the Stem-Verb (3rd person masc. sing. and pl.) produces the sound of a lengthened **ħ** (**ħħ**), then the third radical is **għ**. For the assimilation of **għ** + **ħ** see p. 17 (3). Exx. **tefa'** 'he threw' +**ha**, **hom** = **tefagħħa** pronounced **te'faħħa** 'he threw her'; **tefagħħom** pronounced **te'faħħom** 'he threw them'; but **tfieħa** ('**tfiəa**) 'he extinguished her' and **tfieħom** ('**tfiəom**) 'he extinguished them'.

These criteria should be borne in mind in the conjugation of verbs the third radical of which is **għ** or **j**.

PARADIGM OF VERBS
WITH THIRD RADICAL għ

Like the various forms of the Imperfect of the Strong Triliteral Verb, the Perfects of verbs with third radical għ are similarly related to sets of variable forms of the Imperfect. These are:

PATTERN (i)

KaTaGĦ/jaKTaGĦ. Ex. **qala'**/**jaqla'** 'he earned/earns'.

PATTERN (ii)

KeTaGĦ/jiKTaGĦ. Ex. **tefa'**/**jitfa'** 'he threw/throws'.

3rd pers. masc.	(i) **qala'** (for QaLaGĦ) 'he earned'.
(See Remark 1)	(ii) **sata'** (for SaTaGĦ) 'he could'.
3rd pers. fem. (See Remark 1)	(i) **qalgħet** (ii) **setgħet.**
2nd & 1st pers. (See Remark 2)	(i) **qlajt** (ii) **stajt.**

Remark 1: This form is regular like that of **talab** etc.

Remark 2: Note that the regular formation on the analogy of triliteral verbs would be **qlagħt** for QaLáGĦT and **stagħt** for SaTáGĦT. But in verbs the third radical of which is għ the regular combination agħ (remember għ is silent) becomes **aj**.

PLURAL

3rd pers.	(i)	**qalgħu**
(See Remark 3)	(ii)	**setgħu**
2nd pers.	(i)	**qlajtu**
(See Remark 4)	(ii)	**stajtu**
1st pers	(i)	**qlajna**
(See Remark 5)	(ii)	**stajna**

Remark 3: These forms follow the pattern of Strong Triliteral Verbs. Compare TaLBu and QaLGĦu and note the position of the corresponding radicals and vocalic sequence in both verbs.

Remark 4: This form is obtained by the addition of suffix **u** to the first person singular. As a compound verb made up of **qlajt** (first or second person singular) + pronominal suffix **u**, **qlajtu** could mean 'I have earned it'.

Remark 5: This form is obtained by the usual suffix **na**, added to **aj** which is the diphthongal product of agħ.

Imperfect

(i) (**hu**) **jaqla'**; (**hi, int**) **taqla'**; (**jien**) **naqla'**; — (**huma**) **jaqilgħu**; (**intom**) **taqilgħu**; (**aħna**) **naqilgħu**.

(ii) (**hu**) **jista'**; (**hi, int**) **tista'**; (**jien**) **nista'**; — (**huma**) **jistgħu**; (**intom**) **tistgħu**; (**aħna**) **nistgħu**.

Imperative

(i) **aqla'** (sing.)/**aqilgħu** (pl.).

(ii) **sata'** has no Imperative but the form is **iKTaGĦ** /**iKTGĦu**. Exx. **ibża'** (sing.)/**ibżgħu** (pl.) 'fear'; **ibqa'** (sing.)/**ibqgħu** (pl.) 'remain'.

Past Participle

(i) **maqlugħ** (m.) **maqlugħa** (f.) **maqlugħin** (pl.) 'earned'.

(ii) none, but the pattern is **miKTuGĦ** (final għ pronounced like ħ). Exx. **mitfugħ** (m.) **mitfugħa** (f.) **mitfugħin** (pl.) 'thrown'; **mismugħ** (m.) **mismugħa** (f.) **mismugħin** (pl.) 'heard'.

Verbal Noun

(i) **qligħ** 'earning'/**qalgħa** 'an earning, profit'.

(ii) none, /**setgħa** 'power' but the pattern is **KTigĦ** (final għ pronounced like ħ). Exx. **tfigħ** (**tfiəħ**) 'throwing'/ **tefgħa** 'a throw'; **smigħ** (**smiəħ**) 'hearing'.

Qata' 'he cut' follows the pattern of qala' conjugated above. Most other verbs follow the pattern miKTuGH (mik'tuuh) as the form of the past participle or meKTuGH (mek'tuuh) if the first radical is r as in the case of rafa' 'he raised' (merfugħ (m.) + a, f., + in, pl.) and raġa' 'he repeated' (merġugħ (m.) + a, f., + in, pl. obsolete).

Exx. Perfect bala' 'he swallowed'/Imperfect jibla' — past part. miblugħ (m.) (+ a, f., + in, pl.); ġama' 'he collected'/jiġma' — miġmugħ (m.) (+ a, f., + in, pl.); naża' 'he undressed'/jinża' — minżugħ (m.) (+ a, f., + in, pl.); sama' 'he heard'/jisma' — mismugħ (m.) (+ a, f., + in, pl.); tala' 'he ascended'/jitla' — mitlugħ (m.) (+ a, f., + in, pl.); tama' 'he fed'/jitma' — mitmugħ (m.) (+ a, f., + in, pl.); xaba' 'he satiated himself'/jixba' — no past part.; baqa' 'he remained'/jibqa' — no past part.; laqa' 'he received'/jilqa' — milqugħ (m.) (+ a, .f, + in, pl).

Remark 6: Verbs the second radical of which is q preserve the vowel a of the vocalic sequence of the Perfect Tense.

Exx. laqgħet 'she received' (laqa'); baqgħet 'she remained' (baqa'). Other verbs take vowel e in the third person feminine and third person plural.

Exx. refgħet 'she raised', refgħu 'they raised', tefgħet 'she threw', tefgħu 'they threw'.

DERIVED FORMS

These are formed according to the general system explained in Lessons 19 and 20. Of these only the second form has the past participle. The conjugation of the Perfect and the Imperfect is formed regularly by the same set of affixes used for both tenses. Some examples of derived forms:

2nd Form: Perfect bażża' 'he frightened'/Impf. ibażża' — imbażża' (m.) imbażżgħa (f.) imbażżgħin (pl.) (but also with vowel e — beżża' etc.); qatta' 'he

cut'/iqatta' — mqatta' (m.) mqattgħa (f.) mqattgħin
(pl.); samma' 'he made one hear'/samma' — msamma'
(m.) msammgħa (f.) msammgħin (pl.).

3rd and 4th Forms have no examples.

5th Form: Perfect. tbażża' (or tbeżża') 'he was frightened'/ Impf. jitbażża'; tqatta' 'it was cut to pieces'/jit-
qatta'; ittabba' 'it grew stained'/jittabba'.

6th Forms. No verbs in use.

7th Form: Perfect inbala' 'he was swallowed'/Impf.
jinbala'; ingama' 'it was gathered'/jingama'; inqata' 'it
was cut'/jinqata'.

8th Form: iltaqa' 'he met'/jiltaqa'; stama' (also
instama') 'he was heard'/jinstama' (also jinstama').

Remark 7: Final a' + x becomes long stressed a. Exx.
instama'/jinstama'; ma nstamax/jinstamax not ma
nstamagħx, etc.

EXERCISE 21

(a) Give the derived forms of the following verbs
on the patterns of the numbers indicated in brackets, and
attempt a suitable meaning:

qata' (2, 5, 7); bala' (2, 5, 7); ġama' (2, 5, 7); naża'
(2, 5, 7); sama' (2, 5, 7); tala' (2, 5, 7); tama' (2); xaba'
(2, 5); laqa' (2, 8) żaba' (7).

Translate:

(b) He cut the pages (paġna/i, pl.) of his book with
a pen-knife (taljakarti). She cut the letter (ittra) to
pieces (biċċiet biċċiet). They made him swallow the medi-
cine (mediċina). He first (l-ewwel) took off the coat
(ġlekk); then (imbagħad) he took off his shoes (żarbun).
Are you afraid or do you want (trid) to frighten me? He
first received the delegation (delegazzjoni), then met the
workmen. Have you not heard the noise from the garden?
Narcissus (Narċis) collected from the rocks. The worker
is earning seven pounds a (fil-) week.

Lesson 22

CONJUGATION OF VERBS HAVING w AS FIRST RADICAL

(i) **Wasa'** (also **wesa'**) 'it (he) contained'.

(ii) **Wasal** 'he arrived'.

(iii) **Wiret** 'he inherited'.

(iv) **Weħel** 'he failed in an examination' or 'he got stuck'.

Perfect

(i) (**hu**) wasa'; (**hi**) wasgħet; (**int, jien**) wasajt (or **usajt**); — (**huma**) wasgħu; (**intom**) wasajtu (or usajtu) (**ahna**) wasajna (or **usajna**).

Remark 1: Note that the third person masculine and feminine singular and the third person plural are regularly conjugated like those of Strong Triliteral verbs.

(ii) (**hu**) wasal; (**hi**) waslet; (**int, jien**) wasalt (or usalt); — (**huma**) waslu; (**intom**) wasaltu (or usaltu); (**ahna**) wasalna (or usalna).

(iii) (**hu**) wiret; (**hi**) wirtet; (**int, jien**) wiritt (or uritt); — (**huma**) wirtu; (**intom**) wirittu (or urittu); (**ahna**) wiritna (or uritna).

(iv) (**hu**) weħel; (**hi**) weħlet; (**int, jien**) weħilt; — (**huma**) weħlu; (**intom**) weħiltu; (**ahna**) weħilna.

Remark 2: Note that the first vowel of the vocalic sequence of the Stem-Word is retained throughout, so that the initial radical w, as in the case of Strong verbs beginning with għ, is never immediately followed by the second radical.

Imperfect

In the Imperfect, the Past Participle, and the 7th form of the derived verb, note that the first radical w is dropped. A regular conjugation of wasal, wiret etc. should give jawsal, jiwret on the analogy of jaqbad, and jinżel.

(i) (hu) jasa'; (hi, int) tasa'; (jien) nasa'; — (huma) jasgħu; (intom) tasġħu; (ahna) nasġħu.

(ii) (hu) jasal; (hi, int) tasal; (jien) nasal; — (huma) jaslu; (intom) taslu; (ahna) naslu.

(iii) (hu) jiret; (hi, int) tiret; (jien) niret; — (huma) jirtu; (intom) tirtu; (ahna) nirtu.

(iv) (hu) jehel; (int, hi) tehel; (jien) nehel; — (huma) jehlu; (intom) tehlu; (ahna) nehlu.

Imperative

(i)   asa' (sing.)/asgħu (pl.).
(ii) asal (sing.)/aslu (pl.).
(iii) iret (sing.)/irtu (pl.).
(iv) ehel (sing.)/ehlu (pl.).

Present Participle

(i)   wiesa' (m.) wiesgħa (f.) wesġħin (pl.).

Remark 3: This is one of the few exceptions to the rule that only instransitive verbs have the present or active participle. Wasal, on the other hand, though an intransitive verb, has no present or active participle.

Past Participle

Of these only wiret has its past part. form mirut 'inherited' with the first radical w omitted. Other participial forms are: milud (m.) (+ a, f., + in, pl.) 'born' (wildet); miżrugh (m.) (+ a, f., + in, pl.) 'sown' (żara'); miżun (m.) (+ a, f., + in, pl.) 'weighed' (wiżen).

Verbal Noun

(i)   usigħ 'widening'/wesgħa 'extent'.
(ii) usil 'arrival'/wasla 'an arrival'.
(iii) wirt 'inheritance'/wirta 'an inheritance'.
(iv) uħil 'stoppage'/weħla 'an obstruction'.

IRREGULAR FORMATIONS

Waqaf 'he stopped' is conjugated like **wasal** in the Perfect but is irregularly conjugated in its Imperfect and Imperative which are as follows:

Imperfect

(hu) **jieqaf**; (not **jaqaf**); (hi, int) **tieqaf**; (jien) **nieqaf**; — (huma) **jieqfu**; (intom) **tieqfu**; (aħna) **nieqfu**.

Imperative

ieqaf (sing.)/**ieqfu** (pl.).

Present Participle

wieqaf (m.) **wieqfa** (f.) **weqfin** (pl.) 'standing'.

Waġa' the past participle of which is **miġugħ** or **muġugħ** (m.) (+ a, f., + in, pl.) 'it ached' is also conjugated like **wasal**, but it is irregularly conjugated in its Imperfect and Imperative.

Imperfect

(hu) **juġa'**; (hi, int) **tuġa'**; (jien) **nuġa'**; — (huma) **juġġħu**; (intom) **tuġġħu**; (aħna) **nuġġħu**.

Imperative

uġa' (sing.)/**uġġħu** (pl.).

Though like **waqaf**, **waġa'** is an intransitive verb, it has no present participle.

DERIVED FORMS

2nd Form: Perfect. **wassal** 'he accompanied'/Impf. **iwassal**/past part. **imwassal** (m.) **imwassla** (f.) **imwasslin** (pl.); **waqqa'** 'he threw down'/**iwaqqa'** — **imwaqqa'** (m.) **imwaqqgħa** (f.) **imwaqqgħin** (pl.).

3rd Form: **wiegħed** 'he promised'/**iwiegħed** — **imwiegħed** (m.) **imwiegħda** (f.) **imwegħdin** (pl.).

4th Form: A survival of this form is the verb **wera** 'he showed' which is conjugated as follows:

Perfect

(**hu**) **wera**; (**hi**) **uriet**; (**int,jien**) **urejt**; — (**huma**) **urew**; (**intom**) **urejtu**; (**aħna**) **urejna**. Note that initial **u** becomes **w** if the preceding word ends in a vowel. Ex. **huma wrew**, etc.

Imperfect

(**hu**) **juri**; (**hi, int**) **turi**; (**jien**) **nuri**; — (**huma**) **juru**; (**intom**) **turu**; (**aħna**) **nuru**.

Imperative

uri (sing.)/ **uru** (pl.).

Past Participle

muri (m.) **murija** (f.) **murijin** (pl.) 'shown'.

Verbal Nouns

wiri 'showing'/**wirja** 'a show'; **turija** 'a demonstration'.

5th Form: **twaqqaf** 'it was established'/**jitwaqqaf** — no past part.; **twebbes** 'it was hardened'/**jitwebbes**. No past participle. In both cases **imwebbes** and **imwaqqaf** are the past participles of the second form.

6th Form: **twieled** 'he was born'/**jitwieled** — **mitwieled** (m.) **mitwielda** (f.) **mitwildin** (pl.); **twieżen** 'he leaned upon'/**jitwieżen** — **mitwieżen** (m.) **mitwieżna** (f.) **mitwiżnin** (pl.).

7th Form: **intiret** 'it was inherited'/**jintiret** — no past part.; **intiżen** 'he (it) was weighed'/**jintiżen** — no past part. Note that the first radical w is retained in **intwiegħed** 'it was promised' and **intwera** 'it was shown'.

8th Form: No examples.

9th Form: **usiegħ** 'it became wide'/**jusiegħ** — no past part. The only example of the 9th form with **j** as a first radical is **ibbies** 'he grew hard'/**jibbies**, formed from the adjective **iebes** (m.)/**iebsa** (f.) 'hard'.

10th Form: The only example is **stejqer** 'he recovered his strength'/**jistejqer — mistejqer** (m.) **mistejqra** (f.) **mistejqrin** (pl.).

EXERCISE 22

Translate:

(a) **Il-flixkun** (bottle) **jesa' pinta ħalib. Huma wirtu somma** (sum) **kbira ta' flus. Kemm tesa' nbid din il-bittija** (cask)? **Ċensu** (Vincent) **weħel fl-eżami tal-ġografija. Ieqfu! hawnhekk midfuna l-qalbiena ta' Malta. Hawn dentist? Snieni juġgħuni ħafna. Hu wassalni sal-** (as far as) **vapur** (ship) **qabel sifirt. Il-patata ma tintiżenx bil-ħamrija** (soil) **mwaħħla magħha. Il-ħobż niexef** (stale) **jibbies. Il-marida bdiet tistejqer.**

(b) Can you arrive in time (**fil-ħin**)? How much (**kemm**) does the basket (**basket**) contain? It contains two dozen (**tużżana**) eggs. They all (**kollha**) failed in the June examination (**eżami**). What (**fiex**) did they fail in? Some (**uħud**) failed in history (**storja**), some in geography (**ġografija**), but she failed in Latin (**Latin**). They are rich because they inherited £10,235. Stop! danger (**periklu**). He who promises must (**għandu**) give (**jagħti**). The promised land (**art**) of Jerusalem (**Ġerusalem**). Show me the road which leads to Ħal Saflieni. He showed me the Megalithic (**Megalitiku** sing.) Temples (**Tempju** sing.) of Malta and Gozo.

Lesson 23

CONJUGATION OF THE HOLLOW VERB

These are the verbs which begin with the 1st radical and end with the 3rd radical with long **a** or its mutated form **ie** between them, with the 2nd radical **j** or **w** absorbed into it.

Whether the middle radical of the Hollow Verbs is **J** or **W** can be known by the second vowel of the vocalic sequence of the Imperfect. If this vowel is (i) long **u** the medial radical is **W**; (ii) if/it is long **i** it is **J**.

Exx. (i) **dam/idum** 'he took/takes a long time'; first person singular **domt**; **kien/ikun** 'he was/is'; first person singular **kont**. Other verbs with medial radical w are: **sam/isum** 'he fasted/fasts'; **dar/idur** 'he turned/turns'; **far/ifur** 'it boiled/boils over'; **mar/imur** 'he went/goes'; **għam/igħum** 'he swam/swims'; **qam/iqum** 'he rose/rises'; **żar/iżur** 'he visited/visits'; **dieq/iduq** 'he tasted/tastes' (also **daq/iduq**); **miet/imut** 'he died/dies'.

Exx. (ii) **ġab/iġib** 'he brought/brings' first person singular **ġibt**. Other verbs with medial radical j: **biegħ/ibigħ** 'he sold/sells'; **fieq/ifiq** 'he recuperated/recuperates'; **għab/igħib** 'he disappeared/disappears'; **għan/igħin** 'he helped/helps'; **għar/igħir** 'he envied/envies'; **għax/igħix** 'he lived/lives'; **qies/iqis** 'he measured/measures'; **ried/irid** 'he wanted (or wished)/wants (or wishes)'; **sar/isir** 'he became/becomes'; **tar/itir** 'he flew/flies'; **żied/iżid** 'he increased/increases'.

PERFECT

SINGULAR

3rd person masc.	(i) **dar** (from hypothetical `DaWaR) 'he turned' or 'inspected'.
	(ii) **sar** (from hypothetical SaJaR) 'he became' or 'it grew ripe' (fruit) or 'it was cooked' (food).
3rd person fem.	(i) **daret** (for DaWaRet)
(See Remark 1)	(ii) **saret** (for SaJaRet).
2nd person	(i) **dort** (for DaWaRt).
1st person	(ii) **sirt** (for SaJaRt).
(See Remark 2)	

Remark 1: This form is obtained by the addition of suffix **et** to Stem-Word.

Remark 2: This form is obtained by the insertion of vowel **o** when the second absorbed radical is **w**, and vowel **i** when the second absorbed radical is **j** + the usual suffix **t**. As the form is common to the first and second person singular, the person referred to is brought out by the context.

PLURAL

3rd person	(i) **daru** (for DaWaRu).
(See Remark 3)	(ii) **saru** (for SaJaRu).
2nd person	(i) **dortu** (for DaWaRtu).
(See Remark 4)	(ii) **sirtu** (for SaJaRtu).
1st person	(i) **dorna** (for DaWaRna).
(See Remark 5)	(ii) **sirna** (for SaJaRna).

Remark 3: This form is obtained by the addition of suffix **u** to the Stem-Word. As a compound word, independently of this conjugation made up of the Stem-Word (**dar** trans. verb) + pronominal suffix **u**, it can mean also 'I, you (sing.) have inspected it'.

Remark 4: This form is obtained by the addition of suffix **u** to the first or second person singular. Again as a compound verb made up of **dort** (second person sing.) + **u**, **dortu** can mean 'I (or you) have inspected it'.

Remark 5: This form is obtained by the addition of suffix **na** and the vowels **o** or **i** between the first and second radical.

Imperfect

The Imperfect is obtained by the addition of the usual prefixes given in Lesson 16 to the first radical (consonant) of the verb with the stressed long vowel **u** or **i** between the first and third radical according as the medial absorbed radical is **W** or **J** + **u** for the plural. The ascertainment of the medial radical is a matter of usage.

(i) (**hu**) **idur**;   (**hi, int**) **iddur**;   (**jien**) **indur**; —
(**huma**) **iduru**; (**intom**) **idduru**; (**aħna**) **induru**.

(ii)   (hu) isir; (hi, int) issir; (jien) insir; — (huma) isiru; (intom) issiru; (aħna) insiru.

Imperative

The imperative consists of the second syllable of the imperfect + u for the plural.

(i)   dur (sing.)/duru (pl.).

(ii)   sir (sing.)/siru (pl.).

Present Participle

(i)   none.

(ii)   sejjer (m.) sejra (f.) sejrin (pl.) 'going'.

For the use of this participial form as an auxiliary verb, see Lesson 16, p. 138 para. (i). Other participial forms with an adjectival function are: mejjet (m.) mejta (f.) mejtin (pl.) 'dead'; sajjem (m.) sajma (f.) sajmin (pl.) 'fasting';żejjed (m.) żejda (f.) żejdin (pl.) 'superfluous'. Dejjem meaning 'always' is used as an adverb.

The pattern is KeJJeB (m.) KeJBa (f.) KeJBiN (pl.); but not all intransitive hollow verbs have an active participle.

Past Participle

(i)   none.

(ii)   misjur (m.) misjura (f.) misjurin (pl.) 'ripe.'.

N.B. Of all the Hollow Verbs only the following have their past participle:— mibjugħ (m.) mibjugħa (f.) mibjugħin (pl.) 'sold' (biegħ);   miġjub (m.) miġjuba (f.) miġjubin (pl.) 'brought' (ġieb); megħjun (m.) megħjuna (f.) megħjunin (pl.) 'helped' (għan); meqjum (m.) meqjuma (f.) meqjumin (pl.) 'venerated' or 'respected' (qiem);   meqjus (m.) meqjusa (f.) meqjusin (pl.) 'measured' (qies); miżjud (m.) miżjuda (f.) miżjudin (pl.) 'added' (żied); misjub (m.) misjuba (f.) misjubin (pl.) 'found' (sab); midjun (m.) midjuna (f.) midjunin (pl.) 'owing money'.

Less frequently used are: **midjuq** (m.) **midjuqa** (f.)
midjuqin (pl.) 'tasted' (**daq**); **mibjud** (m.) **mibjuda** (f.)
mibjudin (pl.) 'laid' (**biedet** 'she laid eggs').

Verbal Noun

(i) **dawran** (also **dawrien**) 'turning' (ii) **sajran**
'ripening'. Variants (a-ie) = **ħarsien** 'watching'/**ħarsa** 'a
look' (**ħares**) ('**ħaares**); **ħarġien** 'going out'/**ħarġa** 'an
outing' (**ħareġ**).

The following conform to patterns Nos. 7 and 8 in
Lesson 18 but with the second radical w or j.
Exx. (i) **għawm** 'swimming'/**għawma** 'a swim' (**għam**);
sawm 'fasting'/**sawma** 'a fast' (**sam**); (ii) **bews** 'kissing'/
bewsa 'a kiss' (**bies**); **mewt** 'death'/**mewta** 'a death'
(**miet**).

DERIVED FORMS

2nd Form: **qajjem** 'he raised'/**iqajjem** — **imqajjem**
(m.) **imqajma** (f.) **imqajmin** (pl.); **tawwal** 'he lengthened'/**itawwal** — **imtawwal** (m.) **imtawla** (f.) **imtawlin**
(pl.).

5th Form: **tħawwad** 'he was confused'/**jitħawwad** —
imħawwad (m.) **imħawda** (f.) **imħawdin** (pl.); **issejjaħ**
'he was called'/**jissejjaħ** — **imsejjaħ** (m.) **imsejħa** (f.)
imsejħin (pl.), p.p. supplied by Form 2.

Remark 6: Strictly speaking the doubled radical
w or j of the Hollow Verb should appear also doubled in
the 3rd person plural of the Imperfect when the semi-
vowel is followed by a consonant (Exx. **iqajjmu, itawwlu**)
and in the Past Participle (sing. fem. and pl.) Exx. **mqajj-
ma, mtawwla** etc. In the written language, however, one
of the semi-vowels is dropped.

Sometimes this unnecessary departure from the
pattern can lead to a confusion of meaning as in **lewnu**
and **għajru** which can mean 'they have tinted' or
'insulted' when they stand for **lewwnu** or **għajjru** or 'his
colour' or 'his neighbour' when they stand for **lewn**
'colour' or **għajr** 'neighbour' + pron. suffix **u** ('his').

7th Form: **inbiegħ** 'it was sold'/**jinbiegħ** — **mibjugħ** (m.) **mibjugħa** (f.) **mibjugħin** (pl.); **insab** (also **instab**) 'it was found'/**jinsab** (also **jinstab**) — **misjub** (m.) **misjuba** (f.) **misjubin** (pl.).

8th Form: **żdied** 'he increased'/**jiżdied** — **miżjud** (m.) **miżjuda** (f.) **miżjudin** (pl.); **stab** 'it was found'/**jistab** — **misjub** (m.) **misjuba** (f.) **misjubin** (pl.), p.p. supplied by Form 1.

Remark 7: **żdied**, the 8th form of **żied** for **żtied** (stiǝt), is an exception to the general rule explained on pp. 19-20.

9th Form: **twal** 'he grew tall'/**jitwal** — no past part., **xjieħ** 'he grew old'/**jixjieħ** — no past part.

10th Form: **strieħ** 'he rested'/**jistrieħ** — **mistrieħ** (m.) **mistrieħa** (f.) **mistriħin** (pl.) (the only past part. in use); **stagħna** 'he grew rich'/**jistagħna** — no past part.

EXERCISE 23

Translate:

(a) Ibigħ ħut u bajd. L-għonja għandhom igħinu l-fqar. Għex ħames snin Pariġi, sitt snin Londra u ħdax-il sena Malta. Irrid paċi tal-moħħ u tal-qalb. Ix-xemx għebet wara l-għoljiet (hills). Ir-Randan (Lent) huwa żmien (time) meta l-Insara jsumu. Żort il-Kon-Katidral ta' San Ġwann? Le, immur hemm għada. Il-karozza daret fuq ix-xellug u l-vann (van) fuq il-lemin. Il-mejta kienet omm Indri. Iż-żejjed dejjem bla siwi (useless).

(b) When I went to Amsterdam I visited all the museums (**mużewijiet**). Now everyone has ceased (**sar ma**) to think about anything. His father has been dead four years and his mother six. What do you want to become when (**la**) you grow up (**tikber**)? I want to become either (**jew**) a doctor or (**jew**) a priest. In these temples the gods were venerated by our ancient (**qodma**) people. He who seeks finds. This man owes the shopkeeper money. A book translated (**miġjub**) from Maltese into (use prep. **għal**) English. The man is measured in his words; not so the woman. Some (**xi**) birds (**għasafar**) lay white eggs, others (**oħrajn**) greenish eggs. After much turning in narrow (**dojoq**) streets I arrived home tired (**għajjien**).

Lesson 24

THE PARADIGM OF THE WEAK VERB

[*N.B. In these verbs the third radical* **j** *is quiescent. The pron. suffixes which shorten the form of the 3rd pers. masc. are given in Lesson 29 p. 208 (i) & p. 210 (ii)*].

PERFECT

SINGULAR

3rd person masc.
    (i) **qara** or **qra** + pron. suffixes (for QaraJ) 'he read'.

    (ii) **mexa** or **mxie** + pron. suffixes (for MeXaJ) 'he walked'.

    (iii) **beda** or **bdie** + pron. suffixes (for BeDaJ) 'he started'.

    (iv) **rema** or **rmie** + pron. suffixes. (for ReMaJ) 'he threw away'.

3rd person fem.
    (i) **qrat** (for QaRat).

(See Remark 1)
    (ii) **mxiet** (for MeXiet).

    (iii) **bdiet** (for BeDiet).

    (iv) **rmiet** (for ReMiet).

2nd person
    (i) **qrajt** (for QaRaJt).

1st person
    (ii) **mxejt** (for MeXeJt).

    (iii) **bdejt** (for BeDeJt).

(See Remark 2)
    (iv) **rmejt** (for ReMeJt).

Remark 1: This form is obtained by the elision of the first vowel of the Stem-Word, the change of the second vowel to **ie** in **mxiet, bdiet** and **rmiet** and long **a** in **qrat** + usual suffix **t**.

Remark 2: This form is obtained by the omission of the two vowels in the Stem-Word and the addition of the diphthong **ej** in **mexa, beda** and **rema** and **aj** in **qara** + suffix **t**. The vowel a is favoured by the consonant **q** (glottal stop).

PLURAL

3rd person	(i) **qraw**	(for QaRaW).
(See Remark 3)	(ii) **mxew**	(for MeXeW).
	(iii) **bdew**	(for BeDeW).
	(iv) **rmew**	(for ReMeW).
2nd person	(i) **qrajtu**	(for QaRaJtu).
(See Remark 4)	(ii) **mxejtu**	(for MeXeJtu).
	(iii) **bdejtu**	(for BeDeJtu).
	(iv) **rmejtu**	(for ReMeJtu).
1st person	(i) **qrajna**	(for QaRaJna).
(See Remark 5)	(ii) **mxejna**	(for MeXeJna).
	(iii) **bdejna**	(for BeDeJna).
	(iv) **rmejna**	(for ReMeJna).

Remark 3: This form is obtained by the omission of the two vowels of the vocalic sequence + diphthong **ew** for **mexa, beda** and **rema** and **aw** for **qara**.

Remark 4: This form is obtained by the addition of suffix **u** to the second or first person singular. As a compound verb, **qrajtu** (**qara** being a transitive verb) could be made up of **qrajt** 'you have read' + pronominal suffix **u** 'it' = 'I (you) have read it'.

Remark 5: This form is obtained by the omission of

the two vowels of the vocalic sequence of the Stem-Word. This brings the first two radicals together + the addition of suffix **ej** or **aj** which are characteristic of the first and second person singular + usual suffix **na**.

Imperfect

(i) (hu) **jaqra**; (hi, int) **taqra**; (jien) **naqra**; — (huma) **jaqraw**; (intom) **taqraw**; (aħna) **naqraw**.

(ii) (hu) **jimxi**; (hi, int) **timxi**; (jien) **nimxi**; — (huma) **jimxu**; (intom) **timxu**; (aħna) **nimxu**.

(iii) (hu) **jibda**; (hi, int) **tibda**; (jien) **nibda**; — (huma) **jibdew**; (intom) **tibdew**; (aħna) **nibdew**.

(iv) (hu) **jarmi**; (hi, int) **tarmi**; (jien) **narmi**; — (huma) **jarmu**; (intom) **tarmu**; (aħna) **narmu**.

Imperative

(i) **aqra** ,sing.)/**aqraw** (pl.)

(ii) **imxi** (sing.)/**imxu** (pl.).

(iii) **ibda** (sing.)/**ibdew** (pl.).

(iv) **armi** (sing.)/**armu** (pl.).

Present Participle

Of all the verbs conjugated, only **mexa** as an intransitive verb has the present participle, **miexi** (m.) **miexja** (f.) **mexjin** (pl.) 'walking'.

Remark 6: Note that the omission of **e** from the feminine participial forms having **ie** after the first radical in some cases converts these forms into nouns of unity i.e. nouns indicating one object or one occurrence.

Exx. **nieżla** (f.) 'descending', **niżla** 'a descent'; **liebsa** (f.) 'dressed', **libsa** 'a suit'; **ġierja** (f.) 'running', **ġirja** 'a run'.

Past Participle

(i) **moqri** (m.) **moqrija** (f.) **moqrijin** (pl.) 'read'.

(ii) No past part.

(iii) **mibdi** (m.) **mibdija** (f.) **mibdijin** (pl.) 'started'.

(iv) **mormi** (m.) **mormija** (f.) **mormijin** (pl.) 'thrown away'.

The past participle of this class of verbs is formed by prefixes (i) **mi** (ii) **me** (iii) **mo** added to the first of the two radicals, the second of which is followed by unstressed vowel **i** for the masculine gender + **ja** for the feminine gender. Other examples: (i) **mikri** (m.) **mikrija** (f.) **mikrijin** (pl.) (**kera'** 'he rented'); **mimli** (m.) **mimlija** (f.) **mimlijin** (pl.) (**mela** 'he filled'); (ii) **merħi** (m.) **merħija** (f.) **merħijin** (pl.) (**reħa** 'he let go' — the only example); (iii) **moħbi** (m.) **moħbija** (f.) **moħbijin** (pl.) (**ħeba** 'he hid'); **moħli** (m.) **moħlija** (f.) **moħlijin** (pl.) (**ħela** 'he wasted'); **mogħti** (m.) **mogħtija** (f.) **mogħtijin** (pl.) (**ta** 'he gave').

Remark 7: Note that the prefix **mo** is favoured by Stem-Words which begin with **ħ**, **għ**, **q** and less frequently with **r**.

Verbal Noun

(i) **qari** 'reading'.

(ii) **mixi** 'walking'.

(iii) **bidu** 'beginning'.

(iv) **rimi** 'throwing away'.

Verbs which follow the conjugation of (i) **qara/jaqra**: **rama/jarma** 'he harnessed/harnesses' (the horse); (ii) **mexa/jimxi**; **kera/jikri** 'he hired/hires'; **bena/jibni** 'he built/builds'; **feda/jifdi** 'he redeemed/redeems'; (iii) **beda/jibda**: **mela/jimla** 'he filled/fills'; **sewa/jiswa** 'it was worth/it is worth'; (iv) **rema/jarmi**: **ħeba/jaħbi** 'he hid/hides'; **ħela/jaħli** 'he wasted/wastes'; **ħema/jaħmi** 'he baked/bakes'; **qeda/jaqdi** 'he served/serves'.

Remark 8: Because the verb **rama** is of Italian origin (*armare*), it reserves the first vowel in the Perfect tense. Ex. **armajt**, **armat** not **rmajt**, **rmat**.

DERIVED FORMS

2nd Form: **mexxa** 'he guided'/**imexxi** — **immexxi** (m). **immexxija** (f.) **immexxijin** (pl.); **semma** 'he mentioned'/ **isemmi** — **imsemmi** (m.) **imsemmija** (f.) **imsemmijin** (pl.)

3rd Form: **miera** 'he contradicted'/**imieri** — no past part., but one often hears hybrid **merut** (**ut** is an Italian suffix) and hybrid adjective **meruż** 'contradictious'.

5th Form: **issemma** (for **t** + **semma**) 'he was mentioned'/**jissemma** (for **jit** + **semma**) — **imsemmi** (m.) **imsemmija** (f.) **imsemmijin** (pl.); **trabba** 'he was brought up'/**jitrabba**; **mrobbi** (m.) **mrobbija** (f.) **mrobbijin** (pl.) — p.p. supplied by Form 2.

6th Form: **tkaża** 'he mocked'/**jitkaża** — no past part.

7th Form: **inbeda** 'it was begun'/**jinbeda** — no past part.; **inqara** 'it was read'/**jinqara** — no past part.

8th Form: **imtela** (pronounced **intela** by dissimilation of m) 'it was filled/**jimtela** (**jin'tela**) — no past part.; **intesa** 'it was forgotten'/**jintesa** — no past part.; **xtara** 'he bought'/**jixtri** — **mixtri** (m.) **mixtrijia** (f.) **mixtrijin** (pl.).

10th Form: **staħa** 'he was ashamed'/**jistħi** — **mistħi** (m.) **mistħija** (f.) **mistħijin** (pl.); **staħba** 'he hid himself'/**jistaħba** — **mistoħbi** (m.) **mistoħbija** (f.) **mistoħbijin** (pl.); **staqsa** 'he asked'/**jistaqsi** — **mistoqsi** (m.) **mistoqsija** (f.) **mistoqsijin** (pl.).

Remark 9: **Mistoqsija, mistħija** and **mistoħbija** are also used as nouns meaning question, bashfulness and hide-and-seek (children's game).

EXERCISE 24

Translate:

(a) **Xi** (what) **ktieb bil-Malti qrajt illum? Bdejt "Nazju Ellul", rumanz** (novel) **ta' Ġużè** (Joseph) **Muscat Azzopardi, u "Ineż Farruġ", rumanz ta' A.E. Caruana.**

L-omm tmexxi t-tarbija meta din tibda timxi. Kienu qed
isemmu l-qtil li (which) sar is-sena l-oħra (last year).
Ħwejjeġ (clothes) qodma mormija fit-triq. Dawn it-tfal
trabbew fil-faqar u t-tbatija (suffering).   M'għandniex
x'naħbu. Kull bidu tqil. Il-mixi jagħmel tajjeb (is good
for) għas-saħħa. Bil-qari titgħallem (you learn) tikteb.
Meta ċanfartha (reprimanded), stħat ħafna.

(b) Answer (wieġeb) when you are asked. The build-
ing of the chapel (kappella) was begun in 1063. The jar is
filled drop by drop. Who mentions my name? The name
of God must be mentioned with reverence. This house
costs £4,631. Don't waste your (sing. and pl.) money if
(jekk) you don't want to become poor. I built a small
house at St. Paul's Bay (San Pawl il-Baħar). Throw this
rubbish (żibel) into the pail (barmil). We walked 5 miles
(mili) but they walked 13 miles.

Lesson 25

THE PARADIGM OF THE DOUBLED VERB

THE PERFECT

The characteristic feature of this geminate verb is
that the second and third radicals are identical forming
one assimilated sound with either vowel a or e between
it and the first radical.

SINGULAR

3rd person masc.   (i) **radd** (for full pattern RaDaD)
                          'he restored'.

                          (ii) **mess** (for   MeSeS)   'he
                          touched'.

3rd person fem.	(i)	**raddet**.
(See Remark 1)	(ii)	**messet**.
2nd & 1st person	(i)	**raddejt**.
	(ii)	**messejt**.
(See Remark 2)		

Remark 1: This form is obtained by the addition of suffix **et** to the Stem-Word.

Remark 2: This form is obtained by the addition of suffix **ejt** to the Stem-Word. If these were regularly formed like **tlabt** (from TaLaB), the regular form would have been **rdadt** (short for RaDaDT) and **msest** (short for MeSeST).

PLURAL

3rd person	(i)	**raddu** or **raddew**.
(See Remark 3)	(ii)	**messu** or **messew**.
2nd person	(i)	**raddejtu**.
(See Remark 4)	(ii)	**messejtu**.
1st person	(i)	**raddejna**.
(See Remark 5)	(ii)	**messejna**.

Remark 3: This form is obtained by the addition of suffix **u** or stressed **ew** to the Stem-Word. In the case of **raddu, messu**, independently of this · conjugation, these could be compound formations made up of **radd** 'he restored' and **mess** 'he touched' + pronominal suffix **u** 'it' meaning 'he restored (touched) it'.

Remark 4: These forms are obtained by the addition of suffix **u** to the first form of the first person singular.

Remark 5: This form is obtained by the addition of **ejna** to the Stem-Word.

Imperfect

(i)   (**hu**) **irodd**;   (**hi**, **int**) **trodd**;   (**jien**) **inrodd** or

irrodd; — (**huma**) **iroddu**; (**intom**) **troddu**; (**aħna**) **in-roddu** or **irroddu**.

(In the 1st pers. sing. and pl. note assimilation of **n + r = irr**).

(ii) (**hu**) **imiss**; (**hi, int**) **tmiss**; (**jien**) **immiss**; — (**huma**) **imissu**; (**intom**) **tmissu**; (**aħna**) **immissu**.

(In the the 1st pers. sing. and pl. note assimilation of **n + m = imm**).

Imperative

(i) **rodd** (sing.)/**roddu** (pl.).

(ii) **miss** sing.)/**missu** (pl.).

Past Participle

(i) **mirdud** (also **mardud**) (m.) **mirduda** (or **mar-duda**) (f.) **mirdudin** (or **mardudin**) (pl.) 'restored'.

(ii) **mimsus** (m.) **mimsusa** (f.) **mimsusin** (pl.) 'touched'.

Verbal Noun

(i) **radd** 'restoration'.

(ii) **mess** 'touch(ing)'.

Mess/Imiss — Idiomatic Usages

(i) **Mess** + direct pron. suffixes + Perfect or (ii) **Imiss** + pron. suffixes + Imperfect, besides the literal meaning, expresses also Eng. 'ought to' or 'should'.
Exx. **messek** (**ma messekx**) **tkellimt qabel**, 'you should (shouldn't) have spoken before'; **imissek tistħi minnek in-nifsek** 'you should be ashamed of yourself'; **qatt ma messha** (**messhom**) **għamlet** (**għamlu**) **dan** 'she (they) should have never done this'.

Another idiomatic usage: **mess/imiss** + direct or in-direct pron. suffixes = Eng. it was/is my, your etc. turn.

Exx. **int imissek** or **imiss lilek** 'it is your turn' or **mess lilek** 'it was your turn'; **min imissu?** 'whose turn is it?'

The following are patterns of Perfect/Imperfect correlatives:

Patterns	Vocabulary
1. KaTT (Per.)/ iKeTT (Impf.)	Exx. **qarr** 'he went to confession'/ **iqerr**; **raqq** 'he became thin'/**ireqq**; **saħħ** 'it (event) materialised'/**iseħħ**; **xaħħ** 'he was stingy'/**ixeħħ**. No past part.
2. KaTT/iKoTT	This is the most common pattern.

Exx. **damm** 'he strung together'/**idomm** (p.p. **midmum**); **daqq** 'he sounded or played' (an instrument)/**idoqq** (p.p. **midquq** unused); **ġarr** 'he carried'/ **iġorr** (p.p. **miġrur**, unused); **ħakk** 'he scratched'/**iħokk** (p.p. **maħkuk**); **ħall** 'he loosened'/**iħoll** (p.p. **maħlul**); **ħass** 'he felt'/**iħoss** (p.p. **maħsus**); **ħatt** 'he unloaded'/ **iħott** (p.p. **maħtut**); **għażż** 'he cherished'/**igħożż** (p.p. **magħżuż**, unused); **rass** 'he pressed' **iross** (p.p. **marsus**); **sadd** 'he plugged'/**isodd** (p.p. **misdud**); **xaqq** 'he cracked'/**ixoqq** (p.p. **mixquq**); **żamm** 'he held'/**iżomm** (p.p. **miżmum**).

3. KeTT/ (i) iKeTT or (ii) iKiTT:

Exx. (i) **leqq** 'it glittered'/**ileqq** (no p.p.); **temm** 'he finished'/**itemm** (p.p. **mitmum**); (ii) **bell** 'he wetted'/**ibill** (p.p. **miblul**); **bexx** 'he sprinkled'/ **ibixx** (p.p. **mibxux**, unused); **ġeżż** 'he sheared'/**iġiżż** (p.p. **miġżuż**); **kedd** 'he vexed'/**ikidd** (p.p. **mikdud**); **mess** 'he touched'/**imiss** (p.p **mimsus**).

DERIVED FORMS

2nd Form: **ġedded** 'he renewed'/**iġedded** — **imġedded** (m.) **imġedda** (f.) **imġeddin** (pl.) **ħabbeb** 'he reconciled'/ **iħabbeb** — **imħabbeb** (m.) **imħabba** (f.) **imħabbin** (pl.).

3rd Form: **qarar** 'he heard confession'/**iqarar** — ınqarar (m.) **mqarra** (f.) **mqarrin** (pl.).

5th Form: **thabbeb** 'he made friends with'/**jithabbeb** —no p.p.; **issaddad** (for **t + saddad**) 'it grew rusty'/**jis-saddad** — no past part.

7th Form: **inhass** (also **inthass**) 'it was felt'/**jinhass** (also **jinthass**)— no p.p.; **inghadd** (or **intghadd**) 'it was added'/**jinghadd** (or **jintghadd**) — no past part.

8th Form: **imtedd** 'he lay down'/**jimtedd** — no p.p.; **stadd** 'it was blocked up'/**jistadd** — no past part.

9th Form: **mrar** 'it became bitter'/**jimrar** — no p.p.; **rqaq** 'he grew thin'/**jirqaq** — no past part.

10th Form: **stkenn** 'he took shelter'/**jistkenn** — **mistkenn** (m.) **mistkenna** (f.) **mistkennin** (pl.); **stqarr** 'he confessed'/**jistqarr** — **mistqarr** (m.) **mistqarra** (f.) **mistqarrin** (pl.).

EXERCISE 25

Translate:

(a) **Iż-żiffa nhasset bierda** (cool) **u friska** (fresh). **La** (don't) **timteddx għall-qiegħa ta' l-art** (floor) **kiesħa** (cold). **Is-sikkina** (knife) **u l-furketta** (fork) **ssaddu. Il-qassis qararha qabel mietet** (died); **ma kinetx ilha ma tqerr. Meta tagħmel ix-xita stkenn taħt l-umbrella. Hu għamel ħbieb ma' sid id-dar. Geddu l-wegħda** (vow) **tagħkom 'l Alla. Irqaqet ħafna. Il-flus ingħaddu quddiemi. Temm il-ktieb f'ġimagħtejn.**

(b) The workers unloaded the cars (**karrozzi**) and the waggons (**karru** sing.), then they carried them to the stores (**maħżen** sing.). The raindrops (**qtar tax-xita**) glitter on the green (**aħdar**) leaves of the old (**xiħ**) trees. In summer the shepherd (**ragħaj**) shears the sheep (**ngħaġ**). Cherish your faith (**fidi**) and your parents (**ġenituri**). I like (**inhobb**) grated cheese on spaghetti (spagetti) with sauce (zalza). They held the child by its arm (driegħ). He held the horse by the reins (riedni). In Spring we feel the soft (artab) breeze of the sea. Don't vex your sister. She lay down tired on her bed (sodda).

Lesson 26

THE QUADRILITERAL VERB

Quadriliteral verbs consist of four radicals represented by √ K-T-B-L with one of the following five vowel sequences (i) a-a (ii) a-e (iii) e-e (iv) e-a (v) i-e with the second and third radicals between them.

They can be formed by (i) a repetition of a biradical base (ex. karkar [kar + kar] 'he dragged'; (ii) four different radicals (ex. maqdar 'he despised'; and (iii) four radicals in the case of verbs with vocalic sequence a-a or e-e, of which the first and third or the third and fourth are identical (exx. sensel 'he strung together'; lembeb 'he rolled pastry (with a rolling pin, lembuba)'.

Patterns	Vocabulary
1. KaTBaL:	Exx. (a) *repetition of a biradical base*: qaħqaħ 'he hacked'; dardar 'he made turbid (liquid)' or 'it upset the stomach'; farfar 'he shook off the dust'; (b) *four different radicals*. ħarbat 'he routed'; każbar 'he reviled'; bandal 'he swung'.
2. KaTBeL:	Exx. qarmeċ 'he crunched'; ħawtel 'he was diligent' or 'hard-working'.
3. KeTBeL:	Exx. (a) *repetition of a biradical base*: kexkex 'he shocked'; petpet 'he blinked'; temtem 'he stuttered'; (b)

four *different radicals*: **xeblek** 'he twined'; **xengel** 'he swung'; **ċempel** 'he rang'; (c) *four radicals of which two are identical*: **dendel** 'he hung'; **gerbeb** 'he rolled'.

4. KeTBaL: Exx. **fesdaq** 'he shelled (peas)'; **tertaq** 'he shattered': **werżaq** 'he screamed'.

5. KiTBeL: Exx. **fixkel** 'he obstructed'; **bixkel** 'he cheated'.

THE PERFECT AND IMPERFECT OF QUADRILITERALS

The Perfect and Imperfect of Quadriliterals are formed by the addition of the usual prefixes and suffixes respectively to the quadriliteral Stem-Word which is grammatically also the form of the Singular Imperative, the plural of which is obtained by suffix **u** and the omission of the second unstressed vowel of the Stem-Word.

PERFECT

SINGURAL

Verbal quadriliteral Stem-Words with their five different vocalic sequences.

3rd person masc. (i) **dardar** (ii) **qarmeċ** (iii) **kexkex** (iv) **tertaq** (v) **fixkel**.

3rd person fem. (i) **dardret** (ii) **qarmċet** (iii) **kexkxet** (iv) **tertqet** (v) **fixklet**.

2nd person & (i) **dardart** (ii) **qarmiċt** (iii) **kexkixt**
1st person (iv) **tertaqt** (v) **fixkilt**.

PLURAL

3rd person (i) **dardru** (ii) **qarmċu** (iii) **kexkxu** (iv) **tertqu** (v) **fixklu**.

2nd person	(i) **dardartu** (ii) **qarmiċtu** (iii) **kex-kixtu** (iv) **tertaqtu** (v) **fixkiltu**.
1st person	(i) **dardarna** (ii) **qarmiċna** (iii) **kex-kixna** (iv) **tertaqna** (v) **fixkilna**.

Imperfect

(i) (hu) **idardar**; (hi, int) **iddardar**; (jien) **indar-dar** — (huma) **idardru**; (intom) **iddardru**; (aħna) **indardru**.

(ii) (hu) **iqarmeċ**; (hi, int) **tqarmeċ**; (jien) **inqar-meċ**; — (huma) **iqarmċu**; (intom) **tqarmċu**; (aħna) **inqarmċu**.

(iii) (hu) **ikexkex**; (hi, int) **tkexkex**; (jien) **inkex-kex**; — (huma) **ikexkxu**; (intom) **tkexkxu**; (aħna) **inkexkxu**.

(iv) (hu) **itertaq**; (hi, int) **ittertaq**; (jien) **inter-taq**; — (huma) **itertqu**; (intom) **ittertqu**; (aħna) **inter-tqu**.

(iv) (hu) **ifixkel**; (hi, int) **tfixkel**; (jien) **infixkel**; — (huma) **ifixklu**; (intom) **tfixklu**; (aħna) **infixklu**.

Imperative

(i) **dardar** (sing.)/**dardru** (pl.).

(ii) **qarmeċ** (sing.)/**qarmċu** (pl.).

(iii) **kexkex** (sing.)/**kexkxu** (pl.).

(iv) **tertaq** (sing.)/**tertqu** (pl.).

(v) **fixkel** (sing.)/**fixklu** (pl.).

Past Participle

(i) **imdardar** (m.) **imdardra** (f.) **imdardrin** (pl.) 'upset (stomach)'.

(ii) **imqarmeċ** (m.) **imqarmċa** (f.) **imqarmċin** (pl.) 'crunched'.

(iii) **imkexkex** (m.) **imkexkra** (f.) **imkexkxin** (pl.) 'shocked'.

  (iv) **imtertaq** (m.)   **imtertqa** (f.)   **imtertqin** (pl.) 'shattered'.

  (v) **imfixkel** (m.)   **imfixkla** (f.)   **imfixklin** (pl.) 'obstructed'.

Verbal Noun

  (i)   **dardir** 'upset of the stomach'.

  (ii) **tqarmiċ** 'crunching'.

  (iii) **tkexkix** 'shivering'.

  (iv) **tertiq** 'shattering'.

  (v) **tfixkil** 'obstruction'.

It will be noted from the foregoing examples that the verbal nouns of quadriliteral verbs are formed with (i) the prefix **t** or (ii) without it. Without it are formed quadriliteral verbal nouns beginning with **ċ, d, ġ, s, x, ż, z,** with which **t** would otherwise assimilate.

These verbal nouns are formed by retaining the first vowel of the vocalic sequence of the Stem-Word and changing the second vowel of the Stem-Word to long **i**. The addition of suffix **a** (pl. **iet**) turns the verbal noun into the noun indicating a single action or occurrence. Other examples:— (i) **tbandil** 'swinging' **tbandila** 'a swing' (**bandal**); **tgergir** 'grumbling' **tgergira** 'a complaint' (**gerger**); (ii) **ċapċip** 'clapping' **ċapċipa** 'an applause' (**ċapċap**); **żaqżaq** 'creaking' **żaqżiqa** 'a creak' (**żaqżaq**).

DERIVED FORMS

Quadriliterals have only one derived form which is formed by prefixing **t** to the first radical, a consonant which, as already explained, is assimilated to **ċ, d, ġ, s, x, ż,** and **z.** The derived form is reflexive or passive.

Exx. **bandal** 'he swung' **tbandal** 'he was swung'; **ċarċar** 'he spilled' **iċċarċar** (for **t** + **ċarċar**) 'it was spilt'.

EXERCISE 26

Translate:

(a) **La ddardarx ilma li trid tixrob minnu. Dendel dil-libsa fix-xemx biex tinxef** (to dry). **Il-ħin kollu jisgħol u jqaħqaħ. 'L ommi ħallejtha** (left her) **d-dar tfesdaq il-piżelli** (peas). **Tfixklet fl-eżami u weħlet minn ħames suġġetti** (subjects). **Qarmċu snienhom** (their teeth) **bir-rabja** (anger). **Ma nixrobx ilma mdardar għax għandi l-istonku juġagħni. Wara l-ewwel xita l-ilma talbjar jiddardar. Iltqajt ma' ħafna tfixkil u smajt ħafna tgergir. Fil-gwerer jiċċarċar ħafna demm għal xejn.**

(b) Ring the bell and see who is there. When I heard of (**bi**) the murder I was shocked. They are obstructing our work. Why is she screaming as if she were mad? They clapped their hands when he finished his talk (**taħdita**). The children are swinging themselves on the swing (**bandla**) in the garden. Why are you always grumbling? The knights' (**tal-kavalieri**) blood was spilled (shed) on the bastions for the defence (**difiża**) of Malta. Rock (swing) the cradle and put the baby to sleep. Remove (**warrab**) all obstruction.

Lesson 27

THE IRREGULAR VERBS

Irregular verbs are those which for one reason or another do not follow the rule in part or in whole either because of the loss of one or more radicals in the Stem-Form or because of incomplete or mixed conjugation. These are the following given with their conjugations:

CONJUGATIONS

(1) Ta 'he gave'

Perfect

(hu) ta; (hi) tat; (jien, int) tajt; — (huma) taw; (intom) tajtu; (aħna) tajna.

Imperfect

(hu) jagħti; (hi, int) tagħti; (jien) nagħti; — (huma) jagħtu; (intom) tagħtu; (aħna) nagħtu.

Imperative

agħti (sing.)/agħtu (pl.).

Past Participle

mogħti (m.) mogħtija (f.) mogħtijin (or mogħtija) (pl.) 'given'.

Verbal Noun

għati (also għoti) 'the act of giving'/għatja (also għotja) 'a donation'.

7th Form Perfect

(hu) intgħata (or ingħata); (hi) intgħatat (ingħatat); (int,jien) intgħatajt (ingħatajt); — (huma) intgħataw (ingħataw); (intom) intgħatajtu (ingħatajtu); (aħna) intgħatajna (ingħatajna).

Imperfect

(hu) jintgħata (or jingħata); (hi, int) tintgħata (tingħata); (jien) nintgħata (ningħata); — (huma) jintgħataw (jingħataw); (intom) tintgħataw (tingħataw); (aħna) nintgħataw (ningħataw).

(2) Ħa 'he took' or + object 'he married'

Perfect

(hu) ħa; (hi) ħadet; (int,jien) ħadt; — (huma) ħadu; (intom) ħadtu; (aħna) ħadna.

Imperfect

(hu) jieħu; (hi, int) tieħu; (jien) nieħu; — (huma) jieħdu; (intom) tieħdu; (aħna) nieħdu.

Imperative

ħa (or ħu but ħud if + pron. suffixes) (sing.)/ ħudu (pl.).

Past Participle

meħud (m.) meħuda (f.) meħudin (pl.) 'taken'.

Verbal Noun

uħid 'the act of taking'/uħida 'a harvest' lit. 'one taking'.

6th Form *Passive Sense*

ittieħed 'it was taken' or 'it was infected'.

(3) Ra 'he saw'

Perfect

(hu) ra; (hi) rat; (int, jien) rajt; — (huma) raw; (intom) rajtu; (aħna) rajna.

Imperfect

(hu) jara; (hi, int) tara; (jien) nara; — (huma) jaraw; (intom) taraw; (aħna) naraw.

Imperative

ara (sing.)/araw (pl.).

Past Participle

muri (m.) murija (f.) murijin (pl.) 'seen'.

Verbal Noun

raj 'way of seeing, opinion, judgement'.

(4) Jaf 'he knows' abridged form of jagħraf
'he recognises'

Perfect

kien (kienet etc) + Imperfect.

Exx. (hu) kien jaf (he knew); (hi) kienet taf; (int) kont taf; (jien) kont naf; — (huma) kienu jafu; (intom) kontu tafu; (aħna) konna nafu.

Imperfect

(hu) jaf; (hi, int) taf; (jien) naf; — (huma) jafu; (intom) tafu; (aħna) nafu.

Imperative

af (sing.)/afu (pl.) 'know' generally preceded by kun/kunu. Ex. kun af (sing.)/kunu afu (pl.) meaning 'take note'.

(5)   Qal 'he said'

This verb is used in the third person singular masculine and feminine and third person plural of the Perfect only. All the other verbal forms are supplied by the verb għad (unused) 'he said'/ighid 'he says'. The supplemented conjugation is as follows:

Perfect

(hu) qal; (hi) qalet; (int,jien) għidt (or għedt); — (huma) qalu; (intom) għidtu (or għedtu); (aħna) għidna (or għedna).

Imperfect

(hu) ighid; (hi, int) tgħid; (jien) ngħid; — (huma) ighidu; (intom) tghidu; (aħna) ngħidu.

Imperative

għid (sing.)/għidu (pl.) 'say'.

Verbal Noun

għajdut or għajdun 'the act of speaking'.

Derived Forms

intqal, ingħad (both 7th form) 'it was said'.

(6)   Ġie 'he came'

Perfect

(hu) ġie; (hi) ġiet; (int, jien) ġejt; — (huma) ġew; (intom) ġejtu; (aħna) ġejna.

Imperfect

(hu) jiġi; (hi, int) tiġi; (jien) niġi; — (huma) jiġu; (intom) tiġu; (aħna) niġu.

Imperative

ejja (sing.)/ejjew (pl.) 'come'.

(Different forms from different roots).

Present Participle

ġej (m. sing.), ġejja (f. sing.), ġejjin (pl.).

Derived Nouns

miġi 'arrival, coming'; miġja 'an arrival'.

(7) **Mar** 'he went'

The verb is conjugated partly like a hollow verb and partly like a doubled verb.

Perfect

(hu) mar; (hi) marret (int, jien) mort; — (huma) marru; (intom) mortu; (aħna) morna.

Imperfect

(hu) imur; (hi, int) tmur; (jien) immur; — (huma) imorru; (intom) tmorru; (aħna) immorru.

In the 1st pers. sing. and pl. note assimilation nm = imm.

Imperative

mur (sing.)/morru (pl.) 'go'.

Verbal Noun

mawrien 'the act of going'; mawra 'a walk'; lit. 'a going'.

(8) **Idda** 'it shone'

Perfect

(hu) idda; (hi) iddiet; (int, jien) iddejt; — (huma) iddew; (intom) iddejtu; (aħna) iddejna.

Imperfect

(hu) jiddi; (hi, int) tiddi; (jien) niddi; — (huma) jiddu; (intom) tiddu; (aħna) niddu.

Imperative

iddi (sing.)/iddu (pl.) 'shine'.

Past Participle

middi (m.), middija (f.), middijin (pl.) 'glittering', 'shining'.

Verbal Noun

dija 'shining', 'brightness'.

(9) **Iżża** (always + ħajr) 'he gave (thanks)'

Perfect

(hu) iżża (ħajr); (hi) iżżiet (ħajr); (int, jien) iżżejt (ħajr); — (huma) iżżew (ħajr); (intom) iżżejtu (ħajr); (aħna) iżżejna (ħajr).

Imperfect

(hu) jiżżi (ħajr); (hi, int) tiżżi (ħajr); (jien) niżżi (ħajr); — (huma) jiżżu (ħajr); (intom) tiżżu (ħajr); (aħna) niżżu (ħajr).

Imperative

iżżi (ħajr) (sing.)/iżżu (ħajr) (pl.) 'give (thanks)'.

(10) **Emmen** 'he believed'

Perfect

(hu) emmen (hi) emmnet; (int, jien) emmint; — (huma) emmnu; (intom) emmintu; (aħna) emminna.

Imperfect

(hu) jemmen; (hi, int) temmen; (jien) nemmen; — (huma) jemmnu; (intom) temmnu; (aħna) nemmnu.

Imperative

emmen (sing.)/emmnu (pl.) 'believe'.

Past Participle

mwemmen (m.), **mwemmna** (f.), **mwemmnin** (pl.) 'believed'.

Verbal Noun

twemmin 'believing' or 'faith'.

5th Form

twemmen, jitwemmen 'it was/is believed'.

(11) **Kellu** + Noun 'he had' + Verb 'he had to'

This composite verb already given on p. 109 (Lesson 12) is formed from **kien** 'it was' + **l** 'to' + pron. suffix.

Perfect

(hu) **kellu**; (hi) **kellha**; (int) **kellek**; (jien) **kelli**; — (huma) **kellhom**; (intom) **kellkom**; (aħna) **kellna**. (pronounced **'kenna**).

Imperfect

(Generally with a future sense)

(hu) **ikollu**; (hi) **ikollha**; (int) **ikollok**; (jien) **ikolli**; — (huma) **ikollhom**; (intom) **ikoilkom**; (aħna) **ikollna**.

(12) **Waqaf** 'he stopped'

This verb is irregular only in the (i) Imperative and (ii) the Imperfect. Exx. (i) **ieqaf** (sing.)/**ieqfu** (pl.) 'stop', (ii) **jieqaf** 'he stops', **tieqaf** 'she stops' etc.

(13) **Jisem** 'it is named'

This form is used only with the verbal pronominal suffixes attached to it.

Exx. (hu) **jismu**; (hi) **jisimha**; (int) **jismek**; (jien) **jisimni**; — (huma) **jisimhom**; (intom) **jisimkom**; (aħna) **jisimna**. **X'jismek?** 'What is your name?'. **Jisimni Ġużè Saliba** 'My name is Joseph Saliba. **X'jisimhom martek u bintek?** 'what is the name of your wife and your daughter?'; il-mara jisimha **Rita** u t-tifla **Karmena**, 'my wife's name is Rita and my daughter's is Karmena'.

The past tense of this impersonal verb is expressed by adding before it **kien** invariable for the singular and plural and both genders. Exx. **Kien jismu Fredu** 'his name was Alfred'; **kien jisimha Gerita** 'her name was Margaret'; **il-bniet kien jisimhom kollha Marija u s-subien kollha Ġużeppi** 'the name of all the girls was Mary and of the boys was Joseph.'

EXERCISE 27

Translate:

(a) **Min jagħti jieħu; min ma jagħtix ma jeħux. Ma jiniex narahom għax qiegħda 'il bogħod (far) wisq. Kont taf li ħuk qal dan? Aħna ngħidu dan. X'qal ħuk ma nafux. Huma ġew ilbieraħ. Int meta ġejja? Jien niġi pitgħada. Fejn marret martek? Marret fejn mort jien u fejn mortu intom. In-nida (dew) jiddi fuq il-weraq tassiġar tal-luq (poplar). Ma stajtx nemmen 'l għajnejja. Ma kontx naf x'jismu s-suldat li rajt wieqaf fejnek.**

(b) How many books did you have in your shop? Where is their home? His name was Peter (**Pietru**). Give me water and bread. They took my money and ate my bread. When did she see us last (**l-aħħar**)? She said she did not know. Come (sing. and pl.) here and tell me what happened (**x'ġara**). You who believe in God give thanks to Him for today's food (**ikel**) and health. I stop here beside the grave (**qabar**) of my dead friend.

Lesson 28

THE CONJUGATION OF VERBS OF FOREIGN ORIGIN

Maltese, like English, has a considerable number of loan-words largely from Sicilian, old and modern Italian and more recently also from English.

1. Except for a few loan-words, the pattern of which
has been assimilated to that of strong triliteral or quadriliteral verbs and are conjugated regularly, all verbal
loans end (i) in **a** in open syllable except (ii) those
derived from English which end in **ja**.

Exx. (i) **storda** 'he got dizzy' (It. *stordire*); **obda** 'he
obeyed' (It. *obbedire*); (ii) **skorja** 'he scored' (Eng. [to]
score) and **ixxuttja** 'he shot' (Eng. [to] shoot), two foot-
ball terms; **skiddja** 'it (car) skidded' (Eng. [to] skid).

2. These verbs are conjugated like the Weak Verbs
having **J** as their third radical (Lesson 24) with some
differential characteristics in the composition of the
words the syllabic units of which are determined by the
original word-pattern not completely assimilated to the
native pattern in every detail.

3. No foreign verb has a present participle. Its
function is expressed by the Imperfect. Ex. **tifel jobdi** lit.
'a boy (who) obeys' for 'an obedient boy'. (See Lesson 31).

4. These foreign verbs can be classified into five
classes, the grouping being decided by the related combination of the vocalic sequences for the Perfect and
Imperfect Tense, especially the vocalic ending of the latter,
which decides the pattern group. The following illustra-
tions include the Perfect (3rd person masc. sing.), Imperfect tense (3rd person masc. sing.), the Imperative and
the Past Participle.

(i) *Dissyllabic*: **salva/isalva** 'he saved/saves'; **salva**
(sing.) **salvaw** (pl.) 'save' (Impv.) **salvat** (m.) (a, f. +
i, pl.) 'saved' (p.p.).

Remark 1: These verbs in Italian have their infinitives
in **are**, Past Part. **ato** (m.) **ata** (f.) **ati** (m. pl.) **ate** (f. pl.).
Other examples: (a) *dissyllabic*: **kanta** 'he sang'; **stona**
'he was out of tune'; **studja** 'he studied'; (b) *trisyllabic*:
intaxxa 'he taxed'; **imballa** 'he packed'; **invaża** 'he (devil)
possessed'; **infama** 'he defamed'; **ikkmanda** 'he com-
manded'.

(ii) **ittratta/jittratta** 'he treated/treats'; **ittratta** (sing.)/**ittrattaw** (pl.); **ittrattat** (m.) (+ a, f., + i, pl.); **iddajvja/jiddajvja** 'it dived/dives (aeroplane)'; **iddajvja** (sing.)/**iddajvjaw** (pl.). No Past Part., but transitive verb **ittajpja** 'he typed' has Past participle **ittajjpjat** (m.) (+ a, f., + i, pl.). 'typed'.

Remark 2: These are verbs from Italian or English which in the original language begin with (i) one consonant or (ii) more than one consonant or (iii) a vowel plus two consonants or a doubled (long) consonant. These and their Maltese adaptations require euphonic vowel **i** to make the initial double consonant pronounceable.
Exx. (i) **irbatta** 'he riveted' (It. *ribattere*); **ixxala** 'he made merry' (It. *scialare*); **iffittja** 'he fitted' (from Eng. [to] fit); (ii) **ittrenja** 'he trained' (Eng. [to] train); **ibblakka** 'he polished shoes' (from Eng. black); (iii) **imbarka** 'he embarked' (It. *imbarcare*); **irkanta** 'he sold by auction' (It. *incantare*); **iffronta** 'he faced a situation' (It *affrontare*); **irrabja** 'to be angry' (It. *arrabiare*).

(iii) **pinġa/ipinġi** 'he painted/paints'; **pinġi** (sing.)/**pinġu** (pl.), **pinġut** (m.) (a, f., + i, pl.); **irċieva/jirċievi** 'he received/receives'; **irċievi** (sing.)/**irċievu** (pl.); **irċevut** (m.) (a, f., + i, pl.).

Remark 3: Verbs belonging to this category other than exceptions in Italian have their infinitive in **ere**, Past Part. **uto** (m.) **uta** (f.) **uti** (m. pl.) **ute** (f. pl.). Other examples: (a) *dissyllabic*: **stenda** 'he extended'; **ċieda** 'he surrendered'; (b) *trisyllabic*: **impona** 'he imposed'; **esprima** (**ruħu**) 'he expressed (himself)'.

(iv) **obda/jobdi** 'he obeyed/obeys'; **obdi** (sing.) **obdu** (pl.); **obdut** (m.) (a, f., + i, pl.).

Remark 4: The infinitive of these verbs in Italian ends in **ire**, Past Part. **ito** (m.) **ita** (f.) **iti** (m. pl.) **ite** (f. pl.), but in **utu, uta, uti, ute** in Sicilian Other examples: *dissyllabic*: **fiera** 'he wounded'; **spieda** 'it was finished'; **forna** 'he furnished'.

(v) **stabilixxa/jistabilixxi** 'he established/establishes'; **stabilixxi** (sing.)/**stabilixxu** (pl.); **stabilit** (m.) (+ a, f., + i, pl.).

Remark 5: Also the infinitive of these verbs ends in **ire** in Italian, with *isci* (iʃʃi) as the verbal ending of the second person singular. Ex. *stabilire* 'to establish'; (*tu*) *stabilisci* 'you (sing.) establish'. Other examples: all *trisyllabic*: **skolpixxa** 'he sculpted'; **iffjorixxa** 'he prospered'; no past part.; **ittradixxa** 'he betrayed' — past part. **ittradut** (m.) (+ a, f., + i, pl.).

SAMPLE CONJUGATION OF SEVEN VERBAL GROUPS

Perfect

(i) (**hu**) **salva**; (**hi**) **salvat**; (**int, jien**) **salvajt**; — (**huma**) **salvaw**; (**intom**) **salvajtu** (**aħna**) **salvajna**.

(ii) (**hu**) **pinġa**; (**hi**) **pinġiet**; (**int, jien**) **pinġejt**; — (**huma**) **pinġew**; (**intom**) **pinġejtu**; (**aħna**) **pinġejna**.

(iii) (**hu**) **obda**; (**hi**) **obdiet**; (**int, jien**) **obdejt**; — (**huma**) **obdew**; (**intom**) **obdejtu**; (**aħna**) **obdejna**.

(iv) (**hu**) **stabilixxa**; (**hi**) **stabiliet**; (**int, jien**) **stabilejt**; — (**huma**) **stabilew**; (**intom**) **stabilejtu**; (**aħna**) **stabilejna**.

(v) (**hu**) **ittratta**; (**hi**) **ittrattat**; (**int, jien**) **ittrattajt**; — (**huma**) **ittrattaw**; (**intom**) **ittrattajtu**; (**aħna**) **ittrattajna**.

(vi) (**hu**) **skiddja**; (**hi**) **skiddjat**; (**int, jien**) **skiddjajt**; — (**huma**) **skiddjaw** (**intom**) **skiddjajtu**; (**aħna**) **skiddjajna**.

(vii) (**hu**) **ittajpja**; (**hi**) **ittajpjat**; (**int, jien**) **ittajpjajt**; — (**huma**) **ittajpjaw**; (**intom**) **ittajpjajtu**; (**aħna**) **ittajpjajna**.

Imperfect

(i) (**hu**) **isalva**; (**hi, int**) **issalva**; (**jien**) **insalva**; — (**huma**) **isalvaw**; (**intom**) **issalvaw**; (**aħna**) **insalvaw**.

(ii) (hu) ipinġi; (int, hi) tpinġi; (jien) inpinġi; — (huma) ipinġu; (intom) tpinġu; (aħna) inpinġu.

(iii) (hu) jobdi; (hi, int) tobdi; (jien) nobdi; — (intom) tobdu; (huma) jobdu; (aħna) nobdu.

(iv) (hu) jistabilixxi; (hi, int) tistabilixxi; (jien) nistabilixxi; — (huma) jistabilixxu; (aħna) nistabilixxu; (intom) tistabilixxu.

(v) (hu) jittratta; (hi, int) tittratta; (jien) nittratta; — (huma) jittrattaw; (intom) tittrattaw; (aħna) nittrattaw.

(vi) (hu) jiskiddja; (hi, int) tiskiddja; (jien) niskiddja; — (huma) jiskiddjaw; (intom) tiskiddjaw; (aħna) niskiddjaw.

(vii) (hu) jittajpja; (hi, int) tittajpja; (jien) nittajpja; — (huma) jittajpjaw; (intom) tittajpjaw; (aħna) nittajpjaw.

Imperative

(i)   salva (sing.)/salvaw (pl.).

(ii) pinġi (sing.)/pinġu (pl.).

(iii) obdi (sing.)/obdu (pl.) .

(iv) stabilixxi (sing.)/stabilixxu (pl.).

(v)   ittratta (sing.)/ittrattaw (pl.).

(vi) skiddja (sing.)/skiddjaw (pl.).

(vii) ittajpja (sing.)/ittajpjaw (pl.).

Past Participle

These are formed on the model of the foreign past participles partly adapted to Maltese word-structure as shown in the foregoing examples.

The foregoing examples show that the Perfect and Imperfect Tense as well as the Imperative are formed by means of the pronominal prefixes and suffixes used for the conjugation of native verbs (Lessons 15 and 16), but they retain the basis of the original form of the foreign Past Participle.

Verbal Nouns

There are no hard and fast rules about their formation which is irregular influenced partly by the form of the verbal noun of the original language and partly by the form of verbal native patterns.

Exx. **salvazzjoni** (salva) 'salvation'; **tpinġija** (pinġa) 'painting'; **ubbidjenza** (obda) 'obedience'; **stabilixxa** has no verbal noun; **trattament** (tratta) 'treatment'; **skiddjar** (skiddja) 'skidding'; **ittajpjar** (ittajpja) 'typing'.

Suffix **ar** of the last two English examples is the ending of the Italian infinitive *are* which is used with a considerable number of other verbal nouns of foreign origin. Other examples: **rikordjar** (irrikordja) 'recording'; **vjaġġar** (ivvjaġġa) 'travelling'; **raġunar** (irraġuna) 'reasoning'; **ippumpjar** (ippompja) 'pumping'.

DERIVED NOUNS

Only a few completely assimilated foreign verbs have their derived forms on the model of the native verbs (Lessons 19 & 20). Here are those more in use with the number of their form-pattern in brackets; (a) *Triliterals*: **fallaz** (2) 'he made false'; **tfallaz** (5) **flaz** (9) 'he became false'; **fannad** (2) 'he deepened'; **tfannad** (5) 'it was deepened'; **fnad** (9) 'it became deep'; **paxxa** (2) 'he delighted'; **tpaxxa** (5) 'he was delighted'; (b) *Quadriliterals*: **partat** (1) 'he bartered'; **tpartat** (2) 'it was bartered'; **fantas** (1) 'he fancied', 'imagined things'; **tfantas** (2) 'he took umbrage'; **bixkel** 'he cheated'; **tbixkel** (2) 'he was cheated'.

The other unassimilated, or only partly assimilated, foreign verbs obtain some of the semantic connotations of the nine derived forms periphrastically by:

(i) **ġagħal** 'he compelled' + Imperfect = causative 2nd form.

Ex. **ġagħalha tkanta** 'he made her sing'.

(ii) Verb + **lilu nnifsu** = reflexive — 5th & 7th forms.

Ex. **abbanduna lilu nnifsu** 'he abandoned himself'.

(iii) **Wieħed** (m.) **(waħda,** f.) **lil ieħor** (m.) **(oħra,** f.) or **lil xulxin** 'each other or one another' = reciprocal 5th, 6th & 7th forms.

Ex. **jistmaw wieħed lil ieħor** (or) **lil xulxin** 'they esteem one another (or) each other'.

(iv) **Kien** or **safa** + past participle = passive 5th and 7th forms.

Ex. **kienet** (or **sfat**) **abbandonata minn uliedha** 'she was abandoned by her children'.

(v) **sar** 'he became' + colour word or word denoting physical quality = 9th form.

Exx. **sar vjola** 'he became livid' (lit. violet); **saru krudili** 'they became cruel'.

EXERCISE 28

Translate:

(a) **Qed nittajpja ittra għall-editur ta' dan il-ġurnal** (paper). **Obdi 'l ommok u 'l missierek. Il-pittur** (painter) **pinġa kwadru** (picture) **sabiħ ħafna. Ma salva ħadd mill-għarqa** (shipwreck). **Dil-mara titfantas mixxejn. L-omm titpaxxa b'uliedha. Ittratta lin-nies tajjeb biex in-nies tittrattak tajjeb. Il-karozza skiddjat u x-xufier weġġa'. Il-vjaġġar minn pajjiż għal ieħor jiswa** (costs) **ħafna flus. Dan raġunar żbaljat** (mistaken).

(b) The plane (**ajruplan**) dived over the city. How did she treat you? The country (**pajjiż**) is in danger. Save it (sing. & pl.). He made us treat our enemies (**għedewwa**) better than we wanted. They deepened the trench (**trunċiera**) and hid themselves in it. God is the salvation of man. No obedience without (**bla**) discipline (**dixxiplina**). Will you please (**jekk jogħġbok**) type these two articles (**artikli**) for me? The car skidded and they hurt themselves. She was treated well (**sewwa**) by her husband (**żewġha**).

Lesson 29

THE VERB WITH PRONOMINAL SUFFIXES

(i) The Direct Suffixes

Pronominal suffixes can be (i) Direct or (ii) Indirect. The direct pronominal suffixes are those which form the direct object of the verb. These are attached (a) to the last radical consonant of the verb or (b) to the second radical in contact with the first radical following the omission of the first vowel if the third radical is un-written **j** in verbs ending in **a** (Lesson 24).

The following verbal suffixes are the same as those used for nouns, except for the first person sing. which is **ni**, not **i**.

Exx. (a) **Warrab** 'he removed', **warrabni** (for **warrab** + **ni**) 'he removed me'; but   (b) **rema** 'he threw away'; **rmieni** (for **rema** + **ni**) 'he threw me away' — stress on the penultimate syllable.

1 sing.	-ni 'me'	1 plural	-na 'us'
2 sing.	-k, -ok, -ek 'you'	2 plural	-kom 'you'
(See Rem. 1)		3 plural	-hom 'them'
3 sing. masc.	-h, -u 'him'		
(See Rem. 2)			
3 sing. fem.	-ha 'her'		

Remark 1: (i) **-k**: This suffix is used if the verb ends in a vowel. It brings the stress on to the last syllable.

Exx. **Jaghtik** (for **jaghti** + **k**) 'he gives you'; **jarmuk** (for **jarmu** + **k**) 'they throw you away'.

(ii)   **-ok**: This is added to verbs ending in a conso-nant, when the first vowel of the first syllable is **o**.

Exx. **Joboghdok** (**jobghod** + **ok**) 'he hates you'; **johorgok** (**johrog** + **ok**) 'he gets you out' — stress on the pen-ultimate syllable.

(iii) **-ek**: This is added to verbs ending in a consonant other than those which take the pronominal suffix
-ok.

Exx. **jiġbdek** (for **jiġbed + ek**) 'he pulls or attracts you';
tlibbsek (**tlibbes + ek**) 'she dresses you' — stress on the
penultimate syllable.

Remark 2: **h** is added to verbs ending in a vowel,
in **w** or in **ie**.

Exx. **Qatlu** 'they killed', **qatluh** 'they killed him' (stress
on the last syllable); **qatel** 'he killed', **qatlu** 'he killed
him'; **nsew** 'they forgot', **nsewh** 'they forgot him'; **nsieh**
'he forgot him' (= **nsie** [for **nesa**] he forgot + **h**).

The addition of these pronominal suffixes moves
the stress from the first vowel of the sequence to the
vowel of the second syllable and, in the case of verbs
the third radical of which is **j**, the first vowel of the
sequence is elided altogether.

If the accent moved one syllable forward falls on
the vowel **e**, this vowel changes into **i**.

Exx. **Sellem** ('sellem) 'he greeted', **sellimli** (sel'limli) 'he
greeted me'. When the pronominal suffixes are added to
a Stem-Word ending in vowel **a**, this vowel is mutated
into **ie**, less frequently long **a** (**aa**) which carries the stress.

Exx. **tefa** 'he extinguished (a lamp)', **tfieha** 'he extinguished it'; **ġara** 'it happened', **ġrali** 'it happened to me'.

An orthographic difficulty which is confusing also
to the native speakers of the language is created by the
addition of the pronominal suffixes third person, feminine and plural (i) to the Stem-Verb (Perfect Tense),
and (ii) to the Imperative ending in vowel **i**. It must be
borne in mind that when these pronominal suffixes are
added to verbal Stem-Words ending in **a** in open syllable, this **a** is changed into **ie**. The difficulty arises when
the same pronominal suffixes are added to the Imperative forms of the verb and those of the Perfect Tense.

Thus **Halla** 'he left' + **ha** or **hom** becomes **ħallieha** or **ħalliehom** 'he left her, them'; but **ħalli** (Impv.) 'leave' + **ha** or **hom** becomes **ħalliha, ħallihom** 'leave her, them'.

In their pronunciation, these forms are homophones, but the grammatical distinction between the two must be maintained in the written language. Other examples: **urieha, uriehom** 'he showed her, them' for **wera** 'he showed' + **ha**, + **hom**, but **uri** (Imperative of **wera**) + **ha** or **hom** becomes **uriha, urihom**, 'show her, them'.

No distinction is made in the written language if the verb ends in **a** in the Perfect and Imperative alike, as in the case of **mela** 'he filled', the Imperative of which is **imla**. Therefore **imlieha, imliehom** can mean both 'he filled her, them' or 'fill her, them' (Imperative). Similarly, **insieha, insiehom** (for **nesa** + **ha, hom**) 'he forgot her, them' or 'forget her, them' (Imperative) for **insa** + **ha, hom**.

As **ie** always carries the accent, when the stress moves one syllable onwards in verbs having vocalic sequence **ie-e** on account of the addition of the pronominal suffix, **ie** becomes **i** or **e**.

Exx. Bierek ('biərek) 'he blessed'; **birikhom** (bi'rikom) or **berikhom** (be'rikom) 'he blessed them'; **ġiegħel** ('dʒiəl) 'he compelled'; **ġegħilha** (dʒe'ila) 'he compelled her'.

With regard to verbs ending in ' for final **għ** in the Stem-Word, remember the general rule, that when the pronominal suffix is attached to it, **għ** is written in full throughout.

Exx. Bażża' 'he frightened', **bażżagħkom** 'he frightened you'; **qala'** 'he uprooted'; **qalagħha** 'he uprooted her'.

(Remember also that the phonetic implication of **għ** + **ha** and **hom** = aħħa, aħħom).

(ii) The Indirect Suffixes

The Indirect Suffixes which indicate the indirect object of the verb are **-li** 'to me'; **-lek** 'to you'; **-lu** 'to him'; -lha 'to her'; -lna 'to us'; -lkom 'to you' (pl.) -lhom 'to them'. Like most of the direct suffixes they carry the stress on to the last syllable but one. All strong verbs drop the 2nd unstressed vowel and insert stressed i before the indirect pronominal suffixes 3rd pers. fem. and the plural forms (for examples see paradigm p. 214). Hollow verbs can insert or omit stressed i before the 3rd pers. fem. and sing. Exx. ġablha/ġablhom but more commonly ġabilha/ġabilhom 'he brought (to) her/(to) them'. Verbs ending in għ (') do not require i before the pron. suffixes. In all such pron. combinations vowel e in verbal sequence a-e becomes stressed i. Ex. għamel ('aamel) 'he made'; għamilli (a'milli) 'he made for me'.

In the case of Weak Verbs ending in a (Lesson 24), the pron. suffixes are attached to the second radical in immediate contact with the first radical, changing short a to long a (aa) but more frequently to ie (iə).

Exx. ġara 'it occurred' or 'happened', ġralha 'it occurred (happened) to her'; tefa 'he extinguished', tfieli 'he extinguished for me'; tfieni 'he outshone me'.

EXERCISE 29

Translate:

(a) Ihobbha daqs dawl għajnejh. Żewġha miet issena l-oħra (last year) u ħallieha armla b'ħamest itfal. Alla jbierkek u jimliek bil-hena (happiness). Beżżagħhom bl-għajat (shouting) tiegħu ta' miġnun. Ix-xkora (sack) l-imqattgħa (torn) itfagħha 'l barra mit-tieqa. Il-lampa tfieha u waqa' dlam kbir fil-għorfa (room of a village house). Bħala (as) tifkira (souvenir) lilek nagħtik żewġ kotba u lilha bizzilla (lace) tal-ħarir. Warrabli das-sakran (drunkard) minn hawn. It-tifla tiegħek imqarba (naughty); kissritilna ħames tazzi godda. Bgħattilhom ċekk (cheque) ta' sitt liri bil-posta (by post).

(b) Remove the table for me and put it in the other room. She wrote us a letter from Rome (Ruma).

If you love her, marry her; if you don't love her, leave
her. He left her alone with her children. He that loves
you gives you and blesses you. She will leave him though
(għalkemm) he loves her. Why have you frightened the
children? I have not frightened them, but you are
frightening them with your screaming (twerżiq). He
forgot them all (kollha); will you also forget them? Who
sent you this book from Japan (Gappun)? Where are
the glasses? Fill them with good wine and drink it.

LESSON 30

PARADIGM OF VERB KITEB 'he wrote' + (i)Direct (ii) Indirect Pronominal suffixes (iii) The Two Combined

A verb may be followed by (i) the direct (ii) indirect
pronominal suffixes which have been dealt with in the
previous lesson. The direct and indirect pronominal suffixes can be combined to express the direct and indirect
objects together. The order is: *the verb + direct pron.
suffix + indirect pron. suffix.*

[Note (i) that when the indirect pron. suffix is added
to the direct pron. suffix ha, a becomes ie (i.e. ha becomes hie); (ii) the direct pron. suffix of the third person masculine singular u becomes hu when followed by
an indirect pronominal suffix. The h in hu like h in hie
is silent. Exx. qatel 'he killed', qatlu 'they killed';
qatluhulha (for qatlu + hu + lha) 'they killed him for
her', qatluhielha (for qatlu + hie + lha) 'they killed her
for her'; ġib 'bring' (impv.), ġibu 'bring him', (for
ġib + u) ġibhuli (for ġib + hu + li) 'bring him for me';
ġabha (for ġab + fem. pron. suffix ha), ġabhielha
(for ġab + hie + lha) 'he brought her for her'].

The paradigm on p. 214 illustrates the verb kiteb 'he
wrote' followed by (i) the direct suffix 'he wrote it' etc.;

(ii) the indirect suffix 'he wrote to (for) him'; etc.; (iii) the two sets of suffixes together 'he wrote it for him' etc., with the stress always on the penultimate syllable. Exx. **kitbuhulu** (**kitbu'uulu**); **kitbuhielha** (**kitbu'iəla**).

Remark 1: Note the transfer of the accent in accordance with the general principle governing the position and movements of the stress explained in Part I on pp. 30-32. The stress falls on the 1st syllable in column (i); on the second syllable in column (ii), and on the 3rd syllable in column (iii) — invariably on the penultimate. When the negative stress-attracting particle **x** is attached to any of these three verbal forms, the accent falls on the last syllable. Exx. **'kitbu** 'he wrote it', **ma kit'buuʃ** 'he did not write it'; **ki'tiblu** 'he wrote to (or for) him', **ma kitib'luuʃ** 'he did not write to (for) him'; **kiti'buulu** 'he wrote it for him', **ma kitibu'luuʃ** 'he did not write it for him'.

Remark 2: Remember that on p. 29 of Part I you learned that when one of the liquid consonants and, by analogy **ġħ**, occurs between two consonants, a euphonic vowel is inserted to break up the three-consonant group. But this rule does not apply to l occurring in double pronominal suffixes. Ex. **ħarbtuhomlkom** (accent on the penultimate) 'they destroyed them for you' and not **ħarbtuhomilkom**.

PERFECT

(i) Direct (ii) Indirect Pronominal Suffixes and (iii) both combined.

[*Note that though in column (iii) of the following paradigm I have used throughout as the direct pron. suffix that of the 3rd person sing. masc. naturally this can be replaced by any of the other direct pron. suffixes, according to the intended meaning.*]

GENDER AND NUMBER CATEGORY OF PRONOMINAL SUFFIXES

(i) & (ii) 3rd Pers. Masc. Sing.

	(i)	(ii)	(iii)
3 masc. sing.	kitbu	kītiblu	kitibhulu
3 fem. sing.	kitbitu	kitbitlu	kitbitħulu
2 sing.	ktibtu	ktibtlu	ktibtħulu
1 sing.	ktibtu	ktibtlu	ktibtħulu
3 plural	kitbuh	kitbulu	kitbuhulu
2 plural	ktibtuh	ktibtulu	ktibtuhulu
1 plural	ktibnieh	ktibnielu	ktibnihulu

(i) & (ii) 3rd Pers. Fem. Sing.

	(i)	(ii)	(iii)
3 masc. sing.	kitibha	kitbilha	kitibhulha
3 fem. sing.	kitbitha	kitbitilha	kitbithulha
2 sing.	ktibtha	ktibtilha	ktibthulha
1 sing.	ktibtha	ktibtilha	ktibthulha
3 plural	kitbuha	kitbulha	kitbuhulha
2 plural	ktibtuha	ktibtulha	ktibtuhulha
1 plural	ktibnieha	ktibnielha	ktibnihulha

(i) & (ii) 2 Pers. Sing.

	(i)	(ii)	(iii)
3 masc. sing.	kitbek	kitiblek	kitibhulek
3 fem. sing.	kitbitek	kitbitlek	kitbithulek
2 sing.	—	—	—
1 sing.	ktibtek	ktibtlek	ktibthulek
3 plural	kitbuk	kitbulek	kitbuhulek
2 plural	—		
1 plural	ktibniek	ktibnielek	ktibnihulek

(i) & (ii) 1st Pers. Sing.

	(i)	(ii)	(iii)
3 masc. sing.	kitibni	kitibli	kitibhuli
3 fem. sing.	kitbitni	kitbitli	kitbithuli
2 sing.	ktibtni	ktibtli	ktibthuli
1 sing.	—		
3 plural	kitbuni	kitbuli	kitbuhuli
2 plural	ktibtuni	ktibtuli	ktibtuhuli
1 plural	—		—

(i) & (ii) 3rd Pers. Plural

	(i)	(ii)	(iii)
3 masc. sing.	kitibhom	kitbilhom	kitibulhom
3 fem. sing.	kitbithom	kitbithilhom	kitbithulhom
2 sing.	ktibthom	ktibtilhom	ktibthulhom
1 sing.	ktibthom	ktibtilhom	ktibthulhom
3 plural	kitbuhom	kitbulhom	kitbuhulhom
2 plural	ktibtuhom	ktibtulhom	ktibtuhulhom
1 plural	ktibniehom	ktibnielhom	ktibnihulhom

(i) & (ii) 2nd Pers. Plural

	(i)	(ii)	(iii)
3 masc. sing.	kitibkom	kitbilkom	kitibhulkom
3 fem. sing.	kitbitkom	kitbitilkom	kitbithulkom
2 sing.	—		
1 sing.	ktibtkom	ktibtilkom	ktibthulkom
3 plural	kitbukom	kitbulkom	kitbuhulkom
2 plural	—		
1 plural	ktibniekom	ktibnielkom	ktibnihulkom

(i) & (ii) 1st Pers. Plural

	(i)	(ii)	(iii)
3 masc. sing.	kitibna	kitbilna	kitibhulna
3 fem. sing.	kitbitna	kitbitilna	kitbithulna
2 sing.	ktibtna	ktibtilna	ktibthulna
1 sing.	—		—
3 plural	kitbuna	kitbulna	kitbuhulna
2 plural	ktibtuna	ktibtulna	ktibtuhulna
1 plural	—	—	—

IMPERFECT

(i) & (ii) 3rd Pers. Masc. Sing.

	(i)	(ii)	(iii)
3 masc. sing.	jiktbu	jiktiblu	jiktibhulu
3 fem. sing.	tiktbu	tiktiblu	tiktibhulu
2 sing.	tiktbu	tiktiblu	tiktibhulu
1 sing.	niktbu	niktiblu	niktibhulu
3 plural	jiktbuh	jiktbulu	jiktbuhulu
2 plural	tiktbuh	tiktbulu	tiktbuhulu
1 plural	niktbuh	niktbulu	niktbuhulu

(i) & (ii) 3rd Pers. Fem. Sing.

	(i)	(ii)	(iii)
3 masc. sing.	jiktibha	jiktbilha	jiktibhulha
3 fem. sing.	tiktibha	tiktbilha	tiktibhulha
2 sing.	tiktibha	tiktbilha	tiktibhulha
1 sing.	niktibha	niktbilha	niktibhulha
3 plural	jiktbuha	jiktbulha	jiktbuhulha
2 plural	tiktbuha	tiktbulha	tiktbuhulha
1 plural	niktbuha	niktbulha	niktbuhulha

(i) & (ii) 2nd Pers. Sing.

	(i)	(ii)	(iii)
3 masc. sing.	jiktbek	jiktiblek	jiktibhulek
3 fem. sing.	tiktbek	tiktiblek	tiktibhulek
2 sing.	—	—	—
1 sing.	niktbek	niktiblek	niktibhulek
3 plural	jiktbuk	jiktbulek	jiktbuhulek
2 plural	—	—	—
1 plural	niktbuk	niktbulek	niktbuhulek

(i) & (ii) 1st Pers. Sing.

	(i)	(ii)	(iii)
3 masc. sing.	jiktibni	jiktibli	jiktibhuli
3 fem. sing.	tiktibni	tiktibli	tiktibhuli
2 sing.	tiktibni	tiktibli	tiktibhuli
1 sing.	—	—	—
3 plural	jiktbuni	jiktbuli	jiktbuhuli
2 plural	tiktbuni	tiktbuli	tiktbuhuli
1 plural	—	—	—

(i) & (ii) 3rd Pers. Plural

	(i)	(ii)	(iii)
3 masc. sing.	jiktibhom	jiktbilhom	jiktibhulhom
3 fem. sing.	tiktibhom	tiktbilhom	tiktibhulhom
2 sing.	tiktibhom	tiktbilhom	tiktibhulhom
1 sing.	niktibhom	niktbilhom	niktibhulhom
3 plural	jiktbuhom	jiktbulhom	jiktbuhulhom
2 plural	tiktbuhom	tiktbulhom	tiktbuhulhom
1 plural	niktbuhom	niktbulhom	niktbuhulhom

(i) & (ii) 2nd Pers. Plural

	(i)	(ii)	(iii)
3 masc. sing.	jiktibkom	jiktbilkom	jiktibhulkom
3 fem. sing.	tiktibkom	tiktbilkom	tiktibhulkom
2 sing.	—	—	—
1 sing.	niktibkom	niktbilkom	niktibhulkom
3 plural	jiktbukom	jiktbulkom	jiktbuhulkom
2 plural	—	—	—
1 plural	niktbukom	niktbulkom	niktbuhulkom

(i) & (ii) 1st Pers. Plural

	(i)	(ii)	(iii)
3 masc. sing.	jiktibna	jiktbilna	jiktibhulna
3 fem. sing.	tiktibna	tiktbilna	tiktibhulna
2 sing.	tiktibna	tiktbilna	tiktibhulna
1 sing.	—	—	—
3 plural	jiktbuna	jiktbulna	jiktbuhulna
2 plural	tiktbuna	tiktbulna	tiktbuhulna
1 plural	—	—	—

IMPERATIVE

(i) & (ii) 3rd Pers. Masc. Sing.

	(i)	(ii)	(iii)
2 sing.	iktbu	iktiblu	iktibhulu
2 plural	iktbuh	iktbulu	iktbuhulu

(i) & (ii) 3rd Pers. Fem. Sing.

	(i)	(ii)	(iii)
2 sing.	iktibha	iktbilha	iktibhulha
2 plural	iktbuha	iktbulha	iktbuhulha

(i) & (ii) 2nd Pers. Sing.

No Imperative.

(i) & (ii) 1st Pers. Sing.

	(i)	(ii)	(iii)
2 sing.	iktibni	iktibli	iktibhuli
2 plural	iktbuni	iktbuli	iktbuhuli

(i) & (ii) 3rd Pers. Plural

	(i)	(ii)	(iii)
2 sing.	iktibhom	iktbilhom	iktibhulhom
2 plural	iktbuhom	iktbulhom	iktbuhulhom

2nd Pers. Plural

No Imperative.

(i) & (ii)1st Pers. Plural

	(i)	(ii)	(iii)
2 sing.	iktibna	iktbilna	iktibhulna
2 plural	iktbuna	iktbulna	iktbuhulna

EXERCISE 30

Translate:

(a) X'ittra sabiħa kitbitlu l-għarusa (bride) lill-għarus! Wasslitli t-tifla l-iskola għax għadha żgħira. Twassalhieli l-iskola? Mela le! (with pleasure). Grazzi ħafna. Qalilhom storja Maltija u qalħa b'sengħa (art) kbira; imma l-istorja l-oħra qalhielhom ħuħ. Għannili għanja Maltija u jien ngħannilek għanja Għarbija. Min silifħulek? Dal-ktieb silifħuli s-surmast (teacher) u dil-pinna silfithieli z-zija (aunt). Reġġagħhulhom (reġġa'

= he returned) **lura u għidilhom ma jibgħatuhulix għal issa. Min kissirhomlna? Il-baħrin** (sailors) **kissruhomlna u rmewhomlna 'l barra.**

(b) She wrote him a very long letter from Madrid **(Madrid)**. Get it done (sing. & pl.) for me as quickly **(malajr)** as you can. Don't send (sing. & pl.) these to them with the messenger **(messaġġier)**. If we shall take her to him, he will send her back **(lura)** to us. You (sing. & pl.) brought it (f.) to us after you (sing. & pl.) had seen it (f.). Shall we write it (masc. & fem.) to (or for) them? As you say; but it is better to send them to us. I ate it (masc. & fem.); did you eat it too **(wkoll)**? Will you write her a nice **(pulita)** letter and tell her that they have sent them to us? What has happened to you (sing. & pl.)? Nothing has happened to me (us); but a misfortune **(disgrazzja)** has happened to her.

Lesson 31

SYNTACTIC FUNCTIONS OF THE TENSES

[*In the examples given in this chapter study very carefully the patterns of phrasal and sentence linking and compare them with the corresponding structures in English. Where such sentences are broken up by literal English meanings in brackets, first read the Maltese structure as a whole then examine the components one by one as explained in the brackets.*]

The Imperfect and the Perfect

(1) The Imperfect, besides its usual verbal function, has also an adjectival function corresponding to an adjectival clause in English.

Exx. **Ġanni jiekol** 'John eats'; **Ġanni raġel jiekol ħafna** 'John is a man who eats very much'; **nies jibżgħu** 'fearful people' but **nies jibżgħu minn dellhom** 'people who are afraid of their own shadow' (a Maltese idiom for "cowards").

(2) The Imperfect or Perfect + Imperfect (i) when the subject of both is the same or (ii) when the subjects are different but the Perfect or Imperfect has the direct pronominal suffix attached to it are equivalent to an English sentence consisting of a principal clause followed by an objective (or accusative) infinitive.

Exx. (i) **Irrid** (I want) or **ridt** (I wanted) **niekol** (I eat) = English 'I want (wanted) to eat', (ii) **irridek** or **ridtek** (I want[ed] you) **timpostali** (you post for me) **ittra** (letter) = English 'I want(ed) you to post a letter for me'.

In other combinations, the Perfect or the first Imperfect is followed by the conjunction **li**.

Exx. **Irrid li int tiekol** (emphatic form of **irridek tiekol**) 'I want you to eat'; **ridt li int timpostali ittra** (emphatic form of **ridtek timpostali ittra**) 'I wanted you to post a letter for me'; **xtaqu li aħna mmorru narawhom** (for less emphatic **xtaquna mmorru narawhom**) 'they wished us to go and see them'.

(3) Time-Word or Time-Phrase + (i) Imperfect or (ii) Perfect = a sentence expressing (i) an action still to be performed (future) (ii) an action already performed (past).

Exx. (i) **Għada** (tomorrow) **nitlaq** (I leave for) **lejn l-Ingilterra** = English 'Tomorrow I shall leave for England'; **fis-sajf** (in summer) **immur** (I go) or (ii) **mort** (I went) **Marsalforn Għawdex** = English 'In summer I go (or went) to Marsalforn in Gozo'.

(4) (i) Imperfect or (ii) Perfect + Imperfect indicates contemporaneous action, (i) in the present (ii) in the past.

Exx. (i) **Jidħol** (he enters) **jidħak** (he laughs) = English 'He enters laughing' (Imperfect + Imperfect) (ii) **daħal** (he entered) **jidħak** (he laughs) **u ħareġ** (he went out) **jibki** (he cries) (Perfect + Imperfect) = English 'He came in laughing and went out crying'.

(5) The second person singular can be used impersonally corresponding to the use of the Infinitive in English as the subject of a sentence.

Exx. **Tgħix** (you live) **waħdek** (alone) **dwejjaq** (annoyance) = English 'It is annoying to live alone'; **tiddejjaq** (you feel annoyed) **tistenna** (you wait) = English 'You feel annoyed to wait'; **tgħix** (you live) **kemm** (how much) **tgħix trid** (you want) **tmut** (you die) = English 'No matter how long you live you must die'.

Remark 1: The second person singular in colloquial, that is non-grammatical, contexts is considered as the equivalent of the infinitive of English and other languages. Exx. **tiekol** 'you eat' is used for the Eng. infinitive 'to eat' and **tmur** 'you go' for 'to go'.

(6) A peculiar usage is the following construction to indicate two contemporaneous actions (i) in the present or (ii) in the past. The construction is a noun or a pronoun or a noun and its pronoun (subject) + conjunction **u** (and) + (i) Imperfect or the Present Participle or (ii) + Perfect, the rest of the completing sentence with its verb in the Perfect or Imperfect according as the action took place in the present or in the past.

Exx. **Id-dgħajsa** (the boat) **hija** (she) **u** (and) **tidħol** (she enters) (or fem. pres. part. **dieħla** 'entering') **għerqet** (sank) (or **tegħreq** 'sinks') = 'The boat, while entering, sank (sinks)'; **hu** (he) **u** (and) **jitkellem** (he speaks) **inħanaq** (or **jinħanaq**) (he grew (or grows) hoarse) **f'daqqa** (suddenly) = 'While speaking he suddenly grew hoarse'.

(7) **Kien** (**kienet** etc.) + (i) Imperfect which may be preceded by **qed** or (ii) + Perfect, indicates action which (i) was taking place in the past or (ii) had already taken place in the past (the Pluperfect).

Exx. (i) **Kont** (I was) **naqra** or (**qed naqra**) (I read) **l-gazzetta** (the paper) **xhin** (when) **wasal** (he arrived) **huk** (your brother) (or **xhin huk wasal**) = 'I was reading the paper when your brother arrived'; (ii) **kont** (I was) **smajt** (I heard) **bl-ahbar** (the news) **jumejn** (two days) **qabel** (before) = 'I had heard the news two days before'.

(8) **Inkun** (I shall be), **tkun** etc. + (i) Imperfect or (ii) + Perfect indicates (i) a future action still to take place or (ii) a future action that had already taken place.

Exx. **Meta** (when) **tiġi** (you come) **nkun** (**qed**) (I shall be) **inlesti** (I prepare) or **lestejt** (I prepared) **il-bagalji** (the luggage) = 'When you come I shall be preparing (or will have prepared) the luggage'.

(9) **Baqa'** and **fadal** used impersonally for both numbers and genders mean 'there remain'.

Ex. **baqa'** (or **fadal**) **għoxrin ktieb mhux mibjugħa** 'there remain twenty books unsold'.

SENTENCE STRUCTURE

1. The general order is (i) Subject + Verb + **lil**, shortened form **'il** (before a consonant) or **'l** (before a word beginning with a vowel) + object.

Exx. **Iħobb** (he loves) **'l** (to) **Alla** (God) **u** (and) **lil** (to) **pajjiżu** (his country) = 'He loves God and his country'. Note that the particle **lil** becomes **lill-** if the object takes the definite article.

Exx. **Igħallem lit-tfal** 'he teaches the children', but **iħobb 'l ommu** not **l-ommu** 'he loves his mother', because a noun having the pronominal suffix does not take the definite article when used as the subject of a sentence.

2. While the general order of a sentence is subject + verb, this order is generally inverted in subordinate

adverbial clauses showing Verb + Subject, though the usual order, less idiomatically effective, is sometimes also used.

Exx. **Jien dħalt meta wasal ħuk** (or **ħuk wasal**) **mill-Ingilterra** 'I arrived when your brother arrived from England'; **irrid naf meta sa tiġi oħtok** (or **oħtok sa tiġi**) 'I want to know when your sister is going to come'.

3. Verbs in Maltese can be used without the subject except in co-ordinate clauses, when the subjects are different.

Exx. **Aħna ġbidna l-ispaga** or **ġbidna l-ispaga** 'we pulled the string' but **aħna ġbidna l-ispaga u huma ġibdu l-ħabel** and not **ġbidna l-ispaga u ġibdu l-ħabel** 'we pulled the string and they pulled the rope'.

4. The Imperative in Maltese is followed by another or more imperatives corresponding to so many infinitives in English. The order or request to be communicated to a third person (sing. or pl.) also corresponding to the use of the infinitive in English, is expressed by the Imperfect.

Exx. **Għaġġel mur ilħqu u għidlu jiġi** (lit. make haste + go + reach him + and tell him + he comes — Imperfect) 'Make haste to reach him and (to) tell him to come'; **mur hu l-kafè** (lit. go + take the coffee) 'Go to take the coffee'; **mur għidilhom jieħdu l-kafè** (lit. go + tell them + they take the coffee' — Imperfect); 'Go and tell them to take the coffee'; **għidilna ngħinuk u aħna ngħinuk** (lit. tell us (ask us) + we help you + and we help you) 'Ask us to help you and we'll help you'.

CONDITIONAL SENTENCES

These are indicated by the invariable words (i) **kieku** or **li kieku** 'if' (apparently shortened from **kien ikun** 'it would be') or (ii) **jekk** 'if' followed by the Perfect or Imperfect. The following examples illustrate fulfilled or unfulfilled conditions in the past, the present and the future and the combined structures of the sentences expressing a condition *(protasis)* and the consequence thereof *(apodosis)* which can often change position, that is the *protasis* can come before the *apodosis* and viceversa as in li għidtli li **tixtieq tiġi/kont nistiednek** 'If you told me that you wished to come/I would have invited you' or **Kont nistiednek/li għidtli li tixtieq tiġi** 'I would have invited you if you told me you wished to come'.

Exx. **Kieku dħaktilha kienet tkellmek** 'if you had smiled at her, she would have spoken to you'; **kieku qed jaqla' l-flus kieku** (can be omitted) **mhux qed jittallab** 'if he was earning money he would not be begging'; **jekk għamlet is-sħana il-ħwejjeġ nixfu** 'if it (the weather) was hot, the clothes are dry'; **jekk nieżla x-xita, il-ħwejjeġ qed jixxarbu** 'if it is raining, the clothes are getting wet'; **jekk tagħmel ix-xita, il-ġnien jissaqqa** or **sa jissaqqa** 'if it rains, the garden gets (or will be) watered'; **kieku kont naf, kieku** (may be omitted) **kont niġi** 'if I knew I would have come'; **li kieku riedet tiġi kienet tgħid** 'if she wanted to come she would have said (so)'; **li ktibtli kont niktiblek** 'had you written to me I would have written to you'; **jekk fetaħ il-kexxun ra x'kien hemm ġo fih** 'if he opened the drawer, he saw what there was in it'; **jekk nieħu l-ewwel premju nsiefer** 'if I win the first prize, I'll go abroad'; **jekk taħseb ma tiżbaljax** 'if you think you won't err'; **jekk tiġi hi nitlaq jien** 'if she comes I'll go away'; **"dwiemes" jew "oqbra" kif kieku konna nsejħulhom illum** "rock-tombs" or "graves" as we would call them today'; **kif għamiltha jien ġiet wisq aħjar milli kieku għamiltha inti** 'as I did it, it has turned out much better than you would have done it'.

(i) *Wishes* (ii) *Imprecations* (iii) *Regrets*.

(i) *Wishes* are expressed by **mhux li** (also without **mhux**) + **kien** + subject with which it agrees in person and number. Ex. **mhux** (can be omitted) **li kont ma narah qatt iżjed!** 'if only (how I wish) I could never see him again!' (ii) *imprecations*: **Nirra** + verbal pron. suffixes (= **min ra** 'would someone saw you, him', etc. Ex. **nirrah**

jikser saqajh! 'may he break his legs!' (iii) *regrets*: for failure to have done something in the past is expressed by **mhux li** + Perfect of the verb. Ex. **mhux li tkellmet (marret)**! 'if only she had spoken (gone)!' These are shortened conditional clauses.

Wishes and supplications can be expressed also by (i) the Imperative (2nd pers. sing & pl.) and (ii) the Imperfect (3rd pers, sing.; 1st & 3rd pers. pl.) + the right intonation to distinguish them from ordinary commands or statements. Exx. (i) **Alla, agħtina** or (ii) **Alla jagħtina l-paċi fi żmienna** (i) 'God, give us or (ii) May God give us peace in our time'. **Nitolbu** 'let us pray'.

EXERCISE 31

Translate:

(a) **Mara tidħaq mix-xejn donnha belha. Raġel jiekol f'saħħtu. Ridtkom tiktbulu ittra u tgħidulu jiġi lura. Ridtuni** (or **ridtu li jien**) **noqgħod nitgħażżen ma nagħmel xejn. La** (since) **ridtek taħdem messek** (you should have) **ħdimt. Rajniehom deħlin jidħku u ħerġin jibku. Dwejjaq** (it is annoying) **ma jkollok xejn x'tagħmel. Hu u dieħel żelaq** (slipped) **u weġġa' siequ. Jekk trid tiġi magħna ħallas** (pay) **sehmek** (your share).

(b) If you have not enough (**biżżejjed** after noun) money, you cannot buy (**tixtri**) the house. He had read the news when you spoke (**kellimt**) to him. You cannot love God without loving your neighbour (**proxxmu**). She wanted to tell her the bad news. We went out singing (**għanna** or **kanta** = he sang) and they entered screaming (**werżaq** 'he screamed'). If I knew, I would not have gone. Edward (**Dwardu**) is a man who knows how to talk. She wanted me to write her two articles for her review (**rivista**). They had left (**telaq** 'he left') when you brought it (fem. and masc.) to them.

PART 4

1a. L-arja; is-shab; id-dlam; il-ksieħ; l-art; il-gżira; il-lvant; ix-xemx; il-qamar; iċ-ċpar; il-glata; is-shana; is-silġ; id-dawl; is-sema; il-beraq; in-natura; it-tramuntana; ix-xita; il-qawsalla; id-dell.

1b. Italy is near Malta. Italian is easy; English is less easy. The Spaniards study English and French. The Maltese study English very much. The snow is white. In England there is much rain, cold and mist (fog). The earth and the sky are in darkness. Malta is a sunny island. The English love the sea. Maltese is a Semitic tongue.

1c. **Mar il-knisja u s-suq. Hu l-ħabs. Il-bniedem mhux etern; Alla biss etern. Il-Vessuvju vulkan f'Napli. M'humiex Insara. Il-Qrendi raħal f'Malta u l-Għarb raħal f'Għawdex. Hi mhix Maltija u hu mhux Franċiż. Ir-Russja art kbira. Malta u Għawdex huma gżejjer.**

2a. A wise man and a wise woman. There is good wine in Malta. A green onion is not good. The flag of Malta is white and red. A large eel and a beautiful cow. The cat is a jealous animal. John is a bachelor. The coffee is bitter. Bitter coffee. A rude man and a fussy woman. The doctor and the sick man are both blind.

2b. **Ix-xadina (ix-xadin) għajjura (għajjur). It-tabib għaref fejjaq il-marid u l-marida. Baqra bajda fost il-ħaxix aħdar ta' l-Olanda. Il-bandiera ta' Malta bandiera qadima. Il-ħall qares. Il-gobon Għawdxi tajjeb. Il-maġġur fqir u xiħ. L-inbid qares isir ħall. It-Taljan mhux tqil. Smajt ħoss kbir.**

3a. The folly of old age and the softness of sloth. Cardinal Newman is a learned writer. The whitewasher is old and the tailor is young. Old age is ugly and sick.

A thievish young man and woman. The scavenger is foolish and quarrelsome, but the gardener is a good worker. The beggar is a liar and a thief. The reader read a new book. The whiteness of clouds in the morning and the redness of clouds in the evening are a beautiful vision.

3b. It-tallab marid u l-ħalliel ħażin u ġelliedi. Il-kelb tal-ħajjat kbir u aħrax. Ġimgħa ta' xogħol iebes u tqil. Il-ħdura tal-ħaxix u s-sbuħija taż-żgħożija. Il-bjuda taż-żahar u l-ħeġġa tat-tfulija huma l-poeżija tal-ħolm. Il-kruħa tax-xjuħija tbażża' ż-żagħżugħa u ddej-jaq ix-xiħa. Is-sbuħija tal-belt imqaddsa ta' Ġerusalem. Il-qattiel qatel il-ħaddiem. Xitla kbira fil-mixtla.

4a. This is good news. The soil (lit. earth) of Malta is fertile. Valletta is the capital of Malta; Victoria (or Rabat) is the capital of Gozo. Maltese and Gozitan (folk) song is not like foreign singing. A stammering and quarrelsome old woman. The diligent worker is the owner of this house. A male budgerigar and a female canary. Salini is a long and sunny road. The thick voice of the bass. A great labour crisis and a complicated financial question.

4b. Ir-raġel kiefer u ġellied, iżda l-mara mistħija u ħabrieka. Is-sema ikħal ta' Malta safi u xemxi. Din (dan) tajba (tajjeb). Ix-xiħ u x-xiħa ġellieda (or ġellidin). It-tifla ħalja imma l-missier għani. Għajnejn ġriżi, ħad-dejn roża u xagħar kannella. Iben għażiż u tifla kiefra. L-artist għandu vuċi ħelwa. Il-mara hija l-omm u t-tifla l-bint. Il-missier huwa s-sid tad-dar qadima.

5a. He drank a glass of milk better than a glass of water. The sultan's wife is very ill. The milkman, the greengrocer, and the butcher are at the market. Your wife bought a rotolo of pork and half a rotolo of beef. Alfred is a man of great strength. Christmas is a day of joy for the Christian wor'd. Għajn Tuta is a place-name in Gozo and Għajn Tuffieħa is a place-name in Malta. For

Christians, Jesus Christ is the Son of God. The door of
the house is shut. Today is her mother's birthday.

5b. Agħtini tazza nbid. Mart is-suldat marida.
Xtrajt lira laħam. Kwarta mixi minn Valletta għall-
Furjana. Mara ta' karattru. Tal-ħalib, tal-ħaxix u tal-
laħam ħbieb. Jitkellem mgħaġġel iżda jikteb sabiħ. Jien
rajt (or just Rajt) il-karozza l-ġdida. Żjara dar dar.
Ftit flus (or flus ftit) għal ħafna xogħol.

6a. An old man and an old woman in a cottage
near the sea. Peter's little garden is larger than John's.
Dante is the greatest poet of the world. (Good) cheap is
dear. My dearest friend emigrated yesterday. The small
(young) one is sweet but the smallest (youngest) is
sweeter. The least hard work is also the easiest. A very
sweet boy and an exceedingly good man. Anthony is as
stupid as a clown. Mary is a woman as clean as a pin.
The best known Maltese poet is Dun Karm Psaila.

6b. Ix-Xlendi huwa bajja sabiħa f'Għawdex. Gnejna
u dwejra Marsalforn, bajja xemxija f'Għawdex. Dit-triq
hija usa' mit-triq qadima tar-raħal tiegħi. Ġanni akbar
minn Toni. Il-Malti bħall-Għarbi, iżda mhux tqil daqs
l-Għarbi. Twieled Malta, imma għex Għawdex. Mara
fqajra u dgħajfa, xiħa għakka. It-tigra eħrex mill-iljun.
Pietru kbir daqs Mikiel. L-isbaħ l-indafa! qal Ġużè.

7a. Two years and two months of hard work. He
had an (one) egg, I had two eggs, but she had four. He
has the strong arms of a giant and the eyes of a hawk.
Two weeks without work are worse than death for a
poor man. Two branches cut from an old tree. Two
qnatar of potatoes and two thousand hens. He spoke
twice; once, for nothing. Ten oranges and seven peaches.
The wings of the bird are broken. Two eggs, two cheeses,
a loaf and a bottle of wine for the worker.

7b. Jien rajt (or simply Rajt) id-dar darbtejn. Jien
irrid (or simply Irrid) ħbiżtejn, badtejn u ġbintejn. Sitt
bajdiet moqlija u disa' ħutiet mixwija. Kelma aħjar minn

kelmtejn. Il-kliem perikoluż. Dirgħajn u riġlejn shaħ għax-xogħol iebes u l-ġiri. Figura sabiħa, spallejn wiesgħa (also wesgħin), għajnejn safja (also safjin) u ħaddejn roża. Qoffa frott għall-iltiema. Frotta ħażina tħassar mija. Il-frott skars fix-xitwa. Ħutha xtrawlha ħuta kbira.

8a. Sqallin; dħulin; ħabsin; barrin; għajjenin; għarwenin; sajmin; deħlin; weqfin; maħrubin; ferħanin; setgħana or setgħanin; smajrin; ġwejdin; nidjin; għaljin; ħatjin; paljijiet; tankijiet; bankijiet or banek; ballijiet; sptarijiet; torġien; għidien; furnara; ħaddieda or ħaddidin.

8b. Is-suldat Sqalli hieni. Fjuri fuq l-altar. L-arġentier xtara siġġu qadim. L-infermiera għajjenin. Is-suldati u l-baħrin intelliġenti ħafna. Il-buqar mimli nbid. Buqari mimlija bl-inbid. L-ommijiet henjin ħafna għax l-aħbar tajba. Irġiel u nisa niżlin il-għolja.

9a. bram; sriep; vrus; ċnus; qrati; swali; baned; bnadi; ktieli; laneċ; faxex; pjazez; niċeċ; birer; pinen; boroż; bolol; koxox; frejjeġ; spejjeż; skejjen; psataż; qlafat; kmamar; qratas; tnabar; staten; twavel; vrieden; dbielet, mniezel.

9b. Id-djar ta' Malta kbar u sbieħ. It-tfal morda. Kotba ġodda u pinen qodma. L-għonja ħorox u l-fqar boloħ. It-tifla belha marida. Iż-żwiemel huma bhejjem tat-tagħbija Malta. L-għożżieb għorrief. Malta għandha knejjes qodma u ġodda. Il-knisja tal-Mosta l-ikbar knisja fil-gżira. Kbar huma d-dwejjaq (or Kbira d-diqa) tal-fqar. Il-kwiekeb bħal-labar jew tikek fis-sema. L-armla żżewġet armel. Il-fwieħa tal-ġonna ta' Malta. Il-Maltin u l-Għawdxin Insara. L-Għarab Misilmin.

10a. magħlaq/mgħalaq; maqgħad/-; masġar/imsaġar; maħbeż/imħabeż; magħġen/mgħaġen; midbaħ/imdiebaħ; mitraq/imtieraq; miġbed/imġiebed; mirkeb/imriekeb; mitħna/imtieħen; mixtla/imxietel; miżbla/imżiebel.

10b. **Fil-Mużew hemm ħafna msiebaħ qodma. Mitħna Maltija u ħafna mtieħen Olandiżi. Mitraħ artab u
mħadda iebsa. Imtieraħ rotob u mħaded ibsin. Ix-xiħa
Għawdxija għandha mkebba u magħżel. Għandi mkebeb
u mgħażel ġodda. Il-mogħdrija u l-imħabba huma r-ruħ
tar-Reliġjon. Il-bidwi għandu moħriet qadim iżda l-im-
ħaret qodma m'humiex tajbin għax-xogħol fl-egħlieqi.
Hemm mixegħla kbira l-Imdina, il-belt qadima ta' Malta.**

11a. I ate a very good Maltese orange. Did you eat
Maltese bread? We ate Maltese bread. I myself and
alone did this. These children are Maltese; the others
are either Italian or French. This is the money with
which I paid the worker. The woman whose son is very
ill is poor and lonely. Whose are this white horse and this
old donkey? My wife is a Maltese woman from Sliema. My
brother and your sister love each other. He took to reading English and French books.

11b. **Il-palazz qadim. Il-palazz qadim? Liema ktieb
hu fuq il-mejda? Marti Maltija; martu Ingliża. Liema hi
martek? Jien stess (or innifsi) rajt dar-raġel miexi ma'
dik il-mara. Dawn huma s-suldati li l-kaptan tagħhom
qatel lilu nnifsu. Dawk huma l-irġiel u n-nisa li telqu lil
uliedhom. Din hija l-pinna li biha kiteb dawn il-kotba.
L-Insara tajba jħobbu lil xulxin; l-Insara ħżiena ma
jħobbux lil xulxin. Ta' min hi did-dar u oħt min hi din?
Waħedha m'Alla.**

12a. There are sixty miles of sea from Pozzallo in
Sicily to Malta. Where is the girl? She is near the children. My house is opposite my brothers' (or sisters') house.
How are you? Well, thank you. Is your father well? No,
he is ill. Your mother? Yes, she is very well. Has your
sister arrived? I have been an hour here, waiting for
her; but they have been longer than two hours alone
near the door of the house. This book is mine; the other
is hers. He came to my house with his dog. How did you
come from Rome? By air or by sea? By sea. Let me see
with what your brother came and why. He looks sick
and she always looks sad.

12b. Fejn hu ħuk? Ma nafx fejn hu. Hemm swar madwar il-Belt Valletta. Sqallija hija gżira mnejn nimportaw frott u ħut. Kemm hemm bniet (or Kemm-il tifla hemm) fil-klassi tiegħek? Mhux twil daqsek. Għadha marida. Oqgħod fejni or ħdejja. It-tifel għandu tliett snin. M'ilnix wisq hawn.

13a. How many people are there in Malta? There are over 300,000 people. How long had it been a British colony before it became independent? Are you thirsty? Here is water. Are you hungry? Here is bread. With whom did your father go? With friends. This woman has a gold ring. A heartless man and a brainless woman. Near Malta there are three islands — Gozo, Comino and Filfla. Filfla is a rock used for firing exercises. A ship between heaven and water (Maltese idiom for 'in the offing'). Turn to the left; to the right. He looked up and down and saw nobody.

13b Din mhix bħal dak. L-iben bħal missieru, imma t-tifla bħal ommha. Arloġġ tal-fidda. Ġie siegħa u nofs wara l-ħin. Għal-lum biżżejjed. Ħdejn il-ħanut tiegħu hemm dar biswit il-palazz tal-Gvernatur. Dan hu l-ħlas għax-xahar. Dan hu premju għal tifla. Agħtih lit-tifla mill-Gżira. L-ewwel mar bil-baħar, imbagħad bl-art.

14a. A basket contains 200 melons. The year 1963 is a year of great events. How many thousands of soldiers died in the Great War of 1914-18? Fifty men and thirteen women together with a hundred soldiers went on strike. Pope Paul VI succeeded Pope John XXIII. He came tenth in class; his sister came fourth and their younger brother came fifth. Five by ten fifty; take off five remain forty five. A **robu** is a quarter of a cow. The flesh of a cow is called beef.

14b. Dawn huma dati ta' min jiftakarhom fl-istorja ta' Malta: Is-sena elfejn u tliet mija — elfejn u mitejn Q.K.: il-miġja tal-bniedem f'Malta. Is-sena elf u erba' mija Q.K.: żmien il-Bronż. Is-sena disa' mija Q.K.:

Żmien il-Ħadid. Is-sena mitejn u tmintax Q.K.: Malta taħt ir-Rumani. Is-sena sittin W.K.: l-Għarqa ta' San Pawl. Is-sena ħames mija u tlieta u tletin: Malta taħt l-Imperaturi tal-Lvant. Is-sena tmien mija u seb-għin: Malta taħt l-Għarab. Is-sena elf u wieħed u dis-għin: Il-bidu tal-ħakma Normanna f'Malta. Is-sena elf mitejn u tlieta u tmenin: Il-ħakma ta' l-Aragoniżi f'Malta. Is-sena elf ħames mija u tletin: il-miġja tal-Kavallieri f'Malta. Is-sena elf ħames mija u ħamsa u sittin: l-Assedju l-Kbir. Is-sena elf seba' mija u tmienja u sittin: il-fondazzjoni ta' Università. Is-sena elf seba' mija u tmienja u disgħin: Napuljun f'Malta. Is-sena elf u tmien mija: il-forzi Franċiżi jċiedu lill-Ingliżi. Is-sena elf tmien mija u erbatax: Malta tidħol fl-Imperu Brit-taniku (more commonly Ingliż). Is-sena elf disa' mija u wieħed u għoxrin: l-ewwel Kostituzzjoni ta' Gvern res-ponsabbli. Is-sena elf disa' mija u erbgħin: It-Tieni Assedju l-Kbir. Is-sena elf disa' mija u tnejn u erbgħin: l-għoti tal-"George Cross". Is-sena elf disa' mija u seba' u erbgħin: ir-radd ta' Gvern responsabbli. Is-sena elf disa' mija u disa' u ħamsin: is-seħħ tal-Kostituzzjoni ġdida flok oħra mneħħija. Is-sena elf disa' mija u sittin: iċ-ċentinarju ta' San Pawl (60 W.K. — 1960). Is-sena elf disa' mija u wieħed u sittin: Malta magħrufa bħala l-Istat ta' Malta. Is-sena elf disa' mija u tnejn u sittin: elezzjoni ġenerali mirbuħa mill-partit Nazzjonalista. Is-sena elf disa' mija u tlieta u sittin: is-Segretarju tal-Kolonji (Duncan Sandys) wiegħed l-Indipendenza lil Malta minn Mejju ta' l-elf disa' mija u erba' u sittin. Malta saret Indi-pendenti fil-wieħed u għoxrin ta' Settembru ta' l-elf disa' mija erbgħa u sittin.

15a. She dreamt an ugly dream indeed. The thief lit the lamp and stole the treasure. We asked (or prayed for) the help of God. The student read the novels of Walter Scott. The sick man grew very thin. When she got near me I recognised who she was. We asked for and chose the best house in Marsaxlokk. I had not recog-nised you since you had not got near enough to me. What

had your brother done for me? My brother had asked
for the necessary help.

15b. Hareġ, mexa u sab triq ġdida għal raħal qadim.
Meta qorob, għarfet il-ħalliel. Serqet lira butir u ġobon.
Fhimna l-lezzjoni. Hu kiser riġlu u hi kisret drieġħha.
Qatlu l-ħalliel li kien seraq il-ġawhar. Aħna ġbidna l-ispaga u huma ġibdu l-ħabel. Int għażilt dar sabiħa ħdejn
l-aktar bajja xemxija f'Għawdex. Il-qattiel kien qatel ix-
xiħa meta l-pulizija waslet (f.) or wasal (or more commonly meta waslet (or wasal) il-pulizija). Talbu tlieta u
għoxrin lira tar-radju.

16a. Your brother shut the drawer. Open the door
and shut the window. Why have you opened the window?
Shut it! Don't oppress the poor. Collect (pick up) the
money from the floor. Work well, but think what you'll
do before you begin. This man is very strong. The
weather began to be cold. The wind blows from amongst
the trees. We have drunk wine; now they (will) drink beer.

16b. Ir-raġel ħabat it-tifel b'bastun. Aħbat (aħbtu,
pl.) it-tifel ħażin bil-bastun. Il-missier twajjeb ma jaħ-
qarx lill-familja tiegħu. Alla ħalaq is-sema u l-art mix-
xejn. Il-bniedem jivvinta iżda ma jaħlaqx. Omxot xagħ-
rek sewwa. Qagħdet ġimagħtejn ma' zijuha. Oqgħod fuq
das- (or dan is-) siġġu u aqra l-gazzetta tal-lum. Hija
dehret quddiem l-imħallef iżda ma setgħetx tifhem l-ak-
kuża. Neħilsu d-dinja mill-biża' u l-faqar.

17a. I have seen a man riding a horse and children
riding an ass. I have been standing a long time. They
had been standing for two hours. Charles, a bachelor,
is asleep alone in the old house. The woman is wearing
a new dress and the children are dressed shabbily. There
is a ghost in this house. I am understanding the paper;
but I am not understanding the book because it is difficult. A washed suit looks new. A rented house near
the sea. An open window: sunlight and fresh air in the
house and good health for the family.

17b. Qegħdin jiktbu ktieb. M'aħniex nifhmu l-lezzjoni. Kienu milqugħin min-nies ta' Malta u Għawdex.
L-għalqa miżrugħa ta' Ganni. Hemm ħares fid-dar ta'
l-għażeb. Kien hemm sitt elef u mitejn suldat maqtulin
f'dik il-gwerra. Il-kotba kienu meħudin minn missierek.
Oħtok kienet liebsa libsa qadima. It-tfal kollha kienu
reqdin. Rajtu wieqaf ħdejn il-ħanut waħdu.

18a. Her father's death was a great loss. Our wish
is the freedom of our people. We danced a folkloristic
dance. The barking of dogs during the night. A long
sleep in the darkness with the window and the door shut.
Entrance on payment and exit without payment. The
city of Valletta is full of downhills and uphills. Poems
about sunrise and sunset. The victory of Malta against
the attacks of the Nazis and Fascists in the last war
for the freedom of the Mediterranean. The gathering of
wheat in July.

18b. Hemm ġemgħa (or ġabra) kotba qodma fuq il-
mejda. Il-ġbir tal-wiċċ tar-raba' jsir f'Ġunju. F'lejla twila
ż-żfin jogħġob liż-żgħażagħ. Hajja ta' ħidma kbira. Is-
sokor ħażin għas-saħħa. L-inbiħ tal-kelb qajjem lit-tfal
reqdin. Dalma kbira waqgħet fuq il-belt Valletta. Qam
minn raqda twila u ħolma kerha. Id-daħk f'ħalq il-boloħ.
Kien hemm ferħ kbir ir-raħal.

19a. The children broke all the trees which were in
the garden. Urge the children to study more. The mother
deprives herself of many things for (the sake of) her
children. What's all this self-conceit for? The door was
broken by the wind. My brother is abroad in America,
and my sister (is abroad) in England. God blesses the
rich and the poor. She became very proud because she
inherited from her uncle. I (or you) borrowed £200 from
a business man. The saint deprives himself of the comforts of life.

19b. Min kisser it-tazza l-ġdida? Liema tazza tkis-
sret (or inkisret) il-bieraħ? Raqqdet lit-tarbija. Inħobb

nixxemmex fuq ix-xtajta ta' l-Għadira. Issellifna mitejn lira mill-bank. Tkabbar wisq (or ħafna). Tgħammidt (or kont imgħammed) f'Sannat Għawdex. Ma sifirtx din is-sena. It-tkissir tal-ħġieġ tat-tieqa. It-tkabbir jeqred lill-bniedem.

20a. He became poor and had to borrow money. The names of the brave are never forgotten. He grew old, ugly and foolish. On the 22nd of June the day grows shorter. There is no reason for all this amazement. She loathed her old and ugly husband. The money was stolen from the drawer. Don't interfere with a married man and woman. Everything is forgotten in this world except what is written. Withered flowers in an old vase.

20b. Il-ħalliel inqabad mill-pulizija. Il-flus insterqu mill-bank. Tbierket (or Kienet imbierka) minn raġel qaddis. Iġġieldu u tqabdu għax ma kellhomx flus. Instabu mejta fit-triq. Dal-ktieb inkiteb mitt sena ilu. Nefqu flushom kollha u ftaqru wisq. Malajr intesa wara mewtu. Ftehmu fuq il-kuntratt. Wiċċha ħmar bil-mistħija.

21a. qatta' 'he tore to pieces', tqatta' 'it was (got) torn', inqata' 'it was cut' (fig. he was taken aback); balla' 'he made someone swallow', tballa' 'he was made to swallow', inbala' 'he was swallowed up'; ġamma' 'he collected', iġġamma' 'it was collected', inġama' 'it was collected'; nażża' 'he undressed', tnażża' 'he was undressed', intaża' 'it was shed off'; samma' 'he made one hear', issamma' 'he listened to, or eavesdropped', insama' or instama' 'he was heard'; talla' 'he raised', ittalla' 'he was raised', intala' 'it amounted to'; tamma' 'he forced to eat'; xabba' 'he satiated' (fig. annoyed), ixxabba' 'it was sated; had enough'; laqqa' 'he brought together', iltaqa' 'he met'; inżebagħ 'it was painted'.

21b. Qata' l-paġni tal-ktieb bit-taljakarti. Qattgħet l-ittra biċċiet biċċiet. Bellgħuh il-mediċina. L-ewwel naża' l-ġlekk; imbagħad naża' ż-żarbun. Qed tibża' jew trid tbeżżagħni? L-ewwel iltaqa' mad-delegazzjoni, imbagħad iltaqa' mal-ħaddiema. Ma smajtx dak il-ħoss mill-ġnien? Narċis migmugħ mill-blat. Il-ħaddiem qiegħed jaqla' seba' liri fil-ġimgħa.

22a. The bottle contains a pint of milk. They inherited a large sum of money. How much wine does this cask contain? Vincent failed in the geography examination. Stop! here are buried the brave ones of Malta. Is there a dentist? My teeth are aching (me) very much. He accompanied me as far as the ship before I emigrated. Potatoes are not weighed with the soil attached to them. Stale bread gets hard. The sick woman began to recover.

22b. Tista' tasal fil-ħin? Kemm jesa' l-basket? Jesa' żewġ tużżani bajd. Kollha weħlu fl-eżami ta' Ġunju. Flex weħlu? X'uħud weħlu fl-istorja, x'uħud fil-ġografija, iżda hi weħlet fil-Latin. Huma għonja għax wirtu għaxart elef mitejn u ħamsa u tletin lira. Ieqaf! periklu! Min iwiegħed għandu jagħti. L-art imwiegħda ta' Ġerusalem. Urini t-triq li tieħu (leads to) għal Ħal Saflieni. Hu wrieni t-tempji megalitiċi ta' Malta u Għawdex.

23a. He sells fish and eggs. The rich must help the poor. He lived five years in Paris, six years in London and eleven years in Malta. I want peace of mind and heart. The sun disappeared behind the hills. Lent is the time when Christians fast. Have you visited St. John's Co-Cathedral? No, I'll go there tomorrow. The car turned to the left and the van to the right. The dead woman was Andrew's mother. What is superfluous is always useless.

23b. Meta mort Amsterdam, dort il-mużewijiet kollha. Illum sar ħadd ma jaħseb xejn. Missieru ilu erba' snin mejjet u ommu sitta. Xi trid issir la tikber? Irrid insir jew tabib jew qassis. F'dawn l-imqades kienu meqjuma l-allat minn niesna l-qodma. Min ifittex isib. Darragel midjun ma' tal-ħanut. Ktieb miġjub mill-Malti għall-Ingliż. Ir-raġel meqjus fi kliemu; il-mara le. Xi għasafar ibidu bajd abjad, oħrajn bajd ħadrani. Wara ħafna dawran f'toroq dojoq wasalt id-dar għajjien.

24a. What Maltese book have you read today? I have begun Nazju Ellul, a novel by Ġużè Muscat Azzopardi, and Inez Farruġ, a novel by A. E. Caruana. The mother guides the child when this begins to walk. They were mentioning the murder which took place last year. Old clothes thrown out in the street. These children were brought up in poverty and suffering. We have nothing to hide. Every beginning is difficult. Walking is good for health. By reading you learn how to write. When I reprimanded her, she blushed very much.

24b. Wieġeb meta tkun mistoqsi. Il-bini tal-kappella nbeda fis-sena elf u tlieta u sittin. Il-ġarra timtela qatra qatra. Min isemmi ismi? L-isem t'Alla għandu jissemma bil-qima. Did-dar tiswa erbat elef sitt mija u wieħed u tletin lira. Taħlix (taħlux) flusek (fluskom) jekk ma tridx (tridux) tiftaqar (tiftaqru). Bnejt dwejra San Pawl il-Baħar. Armi (armu pl.) daż-żibel fil-barmil. Imxejna ħames mili imma huma mxew tlettax-il mil.

25a. The breeze was felt cool and fresh. Don't lie on the cold floor. The knife and the fork have grown rusty. The priest heard her confession before she died; it wasn't long since she had been to confession. When it rains, take shelter under the umbrella. He made friends with the owner of the house. Renew your vow to God. She has grown very thin. The money was counted before me. He finished his book in two weeks.

25b. Il-ħaddiema ħattew il-karrozzi u l-karrijiet, imbagħad ġarrewhom lejn l-imħażen. Il-qtar tax-xita jleqq fuq il-weraq aħdar tas-siġar xjuħ. Fis-sajf ir-ragħaj iġiżż in-ngħaġ. Għożż il-fidi u l-ġenituri tiegħek. Inħobb ġobon maħkuk fuq l-ispagetti biz-zalza. Żammew it-tarbija minn driegħha. Żamm iż-żiemel mir-riedni. Fir-rebbiegħa nħossu ż-żiffa ratba tal-baħar. La tkiddx lil oħtok. Imteddet għajjiena fuq soddtha (also sodditha or is-sodda tagħha).

26a. Don't make turbid the water you want to drink
(from). Hang this suit in the sun to dry. He is all the time
coughing and hacking. I left my mother at home shelling
peas. She got confused in the examination and failed in
five subjects. They ground their teeth in anger. I don't
drink turbid water because my stomach aches (me). After
the first rain the water of wells gets turbid. I met with
great opposition and heard much grumbling. In wars
much blood is spilled in vain.

26b. Ċempel il-qanpiena u ara min hemm. Meta
smajt bil-qtil tkexkixt. Qed ifixklu x-xogħol tagħna.
Għaliex qed twerżaq donnha miġnuna? Ċapċpu idhom
meta temm it-taħdita tiegħu. It-tfal qegħdin jitbandlu
fuq il-bandla fil-ġnien. Għaliex dejjem tgerger? Id-demm
tal-kavalieri ċċarċar fuq is-swar għad-difiża ta' Malta.
Bandal il-benniena u raqqad it-tarbija. Warrab kull
tfixkil.

27a. He who gives takes; he who doesn't give
doesn't take. I am not seeing them because I am too far
away. Did you know that your brother said this? We
say this. What your brother said we don't know. They
came yesterday. When are you coming? I'll come the day
after tomorrow. Where has your wife gone? She went
where I went and where you went. Dew shines on the
leaves of poplar trees. I couldn't believe my eyes. I didn't
know the name of the soldier whom I saw standing
beside you

27b. Kemm kotba kellek fil-ħanut tiegħek? Fejn hi
d-dar tagħhom? Kien jismu Pietru. Agħtini ħobż u ilma.
Ħadu flusi u kielu ħobżi. Meta ratna l-aħħar? Qalet li
ma tafx. Ejja (Ejjew) u għidli (għiduli) x'ġara. Intom
li temmnu f'Alla iżżuh ħajr għall-ikel u s-saħħa tal-lum.
Nieqaf hawn fejn il-qabar tal-ħabib tiegħi mejjet.

28a. I am typing a letter for the editor of this
paper. Obey your mother and your father. The painter
painted a very lovely picture. No one was saved from the

shipwreck This woman takes umbrage for no cause. The mother finds delight in her children. Treat people well so that people will treat you well. The car skidded and the driver was hurt. Travelling from one country to another costs a lot of money. This is mistaken reasoning.

28b. L-ajruplan iddajvja fuq il-belt. Kif ittratta-tek? Il-pajjiż fil-periklu. Salvah (Salvawh). Għaghalna nittrattaw l-egħdewwa tagħna aħjar milli ridna. Fanndu t-trunċiera u nħbew (or staħbew) fiha. Alla huwa s-sal-vazzjoni tal-bniedem. L-ebda ubbidjenza bla (or min-għajr) dixxiplina. Jekk jogħġbok, tittajpjali dawn iż-żewġ artikli? Il-karrozza skiddjat u weġġgħu. Kienet ittrattata tajjeb minn żewgħa.

29a. He loves her as much as (he loves) the light of his eyes. Her husband died last year and left her a widow with five children. God blesses you and fills you with happiness (also optatively 'May God bless you and fill you with happiness'). He frightened them with his mad (lit. madman's) shouting. Throw the torn sack out of the window. He extinguished the lamp and great dark-ness fell in the room. As a souvenir, to you I give two books, and to her silk lace. Remove (for me) this drunkard from here. Your girl is naughty; she broke (us) five new glasses. I sent them a cheque for £6 by post.

29b. Warrabli l-mejda u qegħidha fil-kamra l-oħra Kitbitilna ittra minn Ruma. Jekk tħobbha, iżżewwigħa; jekk ma tħobbhiex itlaqha. Ħallieha weħidha mat-tfal tagħha. Min iħobbok jagħtik u jbierkek. (Sa) Titilqu għal-kemm iħobbha. Għaliex beżżajthom it-tfal? Ma beżżejt-homx; imma int qed tbeżżagħhom bit-twerżiq tiegħek. Insiehom kollha; int ukoll se tinsiehom? Min bagħtlek dan il-ktieb mill-Gapan (also Gappun)? Fejn huma t-tazzi? Imliehom b'inbid tajjeb u ixorbu.

30a. What a fine letter the bride wrote to the bride-groom! She accompanied (for me) my daughter to

school, because she is still young. Will you accompany
her (for me) to school? Of course (or, With pleasure).
Many thanks. He told them a Maltese story and he told
it with great art; but his brother told them the other
story. Sing me a Maltese song and I'll sing you an Arab
song. Who lent it to you? The teacher lent me this book
and my aunt lent me this pen. Return it to them and
tell them not to send it to me now. Who broke them
(for us)? The sailors broke them (for us) and threw
them out (for us).

30b. Kitbitlu ittra twila ħafna minn Madrid. Agħmil-
hieli (agħmluhieli) malajr kemm tista' (tistgħu). (La)
tibgħatilhomx (tibgħatulhomx) dawn mal-messaġġier.
Jekk neħduhielu, jibgħathielna lura. Int (intom) ġibt-
hielna (ġibtuhielna) wara li kont (kontu) rajtha
(rajtuha). Niktbuhulhom (niktbuhielhom)? Kif tgħid;
iżda aħjar tibgħathomlna. Kiltu (kiltha). Kiltu (kiltha)
int ukoll? Jekk jogħġbok tiktbilha ittra pulita u tgħidilha
li bagħtuhomlna? Xi ġralek (ġralkom)? Xejn ma ġrali
(ġralna), iżda lilha ġratilha disgrazzja.

31a. A woman who laughs for no reason looks foolish.
A man who eats is healthy. I wanted you to write him a
letter and tell him to come back. You wanted me to be
idle doing nothing. Since I wanted you to work you should
have worked. We saw them enter laughing and go out
weeping. It's annoying to have nothing to do. While he
was entering he slipped and hurt his foot. If you want
to come with us, pay your share.

31b. Jekk m'għandekx flus biżżejjed ma tistax tixtri
d-dar. Kien qara l-aħbar meta int kellimtu. Ma tistax
tħobb 'l Alla mingħajr ma tħobb il-proxxmu tiegħek.
Riedet tgħidilha l-aħbar ħażina. Hrigna ngħannu (or
nkantaw) u huma daħlu jwerżqu. Li kont naf, kieku ma
kontx immur. Dwardu huwa raġel jaf (or li jaf) jitkellem
Riditni niktbilha żewġ artikli għar-rivista tagħha. Kienu
telqu meta ġibtuhulhom (m.) ġibtuhielhom (f.).